INNER
PERSPECTIVES

Harry Langdon

INNER PERSPECTIVES

Elizabeth Clare Prophet

TEACHINGS OF THE ASCENDED MASTERS

MARK L. PROPHET
ELIZABETH CLARE PROPHET

THE SUMMIT LIGHTHOUSE LIBRARY

INNER PERSPECTIVES
by Elizabeth Clare Prophet
Copyright © 2001 The Summit Lighthouse Library
All rights reserved

Library of Congress Control Number: 2001093401
ISBN: 0-922729-76-X

THE SUMMIT LIGHTHOUSE LIBRARY™

The Summit Lighthouse Library is an imprint of Summit University Press.

SUMMIT UNIVERSITY ☙ PRESS®

Summit University Press, ☙, *Pearls of Wisdom,* Keepers of the Flame,
Church Universal and Triumphant, Science of the Spoken Word, The
Summit Lighthouse and Summit University are registered trademarks.

Image on page 368 of Elizabeth Clare Prophet © 1999 Larry Stanley
Design and production: Lynn Wilbert

Printed in the United States of America

Disclaimer: No guarantee whatsoever is made to anyone by The Summit
Lighthouse Library, Summit University Press or Elizabeth Clare Prophet
that the spiritual system of the Science of the Spoken Word, including
meditation, visualization, dynamic decrees and spiritual healing, embodied
in this book will yield successful results for anyone at any time. The functioning of cosmic law is a direct experience between the individual and his
own higher consciousness. As in Jesus' time, some were healed and some
were not—according to their faith or lack of it. Karma and the Divine
Providence must be the final arbiter of each one's application of the sacred
fire. We can only witness to our personal healing—body, mind and soul—
through the use of the suggested mantras and spiritual disciplines. Each
man may prove or disprove the Law for himself. The practice and proof of
the science of being rests with the individual. No one can do it for another.
These spiritual techniques do not replace medical treatment or diagnosis.

05   04   03   02   01   5   4   3   2   1

THE SUMMIT LIGHTHOUSE LIBRARY

was established to publish the

teachings of the ascended masters

as delivered to their messengers

Mark L. Prophet and

Elizabeth Clare Prophet.

These wisdom teachings,

released from the archives of the

Great White Brotherhood,

are for the new dispensation

of Aquarius.

Contents

Introduction

In the early 1970s, I was one among many disillusioned young people struggling to reconcile an inner awareness of truth, spirituality and justice with the seeming inequities of the times. The inherent contradictions of mainstream religion seemed painfully obvious. How, for example, could the idea of a just God be reconciled with the clear inequities of circumstance into which people are born? Yet despite these and other concerns, I felt I had glimpsed the light and I believed in great possibilities.

The son of a fundamentalist preacher, I had been saturated from childhood with notions of the immutable rightness of divine purpose, which even in my most cynical periods never quite forsook me. One nagging personal question, though, refused to go away: Why couldn't the truth about things divine make sense? By 1975, the attempt to answer that question in a satisfactory way had led me into explorations along the less traveled byways of Christian mysticism, Eastern religion, Theosophy, as well as other systems and teachings. I had become convinced that an ancient wisdom yet survived that could, I believed, successfully answer my questions. But where could I find it?

In the summer of 1975, I left the southern city where I had been a radio newsman and talk show host for several years with the clear intuition that I would find what I was looking for. Two months later on the University of Washington campus, I met a group of people who were studying what they termed "the teachings of the ascended masters" as taught by Elizabeth Clare Prophet. Soon a personal and dramatic episode began to unfold for me. From that time on, the thoroughness with which "the teachings" proceeded to answer my innermost questions and confirm my deepest intuitions was almost eerie.

In July of 1976, I found myself in Washington, D.C., attending a conference entitled "Higher Consciousness," conducted by Mrs. Prophet herself. Within a few weeks I was working full-time for The Summit Lighthouse, a spiritual organization founded in 1958 by Mark L. Prophet, Mrs. Prophet's late husband. Soon I was to have the great good fortune of working closely with her on many projects and becoming well acquainted with one of the most remarkable people of our time.

With an extensive broadcasting background, I naturally believed that a series of radio interviews on the basic precepts of the teachings of the ascended masters would be a good idea. Mrs. Prophet agreed, and in the spring of 1977 we recorded a series of fifteen-minute programs for broadcast every weekday morning for thirteen weeks on KIEV in Los Angeles. The result, I believe, was radio history.

Notwithstanding the time constraints, those remarkable programs covered with thoroughness and clarity a vast array of material, most of which had never been discussed so publicly before. The opportunity to participate in such a groundbreaking project was certainly one of the most memorable experiences of my life. That those interviews can now be offered in the present form is more than I could have hoped for.

In the following pages, you will meet the Elizabeth Clare Prophet who spent so many hours with me in that crowded Pasadena studio shedding light on some of life's deepest mysteries. And I believe that when you do, you will come to see her as I always will, as one of the wisest and most compassionate souls ever to walk among us.

Doug Kenyon
Publisher, *Atlantis Rising Magazine*

1

Awakening to Life's Purpose

∞

- *Who is Elizabeth Clare Prophet and what is her mission?*
- *Who is Saint Germain?*
- *What do Saint Germain and Jesus have in common?*

Mrs. Prophet, the first order of business on this premier program is to answer that important question: Just who is Elizabeth Clare Prophet and what does she have to say to Los Angeles, America and the world?

A: Doug, it's really great to be able to talk to you and to a lot of wonderful people who are seeking the meaning of the inner life. I remember when Gautama Buddha first came on the scene. He was such an extraordinary individual that they didn't ask him, "Who are you?" but they asked him: "What are you? Are you a God? Are you a man? Are you human or divine?" And he gave the simple answer, "I am awake!"

So, rather than talking about who I am or where I came from, I would simply say that I am a devotee of God. And in the devotion that I have found for God, I have discovered that he has a great truth for his people on earth in this hour.

That truth comes from within all of us. It is the truth of the Inner Self and the law of being. I come as a devotee of God to share my devotions, for I believe God has given to us a new science and a new religion whereby we can master ourselves and our age.

Q: I think everybody longs for this point of understanding, but most of us find it quite elusive. How is it that you have come to it?

A: I can remember wondering about God and feeling that I knew him personally when I was a little child the age of two or three. My first recollections are of my meditations upon God.

I believe that all children have that inner contact and that the more we are in this world, the more we lose that contact. But somehow I knew as I was growing up that the most important thing in life for me was to find God and to do a work for him that I knew I had come to do.

Interestingly, this concept is touched on in Maurice Maeterlinck's story *The Blue Bird.* In the play, two children, Tyltyl and Mytyl, are on a quest to find the Blue Bird. They come to a blue palace where little children are waiting to be born and masterful beings are directing them. Father Time comes as the children are about to be born and ushers them onto a ship. As the ship sails away toward earth, one can hear in the distance the voices of expectant mothers singing for the arrival of their children.

Upon interviewing the little children, Tyltyl and Mytyl find that each child is going forth with a mission. The children are not allowed to be born unless they have something special to bring to earth. So they begin to tell Tyltyl and Mytyl what they are going to do: One will become a scientist. One will become the ruler of worlds. One will have remedies for sicknesses.

It is not only my own soul but the soul of each one of us that remembers coming with a mission. And I call that mission the "divine plan" or the "inner blueprint." What people should realize is that I am not an exception but rather the rule and that anything that I discover is a gift of God for everyone else.

The first thing that heals the longing of the soul to find God is the recognition that we were each born with a cosmic purpose and a specific divine plan. The second is the recognition that there are masterful beings functioning just beyond the physical plane, referred to by various names in the scriptures of East and West. These ascended masters are our sponsors and our teachers as we attend earth's schoolroom to work out the problem of being.

Our souls will never be content until we discover the mission and the meaning of our lives. And therefore, we need to learn the rules of the game and follow them under the direct guidance of those who know them (and us) well if we are to meet the great challenge of our evolution on earth.

This is the inner perspective that I would like to convey today and as we proceed with these broadcasts. First and foremost, each one of us must make contact with the Inner Self and, in finding that Inner Self and that reality, discover: Why was I born? Why am I here? And what am I going to do about this commitment that I have made to life and to other parts of life on earth?

Q: Is there anything in your experience that is unique, that gives you this special insight that many of us don't have?

A: I have a deep respect for people who intensely follow a certain calling or who have a particular genius or dedication. It doesn't matter whether it is in science or art or business or law. It doesn't matter whether it is in being a mother or a father or a great singer or a pianist. It is the same flame, the same inner dedication of a soul who has found, if not the entire meaning, a portion of the meaning of his life.

I believe that I made a commitment to give to the world a

synthesis of the teachings of the world's great religious leaders and to provide the children of God with a way out in this hour. It is the hour of transition between the age of Pisces and the age of Aquarius.* The age of Pisces was dominated by the great figure of the Lord Jesus Christ. The age of Aquarius is dominated by the Ascended Master Saint Germain, who embodies the flame of freedom.

In this period of transition as we enter the age of Aquarius, the emphasis is on freedom—freedom of the soul and freedom of consciousness. We find great struggles for freedom being carried on in many nations on earth today. We see the suppression of human rights and that endowment of free will that is inalienable to the soul. In this age when we desire freedom, we have to learn the laws that govern freedom and the great disciplines of love that come to us as the Holy Spirit is released from within.

Q: You mentioned both Jesus and Saint Germain, and that immediately raises a lot of questions. I think probably the most important question is: What do Jesus and Saint Germain have in common?

A: I see these great ones as Sons of God. We are all God's sons and daughters, but these Sons have mastered the challenge of life on earth. They have mastered the self, mastered time and space and returned to the Inner Reality, which is called God.

Jesus demonstrated the nature of this mastery according to the way of the Piscean conqueror and returned to what we call the "white-fire core of being" in the ritual of the ascension at the conclusion of his life.

The process of the ascension is actually an acceleration of consciousness. It is an acceleration of the vibration and frequency

---

*Approximately every 2,150 years the earth passes through an age corresponding to one of the twelve signs of the zodiac. The length of an age is determined by a phenomenon called the precession of the equinoxes. A new age begins when the point of the spring equinox moves from one sign of the zodiac to another.

of the very atoms, cells and electrons that compose our beings.

Jesus is the archetype of those who have reunited with the light of the Christ. He was not the exception but the rule—he was the example. What one son of God can do, every son (and daughter) of God can do! This is the message of Jesus for the Piscean age, and it is also the message of Saint Germain for the Aquarian age.

Saint Germain has figured on earth in many incarnations. At the time of Jesus, he was embodied as Joseph, the protector of Mary and Jesus. We know that many Catholics who have prayed to Saint Joseph have received answers in wonderful and miraculous ways. Prior to his incarnation as Joseph, Saint Germain was embodied as the prophet Samuel. He later embodied as Francis Bacon.

We see, then, in the evolution of this soul one who was prophet as Samuel, one who was the archetype of father as Joseph, and one who was a great author and statesman as Francis Bacon. The acceleration of his consciousness and his return to the white-fire core in the ascension took place in 1684, following his life as Francis Bacon.

Subsequent to that, he was very present and very noticed in the courts of Europe as le Comte de Saint Germain, the "Wonderman of Europe." Isabel Cooper-Oakley wrote a book about him entitled *The Comte de St. Germain.* The Count warned kings and queens of coming calamities. He predicted the French Revolution and attempted to stay the hand of the guillotine.

Saint Germain's desire was to form the United States of Europe. Failing at this, he turned his attention to the United States of America, sponsoring the Constitution and a way of life for people who would come from every nation to pursue the flame of freedom, the flame of the Aquarian age.

Saint Germain figures in our folklore as Uncle Sam—a name

that harks back to his embodiment as the prophet Samuel. So the prophet Samuel in the person of Saint Germain is the one who gives the American people their tremendous zest for freedom, their creative genius and sense of alchemy—their impetus for constant self-evaluation and transformation. Above all, Saint Germain sponsors science, technology and the great inventions that have come forth in America for all peoples.

Saint Germain is the master of the Aquarian age and the one who will teach us to find the Christ as the Real Self in this two-thousand-year cycle. Today I have given you just a glimpse of this cosmic being, but we will be talking more about him in future broadcasts.

Le Comte de Saint Germain

2

Your Divine Blueprint

∞

- *What is the Inner Self?*
- *Was Jesus the only master?*
- *Original sin or original bliss? Which is real?*

Mrs. Prophet, on our last program we spoke about contacting the law of the Inner Self. What is the Inner Self?

A: The Inner Self has been revealed in many forms to those who have sought it. And the forms that the Self has taken have determined the course of the world's major religions.

Gautama discovered that Self to be the Buddha. Jesus discovered that Self to be the Christ. But Moses began with the inner realization of what, for me, is the cause behind the effect—the real Source.

When God appeared to Moses out of the bush that burned but was not consumed and gave him his commission to go and speak to the people of Israel and to rescue them from Egyptian bondage, Moses asked the voice that spoke to him, "Who shall I say sent me?" And the voice of God spoke and gave the identification that has been for time immemorial the source of light to his people. God said, "Tell the children of Israel that I AM hath sent you unto them." And he gave his name as I AM THAT I AM.

This was the declaration of being, and upon that declaration of being was the mission of Moses. It was power. It was energy.

It was consciousness. It was self-awareness. And the LORD said, "And this shall be my name forevermore."

This name of God is not simply a name, but it is a word that comes out of that Word by which all things were made. When we say the name I AM THAT I AM we are confirming that the same God who spoke to Moses stands where we stand.

I think that this is the very beginning of the science of the splitting of the atom, the releasing of the energies of the nucleus of life. And it is also the beginning of the opening of the Inner Self of man and woman.

Q: Everybody says "I am" many times a day. So are you saying that they're actually naming God when they say "I am"?

A: The verb *to be* is the first statement of being, and as God is First Cause, he is Being. Some schools of metaphysics and teachings such as Unity have taught, as has Norman Vincent Peale, that what we affirm in a positive way we bring into our lives, and what we affirm negatively we also bring into our lives.

Some have evolved positive affirmations beginning with "I am": "I am well." "I am happy." "I am whole." And they have cautioned us not to say "I am sick" or "I am tired" or "I am unhealthy." And we find that these affirmations work, not only because of the power of positive thinking but because the very name I AM itself releases the energy of God.

Q: Is the element of ego involved in this? I think to many people it appears that when one says "I am," one is asserting one's ego.

A: It is the Divine Ego of us all who declares within us, "I AM." We can choose to be that I AM. We can choose to be one with that Divine Ego or we can rebel against it and say, "Well, I'm going to be what I want to be." We can affirm a separate identity from that inner I AM, and we can affirm it so long that we eventually lose contact with the inner Divine Ego and we live the life of the human ego.

Q: You have mentioned the teachings of Buddha. Where is the teaching of the I AM found in Eastern religions?

A: In the East the corollary to the I AM THAT I AM is the Om, which is spelled *Om* or *Aum*. The object of religion and of devotion in the East is to go within, to go into samadhi, to go into nirvana. And the going within to the source of energy is reflected in the way of life. For instance, in India, where religion is of major import, the outer conditions of many reflect poverty but the people have a rich inner life.

In the West the goal of contact with God is to go within and draw forth the inner flame for the mastery of the matter plane. And we find that mastery being expressed in our environment.

One of the mantras used in the East to go within is the Om. In the West, God has given us the word *Om* as I AM THAT I AM. When it is repeated as a mantra, "I AM THAT I AM, I AM THAT I AM...," it has the effect of drawing forth energy to meet every challenge of our life.

Q: Can one use it in a broader sense? Is there more that one can do with it other than simply affirming that I AM?

A: Jesus said, "I AM the way, the truth and the life" and "I AM the resurrection and the life." He actually gave many affirmations that have been recorded in scripture, and he gave many more to his disciples that were not recorded. He taught them what we call the science of the spoken Word. That science begins with God and it ends with God, and it places man* in the middle as the one who is the instrument for God becoming God.

---

*Because gender-neutral language can be cumbersome and at times confusing, we have often used *he* and *him* to refer to God or the individual. These terms are for readability only and are not intended to exclude women or the feminine aspect of the Godhead. Likewise, our use of *God* or *Spirit* does not exclude other expressions for the Divine.

Q: What is the relationship between God and his Word?

A: John says that in the beginning was the Word and without the Word was not anything made that was made. We find that the Word was made flesh in the incarnation of Jesus Christ. So the Word figures as the Second Person of the Trinity, the Christ, the Son of God. And the function of the Word is creation, the bringing forth out of the Father and out of his law the physical manifestation for us to behold. Man's lack of understanding of the Word before it is made flesh is that darkness that comprehended not the light.

With the coming of the Son of God, we discover the meaning of the Word as the Christ consciousness, as the very mind of God, of which Paul said, "Let that mind be in you which was also in Christ Jesus." This means that we can all become the incarnation of the Word. We can all attain to the level of Christ consciousness. In fact, it is our soul destiny to do so, and not only to be aware of the Self as God but to be aware of the Self as Father, as Son and as Holy Spirit—or, as the Hindus would phrase it, as Brahma, Vishnu and Shiva.

Q: I suppose it's good to say that everybody can become the Christ, but how many have succeeded? Isn't Jesus the only one?

A: I think that people have an idolatrous sense of Jesus. They worship their own concept of what Jesus was. He is seen as the perfect Master, and he was indeed the perfect Master. But he is depicted in people's minds as someone robotlike, perfected in the flesh, so far above everyone else that no matter how well people do in their daily lives they can never come close to approximating the life of Jesus Christ.

And yet the saints have told us that we must imitate Christ. *The Imitation of Christ* by Thomas à Kempis is an important Christian work because it tells us that we must try to imitate

Jesus' life. Jesus told us, "Be ye therefore perfect, even as your Father which is in heaven is perfect."

Now, many think that it is blasphemy to try to become like Christ. They believe that there was only one Son of God and that no one else can be like him because we are all sinners. It is this concept of original sin carried on and on generation after gen-

eration that makes people not even try to master the basic principles of life that Jesus taught. I believe this to be error and to be anti-Christ, and I believe that it deprives Christians, Jews, Muslims and the whole world of the very essence of the life that Jesus lived.

This essence is expressed in Jesus' statement: "He that believeth on me, the works that I do shall he do also; and greater works

Jesus Christ by Charles Sindelar

than these shall he do because I go unto my Father." This statement is the promise of the Lord Christ himself, and our assignment is to work with him and with the Father and to be an imitator of his work.

If Jesus is giving us this assignment, then he must know that God has placed within us the resources to fulfill it. What are these resources? The basic resource of life is the spark of cosmic consciousness, which is the flame in the heart—the threefold flame of love, wisdom and power. The threefold flame is our inner focal point of the Trinity.

I believe that Christianity, as well as Judaism and Islam, has been stripped of the very meat of the Word because Jesus, Muhammad, Moses and the great prophets have been made an exception to the rule rather than the rule of living for us all.

Now is the hour for the coming of our understanding of God as Mother—a Mother who takes her children by the hand and teaches them the wisdom and the law of the Father, a Mother of consolation who explains the role of the Holy Spirit as the great Comforter and the great forgiver in life.

Our understanding, then, is not of original sin but of "original bliss," as we are born of the Father-Mother God, of Alpha and Omega, the beginning and the ending. As we see our souls coming forth from the Father-Mother God, we realize that we come into the world not with the sin of Adam and Eve but with the original blueprint of our Maker. This divine blueprint endows us with the ability to become joint heirs with Christ, with Moses, with Muhammad and with Gautama Buddha.

3

The Ascended Masters

- *Who are the ascended masters?*
- *Why would someone beyond time and space come back to help us?*
- *What is a dictation?*

Mrs. Prophet, who are the ascended masters?

A: I always like to say that the ascended masters are people like you and me. In fact, they are sons and daughters of God who have realized that they are joint heirs with the Christ. When they were embodied on earth, they determined to master life, to pursue God with a passion through their sacred labor and to reunite with him at the conclusion of their sojourn on earth.

The ascended masters, then, are simply people like you and me who have reentered the consciousness of God. Now they are part of the LORD's hosts and the saints in heaven. They are the hovering presence, the living Spirit of God, that ministers unto God's children on earth.

Q: You mean they actually communicate directly with people on our plane?

A: The ascended masters have been communicating with mankind for thousands of years. When the prophets of Israel delivered their prophecies, they would begin by saying, "The Word of the LORD came unto me, saying. . . . " The LORD God they described was a personification of the Great Spirit, an individualized presence that appeared to them. There are also many descriptions in the Old and New Testaments of angelic presences who came with messages and warnings at certain crucial moments.

We find, then, that the appearance of the ascended masters is not new. But the term *ascended master* is new, and it is something we need to understand as we enter the Aquarian age. The term is actually self-explanatory: *master* is one who has the full faculties of being, who has mastered one or more areas of human endeavor. But in this sense, we are speaking of the master as a teacher and the master of life.

An ascended master is one who has ascended, or reunited, with God. He or she has accelerated consciousness, is free from the rounds of rebirth and does not continue to incarnate in flesh-and-blood form.

Now, we've all heard of masters from the East, the masters of India. We would call them unascended masters because they are teachers who have mastered the energies of life and yet they are still in embodiment.

Q: If someone has mastered time and space and transcended this plane, why should he come back and help us?

A: This is the meaning of love. All the great ones who have come to earth have come because of their great love. They could not bear to leave their brothers and sisters without an understanding of the Path. So the ascended masters are the benevolent ones, the compassionate ones who remain with this planetary home to show us the way out.

Their communication has been very real to me for most of my life. I began feeling the presence of the ascended masters in childhood and in my teenage years, and finally I saw the master

El Morya. He appeared to me when I was in college at Boston University.

El Morya (who was embodied as Saint Thomas More) came to me in answer to my prayers of many years. I had told God that I wanted to be of service in communicating his teachings to his children. El Morya told me that I must be trained to be a messenger so that I could set forth the teachings.

I began my training under Mark Prophet, whom I later married, and in time I was able to receive the dictations and teachings of the ascended masters. Mark and I have set forth these teachings in many books and publications and on audio- and video-cassettes. Essentially they provide that synthesis of the world's religions that I knew as a child I had come to deliver.

This work continues at Summit University, where we present the teachings of the ascended masters to people of all ages. It's rewarding work because it always leads the individual back to the Real Self, the Inner Self. And that is the point of beginning for our life's work and fulfillment.

Q: So are you saying that the ascended masters are communicating with you today in the same way that they once did with the prophets in the Bible?

A: This is true and, of course, I am not the only one. There are others who have heard the Word of the LORD. Joel prophesied that in the last days the LORD God would pour out his Spirit upon all flesh. He said: "Your sons and daughters shall prophesy, your old men shall dream dreams, your young men shall see visions." As that Spirit of the LORD is being poured out upon all flesh, the people of God are realizing the very personal presence of the LORD's hosts.

You see this in the charismatic movement today in the Protestant and the Catholic churches. People are waiting upon the

Word of the LORD. They are calling upon that Spirit, and many are hearing and many lives are being transformed by it.

Q: What you're saying is really amazing and fantastic, and I guess the big question is: How does somebody know that what you're saying is true?

A: There's only one way, and that is by the formula Jesus gave us. He said, "By their fruits ye shall know them." He told us there would be false Christs and false prophets. Hence, if there were to be false Christs and false prophets, we may infer that there would also be true Christs and true prophets.

We know that the coming of the Christ is the coming of the "anointed one." The word *Christ* is from the Greek *Christos,* which means "anointed." The Christ is the Son of God anointed with the Christ consciousness, or with the light of the Word—the Second Person of the Trinity.

Those who come in the spirit of prophecy come with the Holy Spirit. Some are endowed as prophets and some as Christs. Then there are those who are not a part of that dispensation but who enter into practices of black magic and witchcraft. These are the false Christs and the false prophets.

The children of God must test, or try, the spirits, as John said, to see whether they are of God. To try the spirits means to test the vibration, to test the very foundations of truth. This we must do through quiet communion and meditation and through calling upon the name of the LORD, I AM THAT I AM, to give us proof that the word we are hearing is real.

Q: Are you saying that it is possible for anyone to decide whether or not your experience is real just by listening to you?

A: Yes, because we all have God living within us, and the flame of God gives to us that consciousness whereby we can distinguish light and darkness.

Q: I wonder if you can tell us what happens during a dictation. Does the master speak through you? Is he present at the time? Does he inspire you? Or what is the nature of this experience?

A: I have been called a messenger by the masters who deliver their messages through me. The office of the messenger is something that comes by the gift of the Holy Spirit. So too is the gift of prophecy. It is a grace. It is an endowment. It is something that one achieves by walking with God until God calls one to speak to his people.

During a dictation my consciousness is accelerated, or elevated, so that it can mesh with the consciousness of the ascended master who is speaking through me. The sphere of my higher consciousness actually meshes with the sphere of consciousness of the ascended master. In that moment, there is the release of the Word. The master uses my voice as the instrument to bring forth his teaching.

Taking a dictation is a very real experience in the presence of the master. It is like being inside someone's mind. The mind of the master is cogitating through my mind and he is speaking through my mouth. However, I am not in a trance, and I am in full awareness with my full faculties of the Christ mind.

Q: Is this different, then, from what is normally referred to as a psychic involvement?

A: Yes. Psychic channeling, which often comes forth in trance, comes through the subconscious mind. The individual is not in the presence of his own Christ mind, and his body is used by discarnates, disembodied spirits, to convey messages from the departed.

Now, this may have its place for those who desire it, but where I stand as a messenger for the ascended masters it is not permitted. I would lose the gift of the messengership and of prophecy were I to engage in any form of interaction with disembodied spirits.

The ascended masters require that their disciples—and I consider myself a disciple—always be in full command of their faculties when they are in communion with God and that they retain their own reason and judgment and self-discipline.

Q: So there's no point at which your own faculties are suspended?

A: That's correct. And of course there are different methods that the great ones use to convey their concepts. Sometimes taking a dictation is like reading a ticker tape coming across Times Square. It simply is in letters of living fire that can be read and repeated. But this is only one form the masters use.

The meshing of consciousness with the master's consciousness can be compared in the Catholic tradition with the Pope's speaking *ex cathedra*. When it is said that the Pope speaks *ex cathedra* (literally, "from the throne, or chair"), it means "out of the mouth of God." It means that God is speaking through the Pope without any opportunity for the Pope to intrude his own preferences or prejudices, and therefore the word that comes forth under those conditions is accepted as absolute and infallible.

Q: When you speak during a dictation, is the message infallible?

A: I wouldn't say that it is infallible, because I think that's a dangerous conclusion to draw. But I would say that there is less opportunity for error than there would normally be in the course of my giving forth teachings.

4

Your Real Self

∞

- *What is the Chart of Your Divine Self?*
- *Who was Jesus' teacher?*
- *What were the "lost years" of Jesus and how did he learn about the Buddha?*

Mrs. Prophet, thus far we've talked about the nature of the Self, and obviously you have a concept of the Self that is quite different from that of many people. Could you explain in more detail what your concept is?

A: You know, Doug, I think that the understanding of the Self is the most important understanding that the individual can have in life. If we fail to understand the nature of the Real Self, we never really quite gain an orientation or an integration in our life.

The Self begins with that which is the permanent atom of being and the cause out of which the effect proceeds. We call this cause the I AM THAT I AM, the Presence of the I AM, or the I AM Presence.

I find that God by any name can be reduced to this sense of the eternal Presence. It defines being, and I see it as a sphere of intense light that marks the point of my origin. It is the permanent part of me, of which I am very aware, and the point to which I will return at the conclusion of this life.

I have diagrammed this Real Self in relationship to the outer evolving self on a chart that is called the Chart of Your Divine Self (facing page 24). The Chart has three parts and, in a sense, could be called the trinity of our identity. First, there is the upper figure, which is a sphere of light. Then there is the lower figure, which represents the soul evolving in Matter, or in time and space.

Between the sphere of light above and the soul evolving below is the consciousness of the Mediator, or the go-between. The go-between is that portion of the Self that can translate to the soul something of the I AM THAT I AM; it is that portion of one's being that is real enough to yet stand in the Presence of God. We call this Mediator the Christ Self, or the Real Self. It is the Self that we are in a state of becoming through our evolution, through all of our experiences in time and space.

You might say, for example, that the lower figure in the Chart would be the man Jesus. The middle figure would be the Self, the Christ. And the upper figure would be the one whom he called Father. We now see a relationship of Father, or the All-Father, the Son and the soul that is endowed with a flame of the Holy Spirit.

That flame is the spark of life. It is the threefold flame of life—a very real spiritual flame that is focused within the body at approximately the point of the heart. It is sealed in what is called the secret chamber of the heart. This threefold flame endows our being with consciousness, with self-awareness, with all of the faculties that we enjoy that are above the animal kingdom. It is the sacred fire that we are to become and that we are to implement and use as our resource for living and for evolving while we are on earth.

The three figures in the Chart, which are now separate because of our limited consciousness, will one day become one. We see this in the life of Jesus. As he matures from birth to manhood, he walks more and more in the stature of his Real Self, his Christ Self. We find him in the temple discoursing with the doctors at the age of twelve. This is a sign that the Christ Presence, or the Christ Self, is overshadowing him and he is speaking the word of that Christ.

We find him at the age of thirty in the full presence of the Christ so that his disciples recognize him as their master. He calls them away from their nets to become fishers of men. He changes the water into wine, begins to heal, to cast out demons—all this because the man Jesus has merged with the Inner Self, the Christ. He walks the earth for three years performing not miracles but the functions of cosmic law. And then walking up Bethany's hill with his disciples after his resurrection, he disappears from their midst and the cloud receives him out of their sight.

This cloud is the same cloud that appeared to the children of Israel. The pillar of fire and the cloud represent the I AM THAT I AM, the eternal Presence. Jesus accelerated to the level of the Christ; then Jesus, the Christ, accelerated to the level of the I AM THAT I AM. This is the nature, the true nature, of the Three-in-One. And we as heirs of Christ, heirs of Jesus, have come to realize that same oneness—three out of one, one out of three.

Q: **In other words, the Trinity is something that is present in all of us all the time?**

A: The Trinity is anchored in us in this threefold flame of power, wisdom and love. The Father represents the power of the Law, the Son is the wisdom of the Law, and the Holy Spirit is the love-action of the Law. So the Trinity exists in us as potential. Until we realize that potential, our relationship to Christ and to Father remains a separate one. And therefore, on the Chart we depict these three figures—one on earth, one higher above, and one still higher. This distance allows individuals to think in terms of heaven and earth.

Q: Where does an ascended master fall on this Chart?

A: The ascended master is one who has walked as the lower figure in the Chart; he has evolved as a soul who has first realized his Real Self as the Christ (the middle figure), become anointed with that Mediator-Self, and then reunited with the I AM THAT I AM (the upper figure) at the conclusion of his life. Therefore, the ascended master would be beyond the material plane, in the Spirit plane and yet as close as the air we breathe.

Q: When Jesus prayed to the Father, he was actually talking to himself, his Real Self?

A: He was talking to his I AM Presence and he was also talking to his inner teacher. Jesus had a teacher. It is customary for us to think of our inner teacher, or our inner guru, as Father.

The teacher whom Jesus acknowledged on the Path as being one with his I AM Presence was one who is called Lord Maitreya, or Maitreya, the Coming Buddha of the East. Maitreya attained the Christ consciousness many centuries prior to the final incarnation of Jesus. He sponsored Jesus and was the one (in addition to Jesus' own I AM Presence) whom Jesus called Father.

Q: Jesus' life and teachings were in the Middle East. How was it that he was initiated in the teachings of the Far East?

A: The Gospels do not tell us where Jesus was between the ages of twelve and thirty. This was a long period of time for our beloved master, considering what he accomplished in the three short years of his Galilean mission.

Ancient Buddhist manuscripts say that during these seventeen years Jesus traveled to India, Nepal, Ladakh and Tibet, where he was known as Saint Issa. If we could have known Jesus between the ages of twelve and thirty, we would have found him in the Far East studying, practicing and teaching the laws of science and truth that he demonstrated publicly in the final hours of his Galilean mission.

Even when we journeyed to India, we were told by a number of guides that there are records saying that Jesus was there. We also know from our verification by the ascended masters that Jesus was humble and that in preparation for his mission he desired to be trained in the very first steps of initiation.

Many of the teachings that Jesus brought forth—in fact, his mantra "I AM the way, the truth and the life"—are actually taken from the Sanskrit, which comes down to us through India from the ancient continent of Lemuria. It was the language that our early ancestors used to meditate upon God and to practice the science of the spoken Word.

Q: So the Chart of Your Divine Self, in which the Christ that we're familiar with is identified as the middle figure, relates to the teachings of the East. Where would Buddha fall on that same Chart?

A: Buddha, as Siddhartha, the child who was born a prince into wealth and the surroundings of opportunity, becomes the soul who must mature and discover the Real Self. Prince Siddhartha left home to find the cause of suffering but also discovered the Real Self, which he defined as the Buddha.

This is because his meditation was upon God through the crown chakra. We call one who has attained the realization of God through the crown chakra the Buddha, whereas we call one who has realized God through the heart chakra the Christ. In reality, the Christ Self, or the Real Self, contains all elements of consciousness.

Q: What is the crown chakra?

A: *Chakra* is a Sanskrit word. It means "wheel," or "center," and refers to the sacred centers in our temple. The heart is the principal center. Above the heart chakra are the throat, third-eye and crown chakras. Below the heart are the solar plexus, seat-of-the-soul and base-of-the-spine chakras. These seven major centers are seven openings into another dimension, and by meditation upon these centers we can experience God in different planes of consciousness.

Each center, which is depicted as having a different number of petals, has a different frequency or vibration. If we center our meditation in the heart, we commune with love. If we center our meditation in the crown, we are communing in wisdom. If our meditation centers in the third eye, we have the power of concentration in truth. And the throat chakra, the power center, gives us the power to create through the science of the spoken Word.

Q: This seems to imply that Buddha represented a higher evolution than Jesus. Is that true?

A: I don't know that we would call it higher. We would call it the way of the East. Buddha demonstrated the way of self-mastery that was the dispensation for the evolutions of the East. Christ showed it for the evolutions of the West. We've reached a period now where there's an exchange between East and West, and we who live in the West must also pursue the type of mastery that Buddha demonstrated.

The Chart of Your Divine Self

5

The Violet Flame

- *How does the soul become the Christ?*
- *What is the violet flame?*
- *How is the violet flame related to the Holy Spirit?*

Mrs. Prophet, we've talked about the evolving soul and what the soul is destined for in terms of the Christ, but I think the question that's really important is, how does the soul become the Christ?

A: People have tried to get to God by many means. They have followed the path of yoga. They have followed the path of asceticism. And we hear the question: "Canst thou by searching find out God?"

We find that we really do not have the faculties to experience God within our limited consciousness. As Paul says, "Flesh and blood cannot inherit the kingdom of God." Esoterically, the term *kingdom* means "consciousness." So we have to find the point within ourselves that becomes the point of contact with the Real.

In other words, if God had not placed a portion of himself, a portion of the Word, within us to incarnate with us, we would not have an opening to find him. The opening always begins with the flame of the Spirit that is in our heart. We cannot find God by the intellect. We cannot find God by the emotions. We cannot find God by physical austerities, nor can we find him through the subconscious plane. Having exhausted these possibilities, we have to find God through God.

Well, what is the essential nature of God? As recorded in the Book of Deuteronomy, Moses said to the children of Israel: "The LORD thy God is a consuming fire." We see references to God as a fire throughout the Old and New Testaments.

John the Baptist said: "One cometh after me, the latchet of whose shoes I am not worthy to unloose. He will baptize you with the Holy Ghost and with fire." It is this baptism of the sacred fire that we seek, and we always begin seeking it within.

When we meditate upon the sacred fire in the heart, we soon discover that this pulsating light that comes clearly to our consciousness accelerates to a vibration that reads as the color violet—hence, the term *violet flame.* The violet flame has been seen by seers, by mystics and by saints. It is the flame of the Holy Spirit and it is also the flame that is revealed in the Aquarian age. It is the seventh-ray aspect of the Holy Spirit. The time for mankind's realization and application of this flame has come. And the Ascended Master Saint Germain is the one who sponsors its release.

How does your soul get to God? By your invocation of this flame, by your meditation upon the flame, by bathing your consciousness in the flame until you experience that transmutation, that change of energy and consciousness that was so often promised by the Hebrew prophets—the promise of forgiveness, the promise that "though your sins be as scarlet, they shall be white as snow."

The promise of the forgiveness of the Holy Spirit is our only way out of the state of nonalignment, which the Buddha referred to as *dukkha,* or suffering. He taught us that all life is suffering. In other words, when we are out of alignment with the inner law of being, we suffer. That suffering is our sense of sin. We get back into alignment by the power of God to erase sin. Whence comes this power?

The Hindus call the Holy Spirit the Destroyer, Shiva—the

one who breaks down the misqualified energies or the misuses of life that we have brought forth by our misuse of free will. For example, hatred is a misuse of free will. We have free will to qualify God's energy as love or as hatred. If we have qualified it as hatred, that energy rests with us. It remains with us as part of our consciousness until we transmute it by love. The power of the Holy Spirit to transmute hatred into love manifests by this dispensation of the violet flame.

How do we invoke the violet flame? Well, we can give a simple mantra where we affirm the name of God, I AM, and then declare that that I AM is the violet flame right where we are. This is a mantra that I like to give to increase the manifestation of the violet flame in my aura:

> I AM a being of violet fire!
> I AM the purity God desires!

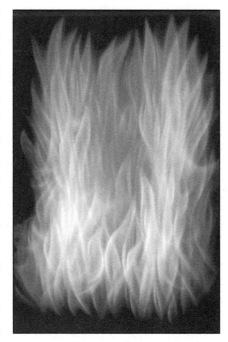

This little mantra becomes a meditation and a visualization that is anchored in the physical temple by the spoken Word. Giving word to our thoughts and our feelings through the throat chakra is the means whereby we gain a new dimension from our prayers, from our mental affirmations, because it is through the throat chakra that we bring into the physical form that which is in the mind and that which is in the heart.

This is why when people begin to give these mantras they experience an immediate acceleration of consciousness. The violet flame, then, is the first step on the path of initiation with the ascended masters, the first step to the point of the soul's return to the Spirit, or to the I AM Presence.

It is interesting to note that the first miracle Jesus wrought was at the marriage feast in Cana of Galilee, where he turned the water into wine. This symbolizes the turning of the water of the human consciousness into the wine of the Spirit. Interestingly, wine itself is a purple or violet color. And this is a clue to those of you who are mystics that Jesus was using the seventh-ray aspect of the Holy Spirit.

When Shakespeare wrote in *The Merchant of Venice:* "The quality of mercy is not strained; / It droppeth as the gentle rain from heaven / Upon the place beneath. It is twice blest; / It blesseth him that gives and him that takes," he was expressing through Portia a key to the alchemy of the seventh age.

The qualities of mercy and forgiveness are the very power of alchemy that is in the violet flame. Mercy is like a cosmic eraser. When we invoke the flame of mercy as the Holy Spirit, it actually erases the cause, effect and memory of sin in our lives. To the Eastern mind, this would be the balancing of karma.

What is karma? Karma is simply cause-effect sequences that we have set up by free will. Jesus taught the apostle Paul: Whatsoever a man soweth, that shall he also reap.

Q: If the violet flame is such a crucial part of the mystic's tradition and experience, why haven't we heard about it before? It seems to me that the Bible makes no reference to it, nor do any other scriptures that I'm familiar with.

A: We remember the words of Paul concerning "unspeakable words which it is not lawful for a man to utter." Over the centuries Jesus Christ, Gautama Buddha and many spiritual teachers have taken certain disciples aside to teach them the inner mysteries. Until this century it was not lawful for those disciples to utter their understanding of the violet flame because, in general, the open use of the violet flame on earth was not allowed.

This was because of mankind's misuse of the law of forgiveness. Man's propensity to petition God for forgiveness and then to go out and repeat the same sin showed that he was still a child and not mature enough to understand that the energy of God is precious and that if God gives his forgiveness, we must go and sin no more.

Q: What's changed in the last hundred years?

A: Every hundred years the LORD God increases his consciousness, his cosmos within us and within the evolutions of earth. We see progress in the field of science, in civilization, in the social order. We are finding that there is also progress in religion. And therefore, we believe in progressive revelation because our God is a God who is continually transcending himself.

This is the nature of a transcendent God. His law remains the same yesterday, today and forever but our awareness of God constantly transcends itself. This is why we need to keep an open heart for God to speak to us. And so in this age, as we enter the age of Aquarius, the dispensation is this gift of the Holy Spirit.

You'll notice that this is reflected in the world's religions. Never has there been such a surge of devotion to the Holy Spirit as there has been in this century, or even in the last two thousand years. It is because the Holy Spirit is the sacred-fire action that culminates in the individual revelation of the violet flame. It is time for the Holy Spirit. It is time for the Comforter. It is time for the violet flame.

Q: You're saying, then, that the violet flame is the key to the unfolding of the New Age?

A: The violet flame is actually the flame of freedom. And unless mankind make use of this flame, they will find themselves so burdened by their own momentum of sin that they will see the increase of mental disease, emotional disease and physical disease in fulfillment of Jesus' prophecy for the end of the age, described in the twenty-fourth chapter of Matthew.

The end of the age he was speaking of was the age of Pisces, the two-thousand-year period of his dispensation. We are in the final hours of that age, and we see how wars and rumors of war and pestilence and famine are upon the earth. It is the violet flame, when invoked by Christians, Jews, Muslims, that will result in the balancing of these energies so that we will not have to pass through a period of intense cataclysm but can make the transition into the new dispensation, the New Age, without the loss of life and limb as the price.

Q: To what extent would the violet flame have to be invoked before it could actually influence what's happening in one's life or what's happening in one's world?

A: Beloved El Morya gave to us the "Heart, Head and Hand Decrees" for the invocation of the violet flame.* These decrees take only ten minutes a day to give. They are mantras. They are fiats. They are meditations. All an individual has to do is to begin to decree just ten minutes a day and he will realize the transformation of his life, so powerful is the Holy Spirit.

---

*See chapter 8.

6

God as Mother

∞

- *What is meant by the Motherhood of God?*
- *What is the role of the divine Feminine?*
- *What is the key to harmony and wholeness in the family?*

Mrs. Prophet, would you tell us what you mean when you talk about God as Mother?

A: Ever since I can remember, I had a feeling that God was both my father and my mother. From the time I was a little child, I had the sense of being comfortable in the arms of this Father-Mother God. As I grew older, I began to study the religions of the East and to realize that for centuries the Hindus have spoken of the World Mother. I remember the first day I heard the term *World Mother.* I had a sense that our earth was enfolded by a presence that could be described as Mother, as a world consciousness and as a world energy.

Since I was not raised Catholic, I did not have the understanding of the devotion to Mary and so I sought this in later years. And I saw clearly that Mary, as the Mother of Jesus, had realized something very special about God as Mother. And I thought she must have had a unique attunement with God as Mother because her concept of Mother enabled her to bring forth the Christ. One day I was looking at her name and it was no longer "Mary," but it just popped out to me as "Ma-ray"—the ray of the Mother.

I saw Mary as the instrument of God as Mother and I began to meditate on that Mother energy. I came to realize that the Mother energy is really a flame. The Hindus call it the Kundalini, or the Goddess Kundalini, which they define as the energy that is locked at the base-of-the-spine chakra. They view it as a feminine principle, a feminine energy. I began to wonder how this energy could be unlocked, and I thought to myself that this energy truly must be in polarity with God as Father.

I remembered hearing the concept of Mary as the bride of the Holy Spirit. Then I thought of the Trinity of Father, Son and Holy Spirit, and I realized that Mother is the aspect of God that unlocks the energies of Father and that the reverse is also true—that the presence of Father would release in us the energy of Mother.

So it came to me that if I would meditate upon God as the masculine principle, that masculine principle intensifying in my life would magnetize the feminine, and that if I would meditate upon the feminine, the presence of the feminine principle would magnify the masculine.

I began to meditate upon the concept of the Tao and on the concept of the T'ai Chi—of all things being in the circle of energy of the plus and the minus, the Alpha, the Omega. I saw this energy as God present within us all. The more I would meditate upon this energy, the more I would feel the wholeness of the presence of the Father-Mother God.

As I studied the world's religions, I realized that mankind have been given the teachings of God in stages, in cycles. For two thousand years we have been given an understanding of God as the Son, and we have come to understand God through the person of Jesus. Prior to that, Moses revealed God as Father, as the Lawgiver, as the very personal representative of the Law.

And in this two-thousand-year period that is beginning, we are finding a tremendous awakening to the energies of the Holy Spirit. People are calling upon the name of the LORD and they are asking God to infill them with that Holy Spirit. This presents a rounding out of the Trinity realized in the consciousness of mankind over several thousand years.

Meantime in the East, the meditation upon that Trinity has been on Brahma, Vishnu and Shiva through many different incarnations of God, all of this bringing us to the climax of realization in the Aquarian age—which is destined to be the age of the rise of the feminine principle—of God as Mother. We see this reflected in social movements and in social upheaval. We see women demanding rights. We see the feminist movement. We see women all over the world coming into their own after thousands of years of not realizing their true identity in a world dominated by the masculine ray.

I came to realize that our devotion to God as Mother will create the balance in the individual and in our civilization that is necessary for the alchemy of self-transformation. Through all of this wondering and this meditating on God and this discovering, I decided that my calling must be to expand the flame of God as Mother so that everyone on earth could do the same, so that woman could realize her role and so that man could realize his role in the perfect balance of the divine union.

Q: **What role does the Mother play in man? I've heard you talk about the divine Feminine. What do you mean by that?**

A: That's an important question. All of us have within us that point of divinity that is the threefold flame in the heart. We know that the threefold flame is the point of realization of the

masculine elements of the Trinity—Father, Son and Holy Spirit.
Now, all of us also have a feminine point of contact, and that
point of contact is the soul, the soul potential of being.

What is the soul? The soul is that substance of identity that
has come forth out of Spirit, or out of the I AM THAT I AM.
The soul, then, is the negative polarity, and Spirit is the positive
polarity of God. The soul is our opportunity to realize God.
However, we read in Ezekiel, "The soul that sinneth, it shall
die." Yet the *Bhagavad-Gita* says, "Never the Spirit was born, the
Spirit shall cease to be never."

The permanent atom of being is Spirit. And the nonpermanent
atom of self, the soul, can become permanent by reuniting with that
Self that is Spirit. So the soul is our consciousness here on earth,
evolving in time and space. The soul in man and woman represents
the feminine principle. And the Spirit, or the I AM Presence,
which we've been talking about, is always the masculine principle.

Q: So everybody is both masculine and feminine at the same time?

A: We are all masculine and feminine in potential. And whether we
are male or female in this incarnation, the goal of life is to balance
these forces. And when we balance these forces within ourselves,
we are able to become one with the cosmos, one with the whole.

Q: It sounds like you're talking about a "holy family." Is it possible
to have a holy family right within oneself?

A: Well, when you put the masculine and feminine forces together, when you have the balance of the Spirit of the living God
and the soul in union with that Spirit, the fruit of the union is the
birth of the Christ consciousness.

Q: Today there seems to be a great deal of attack on the family. How
would you explain that in light of what you've just talked about?

A: It's interesting to think about this in relation to Alpha and Omega, the beginning and the ending. *Alpha and Omega* is simply a synonymous term for the Father-Mother God, the masculine-feminine polarity of the cosmos.

We find that this whole is the source of harmony, joy, bliss, cosmic consciousness and happiness. Whenever we are outside of this whole, we find depression, degeneration, darkness, death, disease. Wholeness is the key to the joy of life. And the resolution of this wholeness becomes the quest of the soul.

We seek that wholeness in the perfect union with someone outside of ourselves with whom we can share our life. The inner wholeness is designed to be reflected in the outer manifestation of the love that we find on earth between man and woman.

So marriage of man and woman is intended to bear, as the fruit of that union, the Christ consciousness in the offspring. The Holy Family, as illustrated by Jesus, Mary and Joseph, is the manifestation of the Trinity and the Mother, and the various members of the family play these roles.

Family life, then, is the foundation not only of the Piscean age but of the Aquarian age. And the destruction of the family is the attack against the twin flames of Gemini, against the wholeness of the Father-Mother God. If this forcefield of our consciousness can be destroyed, if we allow the destructive forces of our civilization to destroy this trust and this tryst, we will be bereft of life's most glorious interchange—the going in and coming out of the Presence of the LORD through daily communion with the Inner Self and with our loved ones.

And so we need to guard the family, and we need to realize that the family becomes a crucible for the testing of our souls on the path of initiation.

Q: Does this mean that one can't find wholeness outside of the family?

A: No, it means that one may choose to find wholeness within oneself through the polarity of Alpha and Omega that God has placed within one's being, or one may choose to find that wholeness in the love experience of man and woman sharing the same goal of creation in life.

Q: Mrs. Prophet, how would you relate these matters to the dilemma of young people today in deciding how to live their lives in regard to love and family, and so forth?

A: I think everyone needs to realize that God, in addition to creating the soul and the Spirit as points of identity, has given to each one of us a twin flame, a counterpart. Twin flames have been in existence ever since the beginning, and so this divine polarity is always present. Every one of us can know that somewhere in the cosmos is the other half of our whole, which represents uniquely the Father-Mother God.

All life, then, is a series of initiations whereby we are walking the Path with Christ and Buddha to return to the wholeness that we share with someone, somewhere—our twin flame. In the interim, while we balance our karma and move in the cycles of life, we may marry, we may have relationships that are beautiful and fulfilling but are not the ultimate relationship. Thus, God has ordained marriage as the matrix for working out this polarity of being.

I would tell young people that it is important to realize that the bringing forth of the Christ consciousness, whether in children or in a creative work, in a career or in something that becomes the dedication of one's life, is the purpose of this energy that we are given, this creative life force—this most sacred fire.

7

Sexuality and Spirituality

∞

- *What is the truth about twin flames and soul mates?*
- *What is the real meaning of sex?*
- *Ultimate bliss—how do you get there?*

Mrs. Prophet, what about soul mates and twin flames?

A: Twin flames are the opposite polarities of the same being. People in love often find that they feel in their oneness that they

are part of each other. And this is the energy of love that comes from God, as God really is the source of love in our relationships.

Twin flames were created by God in the beginning out of the same white-fire sphere of consciousness. Each half of the whole has the same electronic pattern, or blueprint, and that blueprint is not duplicated anywhere in cosmos. Twin flames may often look alike and yet they are often opposite in their manifestations, as they are intended to be the totality of the Father-Mother God in expression.

Soul mates are complementary souls who are working out a polarity of manifestation in one of the planes of consciousness. Their tie is for a particular mastery in time and space, whereas the ultimate union with one's twin flame is for eternity.

The energies that twin flames share are the energies of God, and when these energies are consecrated to the glorification of the Real Self and of Reality, we find that joy and bliss and expansion of consciousness and creativity follow them wherever they go.

Q: How likely is it that a person will find his soul mate or twin flame?

A: It is often very likely. People incarnate and they travel halfway round the world to find that twin flame or they may find him or her living next door. And it is because there is an inner magnet, an inner lodestone, that draws one to one's True Self, one's Inner Self, and to its representative in form. Longfellow's story of Evangeline is the story of the love of twin flames.

Q: There is a lot of discussion about sexual matters these days, and we hear a lot of talk about it being absolutely essential to be free in what one does. How do you feel about that?

A: I look at the word *sex* as an abbreviated term for "sacred energy," or "sacral energy." Sex is the sacred energy of life. And the origin of that energy is in the base-of-the-spine chakra, the focus of the Mother light.

I don't deal with sex as being right or wrong but I deal with God as energy. I understand that the individual has free will, which is the gift from God to determine what he will do with that energy. He has the option to meditate upon the Trinity within the heart

and the magnet of light within the heart to raise the
energy of the sacred fire from the base-of-the-spine
chakra to the upper chakras.

With the raising of the sacred fire, or Kundalini, comes an experience in each succeeding chakra
—in the base of the spine, then the seat of the soul,
the solar plexus, the heart, the throat, the third eye
and the crown. These centers are sacred centers for
God-awareness.

The polarity of the centers is masculine. When
we raise the Mother light, or the feminine energy,
from the base of the spine, there is the fulfillment of
wholeness in each succeeding chakra and we experience the bliss of attunement with the Father-
Mother God and of wholeness.

Sex, then, is much more than a simple experience between man and woman. It is an intimate
experience with God. The individual has been
given a gift of energy; it is a portion of the Godhead. And a portion of that energy is anchored in
each of the chakras.

We have the free will to decide what we will do with this
energy. Many people have seen how easy it is through meditation
and the giving of mantras to raise the sacred fire and to begin to
have deep inner experiences in the mysteries of God.

Alternatively, the use of the sacred fire in sex has its highest
culmination in the bringing forth of children within the circle
of a marriage dedicated to God. When it is not for the purpose
of bringing forth children, it is for the purpose of the balance of
energies between man and woman in the married state.

That balance of energy may also be achieved by the raising of
the energies up the spine and their consecration in each of the

chakras until finally there is the opening of the thousand-petaled lotus through the crown chakra. The bliss of this experience cannot be described and it cannot be compared to any earthly bliss. It is beyond what anyone could even imagine he could experience in this life.

The bliss of that union of the Father-Mother God far outweighs that of any other union. And yet until man and woman have tasted of that fruit, many, of course, prefer the sexual experience.

Q: Are you saying, then, that enlightenment is related to inner wholeness?

A: I would say enlightenment is related to the raising of the energies of the Mother to become one with the Father within the self. Enlightenment comes through contact with God.

Q: Mrs. Prophet, we've talked about the proper use of sexual energies. What about the misuse of sexual energies?

A: The misuse of sexual energies comes about in the overindulgence in sex and its perversions, which, as we are aware, are rampant on earth today. The normal flow of the sexual energies between man and woman united and blessed by their own inner God Presence is certainly ordained by the LORD.

We find that the misuse of sex (and therefore the dissipation of the sacred fire) and its proliferation in promiscuity contributes to untimely diseases, degeneration and disintegration. It also cuts off the natural attunement of the soul with the I AM Presence because the soul requires this sacred fire in order to rise to that higher level of consciousness, which is the union with the Godhead.

We find that people who are overly sensual by nature are very much involved in the things of this world and they deprive themselves of the inner bliss of the heaven-world that is within all of us. The misuse of sex, then, may be at the core of old age, disease and ultimately death. Michelangelo was asked why the face of Mary in the *Pietà* was so young. His reply was that the virtuous woman is always young.

But it is not a matter of sin and virtue. It is not a matter of right and wrong. It is a matter of the conservation of the life force. When you conserve the life force, you have a greater quantity of God manifesting within the temple of your being. And so I think that when individuals by free will misuse sex through overindulgence, they are depriving themselves of cosmic consciousness. This is the great loss, not because of sin or the sense of sin but because this misuse of the sexual experience has become a wedge between the self and the Godhead.

Q: The thrust of so much of what you see in the media and read in books and literature these days seems to be directed toward persuading people to misuse their sexual energies. Why do you think this is happening?

A: I would say that the attempt to keep people in an eternal round of involvement in the things of this world is calculated to deprogram the soul from its natural inclination to rise. It is the soul's natural inclination to seek the inner union with the God Self. The soul yearns for this fulfillment.

Out of a sense of loneliness and because people do not have the Path presented to them, they satiate themselves in the activities of this life to the exclusion of seeking a spiritual path. And they keep themselves going twenty-four hours a day because if everything stopped, they would be left with that gnawing feeling, that loneliness felt by the soul who has not been satisfied through the bliss experience that should be the daily experience of one's meditation.

Q: So you're recommending meditation as an alternative?

A: Yes. I have given courses in meditation and in the use of the science of the spoken Word where I have seen young people and people of all ages raise the energies of the sacred fire naturally into higher chakras. And I have seen the blossoming of life. I have seen joy and health and radiant faces and soul fulfillment that the world could not conceive of. This could be achieved with the mastery of this energy.

Q: In light of what you have said, Mrs. Prophet, what's your advice to young people?

A: I would emphasize the fact that we have all been given this tremendous gift from God that is free will. The second tremendous gift we have been given is the use of God's energy. All energy that we use in thought, in feeling, words and actions and even in our sexual experience belongs to God.

What we have to realize is that we have only so much energy that we have been given and we must decide what we are to use it on. This energy is reflected in the quantity of time and space that is available to us each day. We all experience limitations in what we can accomplish. Multiply this over a lifetime and you see that there is not an infinite portion but a finite portion of energy that is allotted to us.

I would tell young people, then: The sacred fire within you is your creative life force. You can put it to use for the elevation of the entire earth or you can squander it on the immediate indulgences of the senses. Sex in the right context and in balance is a normal part of life on earth. But when it is not in balance it is detrimental and can ultimately lead to the death of the soul consciousness.

I would encourage young people to take up the study of meditation, to study the science of the spoken Word, to experience these sacred energies in all of the chakras and not just in the base of the spine. This is altogether possible and you can begin today. And the experiences that you can have, beginning right now, are phenomenal! There is a world of light and joy waiting for the individual who will just try to enter into meditation and the use of scientific mantras.

Q: How can we learn about meditation and mantras?

A: We've written a number of books and pamphlets that include teaching on the subject, and we have excellent taped meditations. It helps to come in contact with those who are currently demonstrating this science. So I encourage young people to come to our Summit University seminars and retreats, where we practice these meditations and mantras.*

We'd like to invite young people and people of all ages to visit us, to call us up, and just for a moment to consider an alternative way of life, which has actually been lived for thousands of years in previous cultures on earth.

---

*For more information on publications and Summit University seminars, retreats and Internet broadcasts, visit www.tsl.org. Also see pages 366–67 for further information.

8

Energy Is God

∞

- *How do we master our sacred energies?*
- *What does the spoken Word have to do with alchemy?*
- *How can we use the ritual of the heart, head and hand to resolve patterns of consciousness?*

Mrs. Prophet, you've talked a great deal about raising our sacred energies. So now, tell us how.

A: You know, all of life is energy, and I have come to the conclusion that energy is God and God is energy. Everything is made of energy. Everything is made of atomic particles, molecules. And at the core of this energy is Alpha and Omega, the Father-Mother light, the energy that is the source of life on earth.

What to do with this energy has become the great topic of discussion in America in recent years. We have heard talk about an energy crisis and conservation of energy. Well, the great crisis and the great need for conservation is right within the temple of the being of man. And when we master that energy, we will master it in our environment as well.

The way to begin to control this energy is through the discipline of the mind and the discipline of the feelings. Many people in America and on earth today have made some strides along these lines. But the energy of each of the chakras, each of the

levels of consciousness that God has given us to experience, requires a unique mastery.

One of the most important centers that we have is the throat
chakra. It gives us the power to speak and it gives us the power to
release the energy of the Word, or Logos. This gift is unique to
man. And we remember that Jesus said, "By thy words thou
shalt be justified, by thy words thou shalt be condemned." The
Word is energy. Hindus have known this for thousands of years,
hence the Sanskrit mantras that are given by the gurus of India
to their disciples.

Throat chakra

There are also mantras that have been given to us by the ascended masters. And these mantras, which are worded formulas
for the release of God's energy, lead to the raising of consciousness.

The Ascended Master El Morya, Chief of the Darjeeling
Council of the Great White Brotherhood, has dictated a series of
mantras that he has called the "Heart, Head and Hand Decrees."
These decrees represent the steps, or stages, in the disciplines of
the life of Jesus Christ. They begin with the meditation upon the

heart and drawing through the heart the energy that is the violet flame.

The violet flame is the energy of the Holy Spirit, of the sacred fire, for transmutation and forgiveness. It is the gift of the Comforter to us in this century. The violet flame, then, becomes the mercy of forgiveness; and forgiveness is the first step to centering in the heart.

I would like to give this simple mantra of the violet flame. As soon as I begin to give it, my attention is on the heart and I use the power of visualization to see, or to visualize, in my heart this flame of sacred fire of the Holy Spirit. As I am giving through my throat chakra the words of the mantra, I am meditating upon my heart for the release of that energy through the heart center. This is the way it goes:

> Violet fire, thou love divine,
> Blaze within this heart of mine!
> Thou art mercy forever true,
> Keep me always in tune with you.

Those four lines in rhyme represent an alchemical formula just like the matrix of a molecule, the atomic matrix of energy. The visualization is for the drawing forth of the light of the I AM Presence and the anchoring of that light in the heart.

As I give this mantra, I am aware that it is not me giving it but God in me. God in me is the mantra, the energy of the mantra, the voice of the mantra and the person of the mantra. I am simply allowing the free flow of my soul to move with that energy. This mantra can be given once, three times or a hundred times as one goes deeper and deeper into meditation and visualization.

The science of the spoken Word activates the fruit of our meditation upon God and coalesces it in the physical plane. The mantra begins the alchemical change. (Alchemy is a method or power of transmutation, of transformation.) And so as we use the science of the spoken Word, we notice immediate physical changes in our lives, physical changes in our bodies for health, changes in our minds for enlightenment and also in the circumstances of our jobs, our homes, our marriages, our families and our children.

We move from the heart to the head because we are seeking a balance of heart, head and hand in this series of mantras as a balance of the action of the Trinity. So this is the mantra for the head:

> I AM light, thou Christ in me,
> Set my mind forever free;
> Violet fire, forever shine
> Deep within this mind of mine.
>
> God who gives my daily bread,
> With violet fire fill my head
> Till thy radiance heavenlike
> Makes my mind a mind of light.

Now comes the mantra for the hand:

> I AM the hand of God in action,
> Gaining victory every day;
> My pure soul's great satisfaction
> Is to walk the Middle Way.

As we give these mantras, we visualize the violet flame blazing through the heart and the chakras of the head and being released through the hand in action. "Heart, Head and Hand" is a ritual of flow of energy. These mantras will quiet the emotions, they will integrate mind, body and soul, and they are for the fulfillment of the self. They free the energies of life. And the energies that are anchored for this purpose are drawn both from the I AM Presence of life and from the base-of-the-spine chakra.

In the giving of these mantras, there is a clearing of records of centuries of incarnations. There is the clearing of the subconscious mind of those difficulties and problems that everyone has experienced that cause the problems of psychosis and neurosis and all of the diseases to which the race is heir. When these mantras are given, they resolve patterns of consciousness. They develop a flow, an awareness and an attunement with the Inner Self that makes for creativity and a feeling of being alive and well and in action for good on earth.

Q: I suppose the most unusual thing about these mantras is that they are in English. Aren't most people used to hearing mantras in Sanskrit?

A: The ascended masters who have come forward to give the teachings of God in this age have explained that it is important that people understand the meaning of the mantra. English is a peculiar language. It has gone through many histories.

English comes down through the ancient tongues of Atlantis and has a particular vibration and an affinity, believe it or not, to a certain angelic tongue. And therefore there is a special energy for this age that actually comes through the English language. I think this is the real reason for English traveling around the world through the discoveries and explorations of the British Empire. The name of God, I AM THAT I AM, has a vibration and a frequency in English that it does not have in any other Western language.

I recently read a study that indicated that Gaelic and Irish are similar to Hebrew and that the Hebrew patterns were actually transferred by the tribes of Israel as they dispersed throughout the earth. Prior to the Hebrew tongue, there were the tongues that were spoken on Atlantis, and prior to that the languages that were spoken by the early root races on Lemuria. Sanskrit comes down from the early Lemurian tongue.

Q: So it's possible for people who can't speak Sanskrit to benefit from these decrees, I gather?

A: Not only possible, not only probable, but it's happening every day with thousands of students of the ascended masters all over the world!

Q: Would you recommend a particular program of using these decrees?

A: I would say that this science is so dynamic that no one living today should dare bypass the opportunity to experiment with the energy of his own Inner Self through the science of the spoken Word. Because of this, I've published a paperback book on the subject. It's entitled *The Science of the Spoken Word,* and it has in it these "Heart, Head and Hand Decrees" by the beloved Ascended Master El Morya. These decrees can be given in ten minutes. (See pages 366–67 for additional books, tapes and CDs on the science of the spoken Word.)

I have challenged many people who have had problems in life to just take ten minutes a day and give these decrees. And they have transformed their lives by doing this!

It's an amazing thing to think what ten minutes in a twenty-four-hour day, using a certain science of the throat chakra and of the heart and of visualization, can do to put one in tune with one's inner blueprint, the cellular pattern, the frequency of one's own atomic rate, the inner Spirit, this inner Presence. It really is the foundation of life.

9

Commanding God

∞

- *Is it possible to command God?*
- *What is the purpose of ritual?*
- *What do we do when we have a problem forgiving someone?*

Mrs. Prophet, we've been talking about the uses of energy and you've been instructing us on a number of techniques. It's such a fascinating subject. Let's just go a little further into it.

A: My first advice to someone who would begin to use God's energy in a scientific way is that you need to establish a forcefield of protection around your aura and around your chakras because you will now be qualifying the energy of life within you in a different manner than most of the people on earth today.

In addition, our bodies and our minds are constantly subject to all types of energies—energies from earth, radio waves, television waves and rays from the sun. We are all influenced by the mass consciousness, by thoughts and feelings of people near and far. And we have to realize that through the media, through everything that we have eye contact with, from the daily newspapers to the billboards, there is an impression made upon consciousness; and this, too, is the qualification of energy.

If we are going to take dominion within the microcosm of the self, we need to establish a forcefield that is going to protect the new consciousness, the cosmic consciousness that we are in pursuit of and that we desire to experience every day.

There is an energy of white light that we can draw forth from the I AM THAT I AM within us, from this great I AM Presence. This white light of energy is called the tube of light. To visualize this tube of light, you can see yourself standing in a giant glass milk bottle filled with milk.

The top of the milk bottle, as it narrows, is going toward the source of energy, which is the I AM Presence. The energy comes into that giant milk bottle over the crystal cord, which looks like a straw going from the milk bottle straight up to an energy field that is a high concentration of light. (See Chart facing page 24.)

So the invocation of the tube of light is a way of setting your forcefield for meditation, for the science of the spoken Word or just for your daily activities. The "Tube of Light" is the next decree in El Morya's "Heart, Head and Hand Decrees." I would like to give it now. People need to get used to actually vocalizing their mantras and meditations:

> Beloved I AM Presence bright,
> Round me seal your tube of light
> From ascended master flame
> Called forth now in God's own name.
> Let it keep my temple free
> From all discord sent to me.
>
> I AM calling forth violet fire
> To blaze and transmute all desire,
> Keeping on in freedom's name
> Till I AM one with the violet flame.

As I am giving this mantra to God the I AM Presence, I am visualizing myself standing inside this giant tube of light, this giant milk bottle. And around me, within it, I see the energy of the violet flame saturating my form, flowing through my body, blazing through the skin, through the arteries, the veins, the arms, the legs, the extremities. And I am feeling a saturation of my being with the energy of the Holy Spirit. As I give the mantra, I am concentrating on this vision of the Self, and that which I see, the energy I invoke, I will become.

The energy of God will actually coalesce around your visualization. It will also manifest according to the direction of your Inner Self, your Real Self, who is always the director of the mantra and the meditation.

You'll notice how I give this mantra. Mantras are to be given with a certain commanding presence, a certain authority that we use in dealing with God's energy. This is what makes the mantra different from a prayer of supplication. A prayer is a talk with God, a conversation or communion with God, a request. A mantra is a decree of the alchemist—the one we call "the artisan in the temple," the one who is working out the alchemy of the equation of being.

We read in the Book of Job, "Thou shalt decree a thing, and it shall be established unto thee." The alchemist, therefore, sees that the energy of God within himself is his to command. He commands this energy to coalesce in a forcefield that has been predetermined, that has been ordained by God as a forcefield of protection. He then visualizes this and brings it into manifestation by his attunement with the Inner Self, by his oneness with the I AM Presence. This is why we call the mantras that the ascended masters have given us "decrees."

Q: In other words, you're saying that people have the right to order God?

A: People have the right to use God's energy in God's name. It is recorded in the Book of Genesis that when God created male and female he said, "Take dominion over the earth." God gave to us the command, and our answer is to command the energies of earth to come into alignment.

We command energy when we build an airplane or a ship. We command energy when we use advanced technology or split the atom or plant a garden. We are taking dominion over the earth each time we take on a project that is for the general welfare, for the commonweal, for the blessing of all. This is commanding God. Now, that sounds like blasphemy because we have not thought in terms of God being energy, but all of life is God. And this is not pantheism; this is the awareness of the omnipresence of love.

Q: Are you saying that we're taking a shortcut? Instead of spending a great deal of time building our project, we're going directly to the source?

A: Yes, we go to the source. We predetermine what it is we desire to accomplish, we call forth the energy and we seal it in a pattern or a matrix that has already been designed by God and that we are confirming or ratifying by our free will.

Q: The material you have discussed sounds very much like all the ingredients for ritual. Would you talk about the element of ritual in using the science of the spoken Word?

A: That little word *ritual* has an interesting meaning to me. I take it apart and I think of "right-you-all." Ritual, then, whether it is in the laboratory of the scientist or at the keyboard of the concert pianist, is a way of ordering energy for its greatest use by mankind.

Right-you-all means the "righting of the energies." We have all misqualified God's energy. Yesterday we were angry. The day before we were jealous. The day before we had fear and perhaps torment or great grief. These are all misuses of God's energy.

The goal of life is to qualify all energy with the law of perfection and the law of love. This is not impossible but very possible to us because we are the handiwork of God and because we are joint heirs of that consciousness that Jesus knew as the Christ and that Gautama knew as the Buddha.

This use of energy in ritual becomes a daily activity whereby we say: "OK, God has given me so much energy. I'm going to make the maximum use of that energy. Yesterday God gave me some energy that I didn't use very well. He has given me his gift of the Holy Spirit and of sacred fire. So I'm going to call upon his law of forgiveness, his law of transmutation. I'm going to ask God to take his sacred fire and pass it through the energies of yesterday, the energies of hatred, and turn them into love—change the 'water into wine,' change the water of my human imperfection into the wine of God's divine perfection."

In the "Heart, Head and Hand Decrees," beloved El Morya has given to us a mantra for forgiveness. This forgiveness puts us in tune with our inner Real Self, the Christ, who has the authority within our being to forgive sin.

Jesus was the personification of that Christ; and therefore when he went to heal he said, "Thy sins be forgiven thee." In making that statement he caused the alignment of atoms and molecules, and therefore wholeness took place.

The Christ within us is declaring now, "Thy sins be forgiven thee!" In order to accept that forgiveness, we give the following mantra:

> I AM forgiveness acting here,
> Casting out all doubt and fear,
> Setting men forever free
> With wings of cosmic victory.
>
> I AM calling in full power
> For forgiveness every hour;
> To all life in every place
> I flood forth forgiving grace.

Thus as we forgive life, life forgives us. Jesus taught us to pray, "Forgive us our debts, as we forgive our debtors." This mantra for forgiveness demands that we release forgiveness to everyone. Wherever we have the sense of injustice or we have been wronged, we visualize this violet flame of forgiveness going forth from our heart, going forth in this mantra of the spoken Word. We visualize it contacting every individual with whom we have ever had a misunderstanding, and we feel a tremendous peace and love and a resolution of discord in problems that have occurred.

As we send out forgiveness, life sends forgiveness back to us. Ecclesiastes says, "Cast thy bread upon the waters, for thou shalt find it after many days." Our bread is our energy. We cast it forth upon the waters of the human consciousness and, as it is the pure energy of God, it comes back to us. This is the law of the circle, the law of karma, the law of cause and effect, at work in our lives. It is the law that "whatsoever a man soweth, that shall he also reap."

When we sow energy as good vibration, we reap energy as good vibration and we start an upward spiral. The culmination of that spiral is soul liberation, whereby the soul reunites day by day with the Spirit of the living God.

As Paul said, "I die daily," so we say, "I ascend daily." The dying is the putting off of the old man; the ascending is the putting on of the new man. Through the science of the spoken Word we are actually ascending every day.

10

The Law of Abundance

∞

- *How did Jesus work his miracles?*
- *Can we do the same?*
- *Did Jesus use mantras?*

Mrs. Prophet, would you tell us how it was that Jesus was able to perform miracles such as the coin in the mouth of the fish, the feeding of the five thousand and numerous healings?

A: Doug, the most interesting thing about the life of Jesus is that as you study it you come to realize that his miracles were not miracles at all; they were the outworking of cosmic law. He was the greatest scientist of the age, greater than all scientists who have ever followed him on the path of initiation.

Jesus was the master of the use of God's energy. He came to demonstrate the mastery of energy. He came to show us how and to set the example. Jesus said, "He that believeth on me, the works that I do shall he do also; and greater works than these shall he do."

I firmly believe that we have come into the age of the Holy Spirit, the promised Comforter, who Jesus said would remind us of everything that he had taught us and would bring to our remembrance from the Inner Self this science that he had demonstrated.

The multiplication of the loaves and fishes was Jesus' demonstration of a law of Alpha and Omega and the use of the white-fire core of the atom, the nucleus of the atom. We find that the two fishes and the five loaves symbolize the seven centers, the seven chakras of being, and that the wholeness of that energy in Alpha and Omega was all that was required to make that substance available to one, three, ten, five thousand or more. Jesus could have fed five million from the two fishes and the five loaves!

Abundance is the natural law of life, and Jesus always had the abundance of every good and perfect gift from God. He and his disciples were never wanting and yet they did not live in excess. El Morya, in his "Heart, Head and Hand Decrees," has given us a mantra for our realization of this law of abundance. This is how it goes:

> I AM free from fear and doubt,
> Casting want and misery out,
> Knowing now all good supply
> Ever comes from realms on high.
>
> I AM the hand of God's own fortune
> Flooding forth the treasures of light,
> Now receiving full abundance
> To supply each need of life.

This is an interesting mantra because immediately we take the name of God, I AM, and affirm that being where we stand—where I AM. And we declare that this I AM is free from fear and doubt. Jesus teaches us that fear and doubt are the basic cause of poverty, the poverty consciousness and of want. We cannot draw forth abundance and supply if we have fear at conscious or subconscious levels.

When Jesus walked on the water, Peter asked if he could come and be on the water with his master. Jesus said, "Come," and Peter walked on the water. This transfer of energy came by Peter's attention upon the Christ, his belief on the Christ. As long as Peter had his attention upon Jesus, he was above water. But when he momentarily entered into a vortex of his own fear, he immediately broke the contact and sank beneath the waves. He cried out, "Master, save me!" and Jesus extended his hand and restored the lifeline of energy.

Jesus' body was filled with light, and that light overcame the natural laws of gravity. This was because of Jesus' own consciousness of perfection. He had the awareness of the inner Master as being perfect but he did not hold that law of perfection as exclusive to himself. He taught that the law he demonstrated was available to everyone. He instructed us: "Be ye therefore perfect, even as your Father which is in heaven is perfect."

In accord with the life of Jesus, El Morya has given to us a mantra for perfection. This mantra is to help us to realize that we can entertain the law of perfection and the energies of perfection that will transform our lives:

> I AM life of God-direction,
> Blaze thy light of truth in me.
> Focus here all God's perfection,
> From all discord set me free.
>
> Make and keep me anchored ever
> In the justice of thy plan—
> I AM the presence of perfection
> Living the life of God in man!

You'll notice that I AM is used. As I AM is the name of God, when we say that name we are affirming: "I and my Father are one. Where I AM, thou art also." And right where we are, right where we commune with God, there God is.

So in our oneness with God we can declare, "I AM THAT I AM." Whenever we say, "I AM," we are really saying, "God in me is." If we say, "I AM life of God-direction, blaze thy light of truth in me," we are saying, "God in me is the life of God-direction." We not only affirm the presence of that God but we call to that God to "blaze thy light of truth in me."

Finally, in the concluding part of the mantra we say, "I AM the presence of perfection, living the life of God in man!" What we are really saying is, "God in me is the presence of perfection." This is an affirmation, and by cosmic law it must manifest because we have combined it with the name of God, the all-power of a cosmos.

There is a saying that the call compels the answer. When the call is a statement of cosmic law, the answer must manifest—just as a magnet draws the iron filings in their proper polarity.

Q: Did Jesus use mantras?

A: Jesus used mantras and he taught them to his disciples in the Upper Room, but much of this is not recorded in scripture. We read in the Book of John that if everything that Jesus taught were to be recorded, the world could not contain the books that would be written. So we have to realize that a few short books and a few chapters of the Gospels are by no means the fullness of the teachings of Jesus Christ.

Q: If we learn to use the "Heart, Head and Hand Decrees" properly, can we perform the same "miracles" as Jesus?

A: The miracles that manifest in our lives, and that we should be concerned with, are the day-to-day happenings of a greater and greater awareness of God. And this is the goal of decrees—to attain a greater realization of God.

It is also entirely possible—and it has happened in the lives of the saints and the seers of both East and West—that extraordinary manifestations can occur, such as levitation and the stigmata. Many have come with the gift of healing. Aimee Semple McPherson had that gift, as do many others who have the Holy Spirit today. But the world's great mystics have always warned against becoming preoccupied with phenomena, because the goal of the spiritual path is not phenomena but oneness with God.

Q: Mrs. Prophet, do you have some specific advice on how one can integrate mantras and decrees with one's daily activities, say from the time one rises in the morning?

A: The use of mantras is a natural way of life. They don't need to be set aside for a special moment. You can give these mantras in the shower or on the freeway while you are driving to work. They're easily memorized. While you give them, you meditate on the heart. At the same time you can also be performing the necessary preparations of the day. Of course, it is always good to set aside ten minutes for concentration, but if you don't have ten minutes, it's important to give the mantras anyway.

Q: The question right now, then, is what do you do until the doctor comes? In other words, for those who don't already have some printed instruction on decreeing, is there something they can do in the meantime until they get their decree book?

A: You can make up your own decrees spontaneously and begin each fiat of light with the name I AM. (Remember, I AM means "God in me is.") You can get up in the morning and say:

> I AM a son [a daughter] of God!
> I AM full of joy!
> I AM in the action of love this day!
> I AM going forth to conquer my day!
> I AM filled with abundance and every good and perfect gift!

And you can just keep on affirming that the God within you —remembering that that God is energy—is going to manifest in everything that you desire to accomplish. I think it's important to be spontaneous in these fiats and to begin right now to affirm your life as the victorious manifestation of God.

11

Life as a Path of Initiation

- *What is the Path and what did Jesus show us about it?*

- *How can we live on earth and remain in God?*

- *How can we overcome bad habits?*

Mrs. Prophet, will you tell us how the life of Jesus relates to our life today?

A: The life that God has given to us is a life that is intended to be used by our soul to attain reunion with the Inner Self. All else is extraneous and subject to that one goal. If we don't make it in this life, we come again. The soul puts on a new set of "coats of skins," or a new forcefield, and returns once again to the scenes of earth. This is why earth is so familiar to us; it's because we've been evolving here for thousands and thousands of years.

Life, then, is the path of initiation. Jesus, in his great love for the people of earth, came to show us how we could follow the path of initiation and in one concluding lifetime return to the heart of God as he did in the ritual of the ascension.

When we see the life of Jesus as a life marking the stations of our own individual initiation, we look at the birth of Christ as the sign of the birth of our own Christ consciousness—the moment when we determine to manifest the Father-Mother God and to bring forth that Christ light. We have the decision of Jesus to be about his Father's business. We have his decision to discourse with the doctors in the temple, to expound upon the Law. And then between the ages of twelve and thirty, he is in the East preparing for the final three years of his Galilean mission.

One of his first initiations in these three years is the ritual of baptism, an important initiation symbolizing the cleansing and consecration of the soul to the will of God. We have his transfiguration before the disciples. We see his crucifixion, his resurrection. And between the transfiguration and the crucifixion, he works many miracles, so-called, as demonstrations of the science that we must one day prove.

The fact of the matter is that we must affirm that we are being transfigured every day, that we are experiencing the resurrection every day, that we are ascending. Even by a tiny, tiny increment each day we are drawing closer and closer to that energy forcefield that is the white-fire core of the atom of Self.

Continuing in order with the "Heart, Head and Hand Decrees," we find that with each successive mantra we draw forth a greater degree of light. As we become more sensitive, we actually feel this light building within our own bodies. We can begin to feel the burning in the heart, which the disciples felt on the road to Emmaus when they were near the master but did not recognize him.

The burning in the heart indicates the expansion of the threefold flame. It is the sacred fire actually consuming the misqualified energies of fear and hatred and impure motive that often surround the heart. The one pursuing the initiation of the transfiguration, then, gives the following mantra from the "Heart, Head and Hand Decrees":

I AM changing all my garments,
Old ones for the bright new day;
With the sun of understanding
I AM shining all the way.

I AM light within, without;
I AM light is all about.
Fill me, free me, glorify me!
Seal me, heal me, purify me!
Until transfigured they describe me:
I AM shining like the Son,
I AM shining like the sun!

There is a tremendous joy in this mantra of the transfiguration because it represents an influx of light whereby the very cells of our bodies begin to be filled with light and to be flushed of physical as well as mental and emotional toxins. The joy of giving these mantras is the joy of becoming God.

Q: **What is the meaning of the term** *right living?*

A: Right living is one of the requirements of the Eightfold Path of the Buddha, and right living means being obedient to the Inner Self. For thousands of years people have rebelled against the laws of God because they have felt that they were imposed from without as a yoke and as a burden. This rebellion against what seems to be outside of oneself is really the ultimate folly of rebelling against one's own being, one's own True Self.

Moses received the Ten Commandments. Jesus gave us a new commandment. We have received the code of living from all of the great gurus. Confucius' teaching was a very practical wisdom for everyday life. This is really what the great masters have come to show us—how to live on earth and yet to remain in God. And it comes down to a few simple precepts: Love the LORD thy God with all thy heart and all thy soul and all thy mind, and love thy neighbor as thyself.

So right living means being obedient to the highest principles of the religion we were brought up in. Whether we are followers of Muhammad or Zarathustra or Confucius, Lao Tzu or Mother Mary, we must remember that the basic precepts of honesty and right living are a proper and necessary matrix for the science of the spoken Word, this science of alchemy that comes with the Holy Spirit.

Q: Is it true, then, that the science of the spoken Word is in no way a substitute for moral rectitude?

A: Yes. In fact, if the science of the spoken Word is used without the correction of our way of life, it will not be effective because the Law will not work for those who are out of alignment with that Law. If we steal, if we kill, if we partake of substances that we ought not to partake of, we are depriving ourselves of the benefits of the pure energy of the Word.

Lord Maitreya

Q: Is the science of the spoken Word useful in taking care of all the little habits and negative traits most of us are plagued by?

A: That's a very interesting question. The Ascended Master Lord Maitreya has answered that question in his teachings on the overcoming of fear through decrees. He reminds us that Paul expressed the dilemma of these subconscious motivations and momentums when he said, "The good that I would, I do not. But the evil which I would not, that I do."

Maitreya asks: What can the modern-day disciple do to protect himself from evil intent and evil action that he finds manifesting in himself and in the world at large? And he answers the question by talking about the discipline of the controlled use of energy through the science of the spoken Word.

Maitreya compares the momentum of habit to a coil of an electromagnet wound around its core. The number of times that the coil is wound around the core determines the power of the habit and its momentum. In other words, the number of times that the habit is engaged in determines its strength.

We can break that momentum through the use of the science of the spoken Word. As we give the mantras, we break the power of habit. Maitreya tells us that instead of unwinding the coil turn by turn, we can break right through the entire forcefield of that coil and break the habit by the power of God through the science of the spoken Word.

Q: What exactly is meant by the term *initiation*?

A: Initiation is the testing of the soul. It is God's way of determining how we will use the gift of free will. Temptation comes before us; we have to make a decision to walk the path of honor or to walk the path of the compromise of truth. As soon as we demonstrate that we are just stewards of the Law and of the abundance of God, God gives us more. He makes us caretakers of others and of larger fields of energy, more abundance, more supply, more responsibility on earth.

Every day we are receiving initiations and every day we are sending a message to our I AM Presence as to whether or not we are worthy to be counted as joint heirs of the Christ consciousness. Are we worthy to inherit this Christ mind, this mind of the

Buddha, this mind of Confucius? It is ours for the overcoming but we have to pay a price, and that price is to follow the inner law and to be obedient to the inner voice.

Q: So one progresses on the Path by demonstrating one's faithfulness and one's courage, and so forth?

A: In the parable of the talents, Jesus taught, "If thou wilt be faithful over a few things, I will make thee ruler over many." The path of initiation is the only way that God has of determining whether we are ready for an increase of light, of the Holy Spirit, of graces and of the inner keys. There are inner keys that are transferred to the individual by the ascended masters and by his own Inner Self as he passes his tests. And these keys are the very keys that we would have—the keys to the mastery of the science of Matter as well as the science of Spirit.

Q: Such as?

A: The multiplication of the loaves and fishes. We have talked about a mantra that could be used to attain the abundance of God. But there are further keys behind that mantra from which that mantra comes. These are not lawful to reveal because they are the keys that are imparted to the individual by the master himself.

There is an old saying that goes, "When the pupil is ready, the teacher appears." When we show that we are ready because we have been faithful over a few things, we have been willing to discipline our lives and our energies, then we find that the ascended masters approach us.

And as they come—either through a book, through a person, through a teaching, through our hearing about the science of the spoken Word—we begin to pursue the master. We begin to say, "I am going to do what that master says because I want to be like him." So we begin demonstrating the master's techniques and we find that in our own heart of hearts God speaks to us and gives us the key of life.

Q: Is everybody being initiated?

A: Everyone is being initiated. Earth is a schoolroom. The moment you get out of bed in the morning your initiation begins and it doesn't stop till you retire at night! Everybody is making the decision hour by hour to be or not to be in Reality, in Truth, in God.

Q: Does that mean that everybody is on the Path?

A: "The Path" means the path of the ascension. It is the goal of life for everyone to be on that path. But there are a number of tests and a number of challenges that you must meet before you can say you are actually on the path of the overcomers who are tied to the ascended masters. Those who are on that path are daily pursuing the balancing of their karma and the fulfilling of their dharma—the duty to be oneself, to fulfill one's reason for being.

12

Spiritual Resurrection

∞

- *What is the resurrection?*
- *How can we conquer death?*
- *Is immortality possible?*

Mrs. Prophet, you say we're supposed to do everything that Jesus did. How about the resurrection?

A: The resurrection proves Paul's teaching that the last enemy to be overcome is death. The reality of it is that there is no death, but we have to prove that there is no death.

The resurrection is a resurgence of God's energy through our being, through our chakras. It was the drawing forth of the energies of the resurrection from the I AM Presence and from the base-of-the-spine chakra that enabled Jesus to restore life to his temple. By the meditation of his soul upon the Oversoul, or the Higher Self, he overshadowed his body until he restored that body to life.

Now, we begin our resurrection by the restoration of consciousness, of joy, of happiness, of love, of truth. And we keep on increasing and accelerating God's consciousness within us until the ultimate victory over death is a natural conclusion of our soul's quest on the Path and of our soul's reunion with God.

Continuing, then, with El Morya's "Heart, Head and Hand Decrees," we have a mantra for the resurrection—and it can be used every day. As we give this mantra we can say, "I am being resurrected every day! I am overcoming death every day!"

> I AM the flame of resurrection
> Blazing God's pure light through me.
> Now I AM raising every atom,
> From every shadow I AM free.
>
> I AM the light of God's full Presence,
> I AM living ever free.
> Now the flame of life eternal
> Rises up to victory.

We accompany this mantra with the visualization of white light coming through us, rising through us as a white fire pulsating from beneath our feet, through our consciousness and chakras. It is an energy field that can restore us from sickness to health, from depression to wholeness, from anxiety to joy.

There is an alchemy in this mantra and in all mantras whereby through the science of the spoken Word, as in no other form of meditation, misuses of God's energy are transmuted. This process of transmutation means that each time we give mantras that contain the name of God, I AM, we are actually balancing negative karma.

Karma is simply the substance of God's energy that we have qualified either correctly or incorrectly. There is good karma and bad karma, positive karma and negative karma. Our goal is to requalify with light the energy that we have misqualified with darkness. This misqualified energy is stored in a forcefield comparable to the subconscious. When we give these mantras, increments of that energy are returned to the causal body, or the spheres of consciousness that surround the I AM Presence.

So mantras are not given simply for the alteration of a state of consciousness, although they do accomplish this. More importantly, they are always involved in the forgiveness of sin and the balancing of karma. Balancing karma means paying the debt for our misuses of God's light, energy and consciousness.

We give the mantra on the resurrection to remove the consciousness of death. More than we realize, we are burdened by the energies of death on a day-to-day basis. Fear is the beginning of death. Doubt in oneself is the beginning of death. The condemnation or the belittlement of the self is the murdering of the self and its potential to be free. Freedom comes through this resurrection flame.

Q: **Are you saying it would be possible to end physical death?**

A: The termination of death begins in consciousness. Since death is not real, what we see as death is simply the laying down of the body temple by the soul, who then journeys to other planes of consciousness, or other mansions in the Father's house. Jesus said: "In my Father's house are many mansions. If it were not so, I would have told you. I go to prepare a place for you... that where I am, ye may be also."

The mansions are planes of consciousness, and there are many planes of consciousness. The soul journeys to these planes both after the transition called death and during sleep at night. Our souls may depart our body temples and go to other places and other schoolrooms for a learning experience.

Death, then, is the illusion of the cessation of life and it is only real to those who believe that our life is actually in the body. But life is in the flame in the heart and in the soul, and these move on as the path of acceleration continues here and hereafter.

Ultimately the demonstration of the ascension will mean not only the ascension of the soul but also of the physical body. But we have more immediate goals than the overcoming of physical death. Our immediate goal is the resurrection of life as it ought to be lived on earth today.

Q: What about physical healing?

A: Physical healing may come about in the same way—through the use of meditation and the science of the spoken Word and also through the proper diet, which is most important. We can see that light in our body temples brings about a manifestation of healing. Since so many physical conditions are caused by mental and emotional problems, the healing of the mind and emotions and the erasing by the violet flame of records in the subconscious is often all that is required to eliminate physical suffering.

Q: So the first thing you seek to change is consciousness, right?

A: We go to cause behind effect. That doesn't mean to say we don't call upon the medical profession and use medicines and whatever is necessary—surgery, et cetera—for the correction of conditions in the body. But ultimately we seek to manifest the victory wherein the mind of God within us controls the manifestation in matter.

Q: OK, Mrs. Prophet. What happens after the resurrection?

A: You recall that after Jesus' resurrection he came back. He spent forty days with the disciples. He gave them instruction in the Upper Room and told them: "Tarry ye in the city of Jerusalem, until ye be endued with power from on high." And that power from on high descended with the descent of the Holy Spirit on the day of Pentecost.

After the resurrection comes the ascension. We talked about the concept of ascending every day, every hour. The ascension is the acceleration of consciousness. It is actually the increase of the vibratory rate of the electrons as they whirl about and through the nucleus of the atom until ultimately the soul reunites with the I AM Presence, the individualized Presence of God.

The concluding mantra in the "Heart, Head and Hand" series is a mantra of the ascension. As soon as we begin to give it, we are accelerating the white light in our auras, preparing for that ultimate reunion with God at the conclusion of this life or our next life of incarnation. This is how it goes:

> I AM ascension light,
> Victory flowing free,
> All of good won at last
> For all eternity.
>
> I AM light, all weights are gone.
> Into the air I raise;
> To all I pour with full God-power
> My wondrous song of praise.
>
> All hail! I AM the living Christ,
> The ever-loving One.
> Ascended now with full God-power,
> I AM a blazing sun!

The visualization for this mantra is a sphere of white light that now envelops the entire form, the entire being. When we say, "I AM the living Christ," we are affirming, "God in me is the living Christ, and that Christ, which was in Jesus, is now manifesting in me as the fullness of the threefold flame in my heart."

Visualizing the self as a blazing sun gives us the key to the alchemy whereby Jesus disappeared from the people's midst and whereby he could come into the Upper Room right through the wall. That alchemy was simply the rearrangement of the atoms and molecules of his physical body so they could pass through the atoms and molecules of the wall.

The day is going to come in the not-too-distant future when

people on earth will be doing this without difficulty, and it is amazing how quickly this will happen as they begin to understand the science of the Word. Now, when I say, "the science of the Word," I'm talking about *Word* with a capital *W.* I'm talking about the Word incarnate. I'm not just talking about the words that come through the throat chakra in these decrees. I'm talking about the Word as the very energy of creation, which we express when we give a mantra.

Q: The goal of all of this is immortality, right?

A: That goal is something that is near and dear to the people of every religion in the world. Whether it's called soul liberation or the ascension or nirvana, it is the same thing. It's what Paul said: "This corruptible must put on incorruption."

This corruptible must put on incorruption! Paul said that as the very equation of his being bursting from within. His soul was crying out—he knew this as the goal of life. And this is the eternal quest of the overcomers.

Paul also said, "This mortal must put on immortality." This which is temporal in time and space, this soul, which is my option to opt for eternity, must accelerate, must return to the source whence it came—the I AM Presence.

13

Mark Prophet

∞

- *What's it like to contact an ascended master?*
- *Who was Mark Prophet?*
- *Who is the Ascended Master Lanello?*

Mrs. Prophet, you're the head of a growing worldwide movement. Would you just tell us how it all got started?

A: It began with a man and a master, both of whom I was privileged to meet while I was studying at Boston University in 1961. I had been seeking the ascended masters for a full five years. I knew Jesus as the living master of my life, and I understood him to be the Saviour and the open door for the soul's reunion with God.

I was seeking and finding that living relationship with him and in conjunction with that I was seeking the Ascended Master Saint Germain, whom I identified through a picture I had found in an old book in my mother's library. Saint Germain, then, became truly the brother, the "holy brother," which is the meaning of his name—Sanctus Germanus.

And so it was with Jesus and Saint Germain at the forefront of my consciousness that I was pursuing the inner walk with God. Yet finally at the conclusion of my five-year search, it was neither of these who came to me but it was in fact the Ascended Master El Morya. El Morya was to be my guru and the one who would train me to be the messenger for the ascended masters.

I found El Morya through his messenger Mark L. Prophet. Through a strange set of circumstances I had come across a group of devotees in Boston who were students of the ascended masters. I attended one of their meetings one evening and found that Mark Prophet had journeyed from Washington, D.C., to give a lecture and dictation. As I sat in the audience in meditation, I began to be filled with the Holy Ghost.

After Mark concluded his lecture, he delivered a dictation by Michael the Archangel. The dictation came as the dictations came to the prophets of Israel. The Word of the LORD and the Spirit of the LORD truly descended upon this man Mark, whose face I beheld for the first time. As I listened to the Word of the emissary of God, Archangel Michael, I felt the deliverance of this archangel, who is depicted in the Book of Revelation as the one who comes to help the Woman clothed with the Sun and to deliver her and the Manchild from the face of the dragon.

I recognized in Archangel Michael a being whom I had known for many incarnations and who had succored Joan of Arc in the hour of her great triumph and her sacrifice. And I knew that I was meeting one who was to lead me through the wilderness and bring me to my service to the LORD in this hour. And so, Archangel Michael delivered through Mark Prophet the message that set me free to follow the calling from God to be a messenger.

During the months that followed this meeting, I was in communion with my own God Self and with a number of the ascended hosts—not the least of whom was Mary, the mother of Jesus, whom I was just discovering. I found her to be the great Mother, the great Virgin consciousness, and the one who restores in the sons and daughters of God their mission on earth.

Not long after, I was cutting through a park in Boston and there crossed my path the Ascended Master El Morya. He appeared to me in a great light and a great energy. It was not a physical appearance, but I felt a presence and I saw a person with my inner eye, my third eye.

Tall, enturbaned, in a blue robe, he communicated to me the necessity of the mission of communicating to the sons and daughters of God, the remnant of the people of light on earth, the teaching of the Christ and of the prophets of Israel. Some of this teaching had been lost and some of it had not yet been interpreted by the Holy Ghost so as to make it understandable to the children of God in this age.

He gave me my commission and said it had come as the result of my imploring the LORD to fulfill my mission and of my constant prayer to Jesus Christ and to Saint Germain. He told me that I should go to Washington, D.C., to be trained as a messenger for the ascended masters and that he would train me through Mark Prophet. The purpose of his training would be so that I could receive the initiations that would allow me to come into alignment with Jesus and Saint Germain and finally to be anointed by Saint Germain as his messenger.

I obeyed the instructions of El Morya. I prepared to leave Boston and journeyed to Washington, where my training began. It was an arduous training and it has led me across the years to this hour of the fruit of that mission, the movement that is today known as The Summit Lighthouse.

Q: You describe an extraordinary chain of events. Did any of this frighten you at any time?

A: It didn't frighten me because I was like the hound of heaven. I was pursuing the ascended masters from the moment I recognized the portrait of Saint Germain. I remembered that prior to my incarnation I had been in the inner realms of light with the ascended hosts. I had recollections of the plans that the ascended masters had made to bring to fruition in this age the teachings of the two witnesses spoken of in Revelation.

And I was, you might say, chafing at the bit, waiting for the coming of the LORD's hosts. In fact, I was so determined that I would make contact with the Brotherhood of Light that I actually stood on the roof of my apartment in Boston and cried out to God and to Jesus and to Saint Germain to come and get me because I was ready for service!

Q: Were you able to tell anyone else what you were going through?

A: I could only really communicate it to Mark Prophet, who became my close friend and teacher on the Path, the instrument of El Morya and ultimately my husband. I had the privilege of knowing him as friend and as his wife and the mother of his four children.

And so with Mark and then with the growing student body of devotees of the masters, the movement has grown. After we were married, Mark and I served together for just about twelve years and then he took his leave of this plane, as he had told me he would do as soon as he had prepared me to succeed him. He passed on and made his ascension and is now known to us as the Ascended Master Lanello.

Q: What was Mark Prophet like?

A: Mark Prophet was the one I had been searching for in this world. I can remember that from the time I was a little child, wherever I went I would look for a pair of eyes that were full of God and full of the hope of the heaven-world. Everywhere I went, in every church and synagogue where I would go seeking for God, I would be looking for those eyes. And when I was in Boston in that little meeting, I saw him for the first time, and I recognized the eyes of the one for whom I had been waiting.

Mark Prophet was to me, and to all of us who knew him, the living example of one who embodied a tremendous energy of God, a tremendous love and a tremendous wisdom. He was like Abraham; when we were with him it was like living in the bosom of God. He was Father to us. He was Teacher. He was all things. We could see in him Mother and Holy Spirit.

He lived the teachings of the ascended masters and he gave to us a most delicate impartation of the flame of his heart. The flame of the Holy Spirit burned on the altar of his heart. It is through that Holy Spirit that we envision the deliverance of America and the earth.

Q: Does Mark still communicate with you?

A: He is one with the immortals as the Ascended Master Lanello and he is a part of the body of God in heaven communicating to us the true teachings of Christ and Buddha in this age.

14

Mark's Early Life

∞

- *What kind of man remembers being born?*
- *What kind of movement would he start?*
- *How far can you go with a typewriter and a light bulb?*

Mrs. Prophet, tell us more about The Summit Lighthouse and how it all began.

A: It began with the life of Mark Prophet, whose contact with the brotherhood of the ascended masters antedated even his birth in this life. He actually had a conscious awareness of the ascended masters from the moment of his birth on and a continuous awareness of his experiences prior to birth. He remembered seeing his father and mother waiting for him to be born, then passing through the birth canal and the moment of birth.

Mark remembered consciously leaving the body as a little child and communing with the angelic hosts and ascended masters as well as with those souls who were to join him in embodiment to further the movement, including myself. He remembered communing with me on the inner, as I was born a number of years later.

And so as he grew up, Mark was a devout Christian and sought God through the Pentecostal movement. He sought the Holy Spirit and actually received the Holy Spirit when he was in his teens. As a young boy, Mark established a little altar in his attic in his hometown, Chippewa Falls, Wisconsin. There he would go, summer and winter, for hours and hours a day in the heat and cold, praying to God and communing with God.

He was hard working. The family was poor and his father passed on when Mark was nine. His mother also was very devout; later on she took up the study of Unity as Mark moved through various churches seeking truth.

When El Morya appeared to him, Mark was to a certain extent frightened—perhaps *concerned* is the word—to see an Indian master with a turban looking at him and speaking with him. After El Morya had communicated with him a number of times, Mark asked him not to return because he could not reconcile the teachings that he had learned in church with the coming of an Indian guru. El Morya bowed graciously and said to him, "As you wish, my son," and removed himself from Mark's life.

It took a number of years of soul searching before Mark realized that he ought to pursue this great teacher. But not until Mark called upon him again, actually called upon him in the name of Jesus Christ, did El Morya return.

Mark has recounted the story of when he was working on the railroad and he had a communication from El Morya directing him to found The Summit Lighthouse. Morya's communication, encapsulated in a few seconds—in fact, the time it took Mark to raise his arms and bring down again the sledgehammer—was the prophecy of the entire movement and what it would mean to America.

Mark then went through the normal course of events. He served in the U.S. Army Air Corps. His calling ripened and in later years he moved from the Midwest to Washington, D.C., where he founded The Summit Lighthouse under El Morya's direction in 1958.

It began with the publishing of *Pearls of Wisdom. Pearls of Wisdom* are weekly letters from the ascended masters to their chelas, or disciples, throughout the world. They contain necessary teaching and timely instruction for the Path as well as commentary on world conditions. Thousands have found the answers to their personal problems through the *Pearls of Wisdom.*

The *Pearls of Wisdom* have been published by The Summit Lighthouse continuously every week since 1958. Since Mark's ascension in 1973, I have been receiving the dictations for the *Pearls.* We are always happy to share them with anyone who is interested.

In addition to publishing the *Pearls of Wisdom,* The Summit Lighthouse is the sponsoring organization for the Keepers of the Flame Lessons, which are provided to members of the Keepers of the Flame Fraternity. This fraternity is sponsored by the Ascended Master Saint Germain, and the lessons that he provides are intended to give individuals who have had a basic orthodox background in religion, or no background at all, the first steps on the path of self-mastery. The Keepers of the Flame Lessons are sent monthly to members of the fraternity.

Q: Is it true, then, that the beginnings of The Summit Lighthouse were quite modest?

A: Yes, they were. I remember how Mark used to talk about being in a house on Kentucky Avenue in Washington, D.C., with a 300-watt light bulb and a typewriter. He would sit there and type out the dictations from El Morya. He and one devotee of the masters, who became his secretary, printed these messages. Students of the ascended masters began asking for them, and so Mark began to distribute them.

When I arrived on the scene in 1961, also called by El Morya, there were probably no more than several hundred people receiving these letters. Today thousands throughout the world are receiving them.

It is a wonderful experience to be a part of the movement that is sponsored by the ascended masters and to realize that the ascended masters are the true teachers of the age. They are the ones who have perfected their soul consciousness and merged with the I AM THAT I AM. Therefore our contact with the ascended masters is always a contact with the immortals.

In the Old Testament whenever the prophets begin to speak, they say, "The Word of the LORD came unto me...," or "The Spirit of the LORD was upon me...," and then they deliver what the LORD spoke to them. Now, these early prophets of Israel were all messengers for the ascended masters, and the LORD who spoke to them is the LORD that comes in the consciousness of Elohim.

Elohim is a Hebrew word for "God," meaning God in the plural. *Elohim* is a plural noun, a plural form; and that plural form is seen in the Book of Genesis, where it is written that God said, "Let us make man in our image, after our likeness."

The manifestation of God in the hosts of the LORD and in his emissaries is a plurality in a unity. God is one God, and yet his many manifestations as Elohim, angels, ascended masters and other spiritual beings are all a part of God's being. And the LORD that came to the prophets of Israel is the same LORD, or Law, or personification of the Law, that we see in these spiritual beings.

God has never left the earth without the spirit of prophecy, because in the transfer of the spoken Word through the prophets, there is a transfer of energy. This energy is the Holy Spirit and it energizes and vitalizes and nourishes the people of God on earth.

And so Mark and I understand our role to be in the tradition not only of the prophets of Israel and the saints of the Church but also of the great masters who have come out of the East. In every century there are one or more individuals who keep alive this spirit of prophecy. But as Jesus said, there are also false Christs and false prophets.

Ironically, people always ask us the question, "Well, is that your real name? You know, it sounds very contrived, this Mark Prophet." Actually, Prophet is an Irish name and it is Mark's ancestral name. When I married Mark, this became my name also. The name indicates our mission to keep alive the spirit of prophecy.

The ascended masters do speak through us and they envelop us in a mantle, a momentum or matrix, of consciousness. And the speaking through the messenger is the spontaneous coming forth of the Holy Spirit that was prophesied in the Book of Joel.

Q: The movement that began as The Summit Lighthouse in 1958 includes another name now, does it not?

A: The Summit Lighthouse was founded to publish the teachings of the ascended masters. Once these teachings were published and many devotees of the ascended masters began to gather, the demand for a devotional experience, a total religious experience, led to the formation of a church around the teachings.

This church has come to be known as Church Universal and Triumphant. And so The Summit Lighthouse and Church Universal and Triumphant together perform the function of answering the soul needs of the people today.

Q: Could we talk a little bit about the scope of this movement?

A: Its scope includes the defining of Father, Son, Holy Spirit and Mother as the consciousness of God. In fulfillment of the role of Father, we have the teaching as the Law. And so our ministry and our work has been to set forth God's law as people will come to understand it in the two-thousand-year cycle known as the

Aquarian age, which is now beginning.

We are concluding a two-thousand-year cycle known as the Piscean age. Jesus Christ is the Piscean conqueror. He is the master who has shown us the mastery of the water element. Those who are students of astrology understand that Pisces is a water sign. The sign of Jesus is the sign of the fish. It's a unique sign because when we draw a fish symbolically, we see that two arcs form the fish and those two arcs are a hint of the mastery of the energy of the caduceus, or the rising energies of the spine. And that is what Jesus mastered. He mastered the Mother and Father energies of being and performed all of his so-called miracles by that mastery.

In this age of Aquarius we master the air quadrant, or the mind, the mental body. We see this in the technology of the airplane, satellites and the movement of our consciousness—our ability to move quickly on the face of the earth. Our technology, communication and transportation are all moving toward the air quadrant.

This is the sign of Aquarius. And the master, or the one who comes to give us the understanding of the Law in the Aquarian age, is Saint Germain. Saint Germain is an important figure in our movement. He has come to give us the understanding of the Holy Spirit as the violet flame. We use the violet flame as the instrument of the baptism of the sacred fire, the baptism of the Holy Ghost, and the forgiveness of sin, the washing of the waters of the human consciousness by the Word that comes to us.

In our understanding of The Summit Lighthouse, then, we find that the setting forth of the Law for the mastery of the Aquarian cycle is of paramount importance, just as Jesus' teaching was of paramount importance in the establishment of the Piscean age.

15

Education

- *What is education the ascended master way?*
- *How much can you learn about the Path in a retreat at Summit University?*
- *What is the first step for someone who wants to learn more about the ascended masters' teachings?*

Mrs. Prophet, we talked about the role of Father. What about the other three aspects of God—the Son, the Holy Spirit and the Mother?

A: Once the Law is set forth and the teaching is made known, then we need the interpreter of the Word, and this comes through the Second Person of the Trinity, the teacher. And, of course, Christ is ever the teacher, the World Teacher. Buddha is also a World Teacher.

In our movement the teaching arm has been Summit University and Montessori International. Mark and I founded both of these under the sponsorship of the ascended masters. Montessori International actually came first. It was founded in Colorado Springs, where we had our headquarters for a number of years. We envisioned it as a private school based on the principles of Maria Montessori combined with the teachings of the ascended masters.

Our intent was to offer children the freedom of the inner

creativity of the soul together with a certain framework of discipline, enabling them to adapt to the path of initiation and follow Christ and Buddha from a very early age.

Students come to Summit University from all over the world to spend time with us, studying the path of the masters and their teachings. Summit University has a program that teaches the mastery of the threefold flame, the understanding of balancing karma, the sacred labor, the fulfilling of dharma. Dharma is the duty to be oneself, and that duty is most important to the soul.

We find that all of the teachings that we learn here under the ascended masters have one goal, and that goal is for us to be the fullness of the Holy Spirit in action in the community. We see the work of the Holy Spirit as the great activator of good within the world community. And we desire our young people and people of every age to find their niche in society, to get out there where the action is and to help people realize the Inner Self so that they can unlock the energy within to actually change conditions.

We encourage young people to go back to school, to get off drugs, to find the Inner Self and the inner energy and to take up where they left off when they became disillusioned with society. To motivate them to go back and infuse that society with light is our purpose and intent.

So this "action" part of our movement comes under the Holy Spirit. It is love-action that we are interested in and all teaching comes to naught without this love, or this charity, as Paul spoke of it. The Holy Spirit arm of the movement consists of dedicated Keepers of the Flame. A Keeper of the Flame is simply someone who has dedicated his life to the keeping of the flame of God consciousness, or the flame of life itself, and that is always in active service.

Finally, the realization of the Mother within the movement

is the Church itself. The Church has always been known as the Bride of Christ. It is the temple, the tabernacle, the place of the Mother, the home of the Mother, where the children of the Mother—of Mother Mary and of the Woman clothed with the Sun, spoken of in the Book of Revelation—come to pursue the path back to the Father.

And so the Church has its devotional services, its healing services, its initiations and ritual. (Bear in mind that ritual is the means of "right-you-all," the righting of the Law within us.) All of this satisfies the soul's need for a devotional aspect to the teaching. We are not left to a dry, brittle, intellectual experience or a mere emotional experience, but we can experience the self actually merging not only with God but also with all souls on earth who are one in this community of light.

Q: Mrs. Prophet, you've described a rather complex array of activities that one may participate in. I think the question for most is: What's the next step for someone who has decided he's interested in the movement and who is interested in knowing how to begin?

A: I think that everyone should realize that this is not a movement that is concerned with getting members or getting contributions or controlling people's lives. There is definitely a free flow and it is our attempt to just give people the teaching and let them take that teaching and do what they will with it in their lives.

I would suggest that people simply get on the mailing list and receive the *Pearls of Wisdom*. Then they can evaluate the teachings and see how they fit together with their own religion or their desire to be apart from religion. They can then decide what relationship they would like to enter into with one or more of the ascended masters.

Q: There's no obligation, then, to part with one's current religion?

A: No. I think what we need in this age is a reinfusing of the Spirit in the churches and in the synagogues and in the mosques. We need people who will take the new spirit, the new wine, and who will go back and clean house and actually fill the temple with the glory of the LORD. And so I am not concerned that people break away from their old religions. I'm concerned that people realize that they are free to communicate with God and to share that communication with others.

Q: Mrs. Prophet, for people who would like to explore the teachings at home, is there any opportunity available for them?

A: Of course, as I've mentioned, there are the *Pearls of Wisdom.* And then we have a number of books and our main work, *Climb the Highest Mountain,* which presents the Law in several volumes. It's for the serious student and yet it can be understood by anyone. We suggest that you send for our free catalog.*

For those of you who prefer not to read, we have many tape albums of instruction, lectures and dictations, so that you can actually hear in your own home the dictations of the ascended masters and study their teachings and really discover the meaning and the fulfillment of your life.

---

*See page 367 or visit our Web site at www.tsl.org.

16

Spiritual Keys to Healing and Wholeness

- *What do the ascended masters teach on healing?*
- *What are the four lower bodies?*
- *How does the violet flame heal?*

Mrs. Prophet, many people are quite concerned about the matter of healing. What is the ascended master teaching on healing?

A: The teachings of the ascended masters are for wholeness—the wholeness of the soul, the soul's integration with the mind, the heart and the body temple. The ascended masters teach that whatever is manifesting in the physical body is an effect of an inner cause and they show their chelas how to go to the cause behind the effect.

In order that we might understand the levels of causation, the masters teach us that the nature of our being is fourfold. They refer to this fourfold being as the great pyramid of the self. Each of the four sides of the pyramid represents one of man's lower vehicles. These vehicles are the etheric body, the mental body, the emotional body and the physical body. We call these "the four lower bodies."

The etheric body is the fire body. It is the natural envelope of the soul. It has the highest frequency of the four lower bodies and it corresponds to the fire element. Within this etheric envelope, or sheath, God has placed the blueprint of the soul identity, the blueprint that will manifest as consciousness, as mind, as emotion and as the physical matrix itself.

The etheric body actually has two compartments, the higher etheric body and the lower etheric body. The lower etheric body is related to the subconscious mind. The higher etheric body is related to the superconscious mind. And between the two there are the recordings in man's being of his heaven and his earth, so to speak— of the perfection of the soul's origin in God, his heaven-world, and of what he has made of his soul and his consciousness through his many experiences in his incarnations in time and space.

We deal with the subconscious and unconscious mind as the source of man's problems and with the superconscious mind as the great cause behind all effect, which becomes the source of healing. That superconscious mind, of course, is the I AM THAT I AM, the blessed I AM Presence. Actually, the higher etheric body is a reflection and the very repository of this I AM Presence, this I AM THAT I AM.

We find that the key to the healing of the total being of man, the key to wholeness, is in this etheric body. The original purpose of the etheric body was to be the vehicle of the memory of God. This memory is the inner blueprint of the soul as it came forth from the living Spirit. As we study the functions of the four lower bodies, we begin to see how they may be correctly used and how mankind have misused these lower vehicles.

Q: Mrs. Prophet, what are the correct uses of the other three lower bodies?

A: The mental body, the sheath of God's consciousness, is intended to be used as the vehicle of the mind of God and the mind of the Christ and the Buddha. But instead some have taken that precious energy and stamped upon it our version of mind, which has become the carnal mind, or the intellect, and we have used the mental body to be a receptacle of worldly knowledge instead of the knowledge of both this world and the next.

We therefore have made of the mental body a very limited vehicle, when it could be the instrument of the fullness of the mind of God that was manifest in Jesus Christ and Gautama Buddha. We find that the impressions in the mental body have their effects upon the physical body. Where there are impurities in the etheric body, these are reflected in the mental body. Where there are impurities in the mental body, these are reflected in the feeling body. And where there are impurities in the feeling body, these are reflected in the physical body.

The purpose of the feeling body (the desire body) is to express the desire of God. God has only one desire and that desire is to be God. God desiring to be God ought to be the experience of our meditation and our communion.

We ought to use the feeling body, the body of "energy-in-motion," or e-motion, to experience the intense feelings of God as love, as truth, as kindness, as compassion, as purity, and so forth. But instead we have used the emotional body to record the feelings of anger and pride and jealousy and revenge, hatred and intense fear and anxiety, which we find influencing so many of the people today.

Finally, we have the physical vehicle, which was ordained by God to be the temple of the Holy Spirit, the temple of the living God. But we have allowed to come into this temple all manner of perversions of that God—everything from the impurities that we find in our food to the impurity that is reflected from the mental and feeling worlds. And thus the invasion of the body temple has become very great. In the time of Jesus it was seen as demon possession, and the ritual of exorcism, of course, has always been recognized in the Catholic Church.

We find that in order to have healing and wholeness of the four lower bodies, we must set the boundaries of the temple. These four lower bodies, these four sides of our great pyramid of life, are the lines of demarcation that separate us from the mass consciousness. When we have an identity that is clearly defined in God, we can retain the uniqueness of the self in God. When our individuality is not clearly defined, then we tend to float and to drift and to merge with every type of vibration, seen and unseen, and we become nothing more than an amoeba or a jellyfish floating in the sea of the mass consciousness.

When we look for healing, we need to look for wholeness through the integration of the energies of the four lower bodies. That integration takes place through the threefold flame in the heart. The threefold flame of Father, Son and Holy Spirit—of Brahma, Vishnu and Shiva—is the point of contact with our own individual cosmic consciousness.

Through meditation and the use of the science of the spoken Word in the giving of decrees, we make contact with the central flame that burns on the altar of being, this threefold flame of life. And it is by that flame that we invoke the energies of the Spirit of God to descend into the chalice, the matrix, the crucible of the self, the soul evolving in Matter.

Saint Germain, our teacher in the Aquarian age,

teaches us to become alchemists of the sacred fire. You know, the ancient alchemists saw the fourfold nature of life as fire, air, water and earth. In our knowledge of chemistry and physics today we do not consider these to be the proper designations for Matter. But they refer to more than the molecular structure of the elements; they actually refer to planes and frequencies of consciousness.

For instance, the frequency of the etheric body, the fire body, is at a much greater rate, a more intense rate—it is closer to Spirit —than the denser physical vehicle. In fact, its frequency is so different from the physical vehicle that we do not see the etheric body. We only have a sense of its effects because we have a memory, and in moments of meditation the soul remembers its experiences before this incarnation, even when it was "hid with Christ in God" in the very beginning.

The mental body has a different frequency, which corresponds to air and the airlike quality of the mind. It interpenetrates fire and yet remains distinct in its own alchemy.

The feeling, or desire, body is the water body. We associate water with emotion, "energy-in-motion." This water is a tremendous power and a movement and its essential characteristic is that it has no shape. In dealing with the quality of water and its frequency, we come to understand how our emotions can so suddenly come upon us and move so easily in and out of perspective.

Finally, the physical body, which corresponds to the alchemist's earth, is dense, concrete. And it is so concrete that we often mistake the physical body for the actual person, the self. We think that the body is the individual, when actually it is only the house that the soul occupies for a time. And that soul will again occupy other houses, other mansions, until it has fulfilled its course.

Q: What is your advice to someone who is looking for immediate healing?

A: Healing does not begin with an intense anxiety to rid oneself of physical conditions but with the desire to attain wholeness in God. This brings about the healing not only of physical disease but of mental and emotional disturbances as well.

In the Aquarian age, healing and wholeness begin with one's God Self and the invocation of the violet flame. The violet flame is the baptism of the Holy Ghost; it is the law of forgiveness. And when it is invoked it begins, like a cosmic eraser, to consume the cause, the effect, the record and the memory of all imperfections in the subconscious and in the four lower bodies that are bringing distress into manifestation.*

---

*Please note that although spiritual techniques and the violet flame can facilitate our healing at many levels, they are not intended to replace regular medical diagnosis or to be used as a substitute for proper medical care.

17

The Flame in the Heart

∞

- *What is the threefold flame of life?*
- *Why is the flame in the heart important?*
- *How does the violet flame work?*

Mrs. Prophet, we've talked about the four lower bodies. Where do we go from here in healing?

A: Understanding the four lower bodies is obeying the ancient injunction "Man, know thyself." And man must know himself in order to heal himself. The four lower bodies are vehicles. They are interpenetrating sheaths of consciousness, referred to as "coats of skins" in Genesis. (Notice that *coats* is plural and not singular, denoting the four vehicles.) In addition, there are centers of God consciousness that interpenetrate the four lower bodies.

The seven major centers correspond to the seven rays of the Christ and the Buddha. These seven centers are called chakras. A chakra is a wheel, a vortex of light. Its purpose is to take in light as nourishment for the four lower bodies and to give forth light. The sending forth of light is an action of Alpha; the taking in of light is an action, or reaction, of Omega. So, the going out and the coming in of energies within the chakras is another manifestation of the balance of the Father-Mother God within the temple.

The key chakra of the temple is the heart, because within the secret chamber of the heart center is the threefold flame of life.

The threefold flame of life is one with the Father, Son and Holy Spirit at all hours of the day and night. And therefore right within this body temple, upon the altar of the heart, there is burning a flame that is actually God in manifestation. It is through this flame that we can invoke the light of Father, Son and Holy Spirit for the redistribution of energies in the temple when there is disorder or disease (dis-ease) or discord, which is the absence of wholeness.

In our meditation upon Father, Son and Holy Spirit, we visualize the I AM THAT I AM as a great sphere of white light pulsating just above our own being. Coming forth out of this white sphere is all of the energy of God that is necessary for the manifestation of wholeness. We are taught by the Holy Spirit that the violet flame must blaze through and pour through our temple to sweep it clean, to consume the cause and core of our misuse of energy in this and past incarnations.

For the disciple of the New Age—the one entering the age of Aquarius who has sensed the new dispensation, the new energy, but is not quite certain what that energy is—we draw attention to the master Saint Germain. Saint Germain is the one who comes to teach us the alchemy of the violet flame. It is his initiation of his disciples. It is the coming of the promised Comforter.

The beginning of healing is forgiveness. We must call upon the law of forgiveness and use its instrument, the violet flame, to overcome those conditions that have caused us the negative karma that has created disease.

Q: Does this mean that someone can use the violet flame to help heal, say, the common cold?

A: This is certainly a possibility because the common cold can be a manifestation of emotional substance. However, healing comes not only through the violet flame but through the correct balance of energies within the physical body. This is because the cold has been translated from the emotional level to the physical, and so we need to deal with the chemistry of the physical body itself.

Now, this subject of healing is vast. It includes correct diet and the uses of chemistry that are prescribed by physicians. The use of the violet flame, however, is extremely effective, and it can also help us deal with the problems of biochemistry within the physical body.

I'd like to give you another example of how to invoke the violet flame, because it is so necessary in this age and it really is the key to our initiation in this new energy:

> I AM the violet flame
>> In action in me now
> I AM the violet flame
>> To light alone I bow
> I AM the violet flame
>> In mighty cosmic power
> I AM the light of God
>> Shining every hour
> I AM the violet flame
>> Blazing like a sun
> I AM God's sacred power
>> Freeing every one

This mantra comes from the heart of Saint Germain. It uses the name of God, I AM, with a series of affirmations of the sacred fire. Again, we must always bear in mind that when we say, "I AM," we are affirming, "God in me is." We are saying: "The energy of the I AM THAT I AM is qualified now with the violet flame by the action of the Trinity within my heart, which is God's gift to me in the endowment of my very own threefold flame."

In this mantra when we say, "I AM the violet flame in action in me now," we are saying, "God in me is the violet flame in action in me now." We are declaring that where I AM, there God is, and where God is, he is the fullness of this action, this specific action of the violet flame, which is his very own being. It takes understanding of the Law and meditation upon this being of God, who is where I AM, to make the use of the science of the spoken Word effective. We are not absently or vainly repeating words when we give these mantras; we are entering into a very sacred science of the priest of the Order of Melchizedek.

It is a sacred science whereby man voluntarily enters into a oneness with his Creator, becoming co-creator with him as he is ordained to be. The mediator of this co-creation is always the Real Self, the anointed one, the Christ.

As you give this mantra, meditate upon the heart as a white sphere and visualize the greater white sphere of the I AM Presence above the self. The goal of the mantra is to have the sphere within the heart that surrounds the threefold flame converge with the sphere that is the I AM Presence. This convergence of God above with God below is the essence of our healing and our wholeness.

When I give that mantra, it is with a voice that is different from my speaking voice. It is God in me speaking from the very depths of my heart and my soul. I have been decreeing, of course, for many years and when I open my mouth and center my energies in the heart, I am totally surrendering my temple and my being and my centers to God.

This centering allows the energy of the Holy Spirit to use my throat chakra. And the same will happen to anyone who comes to understand the self as the instrument of God.

Q: **Mrs. Prophet, can you tell us what's actually happening when people invoke the violet flame?**

A: Doug, I'd like to read to you from *Climb the Highest Mountain,* where Mark and I have recorded Saint Germain's teaching on the violet flame. The master says:

> The violet flame is the spiritual wine of forgiveness, the quality of mercy that, as Portia said, "is not strained; / It droppeth as the gentle rain from heaven / Upon the place beneath. It is twice blest; / It blesseth him that gives and him that takes."

When you invoke the violet flame for the healing of a specific problem, this is how it works. It envelops each atom of your being individually. Instantaneously a polarity is set up between the nucleus of the atom (which, being Matter, assumes the negative pole) and the white-fire core of the flame (which, being Spirit, assumes the positive pole).

The dual action of the light in the nucleus of the atom and the light in the enveloping violet flame establishes an oscillation that causes the untransmuted densities to be dislodged from between the electrons. As this substance is loosened at nonphysical, or "metaphysical," dimensions of Matter, the electrons begin to vibrate with an increased amount of energy, throwing the misqualified substance into the violet flame.

On contact with this fiery essence of freedom's flame, the misqualified energy is transmuted and God's energy is restored to its native purity. Relieved of the patterns of imperfection and restored to the plus-minus balance of Alpha and Omega, this energy of the Holy Spirit is returned to the individual's causal body, where it is stored until he elects to use it once again to bring forth the noble work of the Christ "on earth as it is in heaven."

18

The Immaculate Concept

∞

- *What are the first steps to healing?*
- *How can one put the immaculate concept to work?*
- *Can you heal yourself by denying that you're ill?*

Mrs. Prophet, your explanation of the violet flame sounds rather complex. Can you simplify it for us?

A: Doug, the violet flame is really a very simple gift of the Holy Spirit. But Saint Germain is the Master Alchemist, and he is the scientist of the age of science. Most inventions, when they are applied, of course, are simple for the everyday man to use. It isn't necessary that we know all of the technical workings of the violet flame to use it every day.

I like the simple mantra to the violet flame "I AM a being of violet fire! I AM the purity God desires!" When you repeat this mantra with great sincerity in the depths of your heart after a period of meditation, you can draw all the energies of your communion with God through prayer and meditation into focus in your heart for the wholeness and the integration of your four lower bodies.

When we say, "I AM a being of violet fire! I AM the purity God desires!" we see the entire body filled with the violet light—crackling, sparkling, leaping violet flame passing through and consuming that substance that is impure. This is the beginning of healing, but there are many steps to healing.

Q: Can you tell us what these steps are, Mrs. Prophet?

A: I think it is important to establish meditation upon one's inner blueprint, upon the soul and its pattern. I call this the science of the immaculate concept. It really is the sacred science of the Mother. A certain understanding of this science has filtered through the metaphysical movements of the past century. The science of the immaculate concept is based on the realization that God has made man in his image and likeness, and therefore behind the outer manifestation there is a perfect reality and a perfect form.

We must have clearly in mind that the natural state of being is wholeness, is oneness with God, is the perfection of the Law. This perfection, this law, this being, is the True Self that exists behind the outer manifestation of an absence of wholeness. In reality, this is the Real Self that we would become.

We can visualize the All-Seeing Eye of God superimposed over our third-eye chakra. Using the gift of God of clear seeing, we behold the perfect Master. We see before us Jesus the Christ. We have his image clearly in mind, as he is a key figure in our overcoming. Or we may visualize the Buddha or Kuan Yin or Mother Mary. We translate the perfection of these sons and daughters of God to our own self, and in the calmness of our meditation upon God we know that this identity is also native to us. Then we begin to mentally affirm that perfection, even as we verbalize that perfection through the science of the spoken Word.

You know, Jesus used a number of mantras in his ministry, but these are taken as simple expressions about himself. He used the word *I AM* to declare, "I AM the way, the truth and the life." Not understanding the use of "I AM" as the name of God, people have thought that he was referring only to the man Jesus. But he was referring to the fact that the God in Jesus is, was and ever shall be the way, the truth and the life.

We as joint heirs with Christ can make that same affirmation. We can declare with Jesus and with Saint Germain, "I AM the way, the truth and the life," as long as we know that we are saying, "God in me, Christ in me, is the way, the truth and the life."

The consequence of that affirmation must be wholeness. If we enter into it as a meditation and really understand it as a mathematical formula, it becomes an equation of being. If God is where I am, if he in truth is congruent with myself here and now, if God is the way, the truth and the life within me, then I too must be that reflection and the fullness of that glory. I too must be whole. This is a natural process of healing that we follow as alchemists of the sacred fire, as we would also become scientists with the great scientist Jesus Christ.

Q: What about the business of simply saying one isn't sick?

A: That gets into denial. It's all right to deny, but you must follow it up by filling your body temple with light. You see, energy can neither be created nor destroyed. When you merely deny that you are sick, you are practicing a form of autohypnosis. You are hypnotizing the self into believing you are not sick but you are not doing anything with the energy.

This energy must be dealt with; it is going to go somewhere. If it is manifesting as disease in the physical body and you deny its presence, it may very well manifest in the feeling body or the mental body or be driven deep into the subconscious.

The ascended masters have told us that if we merely deny disease, we use our free will to alter the working out of karma. Karma is simply the law of cause and effect. All disease is an effect of a prior cause, and usually that cause is some form of mental or emotional discord. That discord eventually works itself out on the physical level and then we are purged of it at every other level.

The cycles of the flow of energy in the four lower bodies always move from the memory (or etheric) body, where everything is recorded at the subconscious level, through the mental body, through the feeling body; and finally the ultimate effects will be in the physical body. Old age, disease, disintegration, decay are all the result of prior causes recorded in the etheric body that have cycled through the mental and emotional bodies. Denying disease, then, can be a form of what I call mental physics. It is using the mind to rearrange matter but it is not getting at the cause behind the effect.

The only energy that can erase those effects is the energy of the Holy Spirit. The Holy Spirit is absolutely essential to our healing and to our wholeness. The specific energy of the Holy Spirit that is required is the violet flame, the light of forgiveness. This is why Jesus said, "Thy sins be forgiven thee." He was invoking by the science of the spoken Word this energy of the Holy Spirit.

We need to be careful that we remove the cause so that we can be forever free from the effects. The ascended masters have taught us that if we, so to speak, shove all effects in our outer world back into the subconscious by simply walking around denying that things exist, we are simply postponing the day of reckoning and in a future incarnation we will have to deal with those subconscious patterns.

However, in the true sense of the word, the action of denying evil has an important part in our demonstration of the science of the Mother. It comes from Jesus' teaching "This kind goeth not out but by prayer and fasting." Prayer and fasting represent the yang and the yin, or the Father and the Mother, the Alpha-and-Omega balance of the science of wholeness. Prayer is the imploring of God for the strength, the energy, the light that is necessary for wholeness. But fasting is the denial—the refraining from the engaging of our energies in evil. (*Evil* is a code name, by the way, for "energy veil.")

So prayer and fasting are like affirmation and denial. We affirm truth, and by the power of that affirmation we can deny the opposite. For instance, we can say, "I AM whole and I AM the manifestation of God." Then we can deny the opposite: "And there is no disease, there is no incompleteness, there is no absence of the fullness of God's being in me!" That denial, when it goes along with the affirmation and is accompanied by the use of the violet flame, represents a more complete formula for healing.

Q: Is instantaneous healing possible? Does it happen often?

A: It certainly is possible. It comes by belief, it comes by the gift of the Holy Spirit. But often the instantaneous healing is a manifestation of the mastery of the healer rather than the one healed. For instance, Lazarus was raised from the dead by Jesus. This was a demonstration of Jesus' mastery over death. Lazarus himself subsequently died; he had not mastered the energies of life over death. Subsequent to his death, he reincarnated and has continued to reincarnate and has yet to prove the law of the ascension.

Q: So it's up to the individual to heal himself in the ultimate sense?

A: The path of the ascended masters is a teaching of "Physician, heal thyself." In the Aquarian age the ascended masters are not so much interested in instantaneous healings whereby the individual does not take the responsibility for his mistakes and errors and misuses of the Holy Spirit. They are more concerned that the individual come to grips with his own karma—the law of cause and effect—and understand that "whatsoever a man soweth, that shall he also reap."

19

Cause and Effect

- *Where does disease come from?*
- *How can Jesus' affirmations help us?*
- *Who are the healing masters?*

Mrs. Prophet, we were talking about taking responsibility in matters of healing. How does one put that into action?

A: The ascended masters are concerned that their chelas put on the mantle of Christ, of Buddha and not merely touch the hem of the garment. There is a big difference here. It's important that we realize that we may be in the presence of Jesus Christ and he may heal us—in fact, he may heal us lifetime after lifetime—but until we actually realize our responsibility in the use of free will and the use of God's energy, we will never be free from the rounds of rebirth.

To gain that freedom we need to begin to ask ourselves, "Well, why do I have this problem?" All of us have a basic awareness of the effects of certain foods upon our bodies. I would not think of asking someone to heal me of a condition in my body that I incurred by knowingly partaking of food that does not help the harmony of my body. I would recognize that I needed to fast for a day and remove from my diet that type of food.

If we study the causes and effects in the physical temple, we realize that indulging in temper tantrums or periods of weeping or prolonged periods of hatred of other parts of life or jealousy also has an effect. We can watch ourselves and see that even dishonesty will result in a certain type of physical disease. Disease may not come immediately, but over the years these energies recycle. We can seek an instantaneous healing of outer symptoms or we can say, "I'm going to take command of my life and I'm going to eliminate the hatred that is causing me this suffering." And so it goes.

Q: How can one identify causes that may have occurred many lifetimes ago?

A: It is not always easy and we don't necessarily have to identify these subconscious momentums. We can know that if we are experiencing a problem in one of the four lower bodies, it is likely an effect of a past misuse of energy.

That misuse of energy may have been as recent as an hour ago when we ate something we shouldn't have eaten or we drank something we shouldn't have drunk, or it may have been fifteen embodiments ago. In either case, the correct use of the sacred fire, the call to the violet flame, the affirmations of Jesus Christ will begin to set God's energy in motion to heal the cause and core of the condition.

Q: Is illness always a manifestation of past misuse of energy?

A: No, not altogether. Illness may be simply the effect of the weight of the mass mind upon an individual. And therefore we need to protect the temple of being. We can begin to have a headache because of very dense energies of confusion or discord manifesting through people close to us or at a greater distance away.

Q: Are you saying we are influenced by people we don't have direct contact with—that is to say, the world at large can affect the way we feel?

A: Yes. We notice this when we're all trying to get out of the city at the same time on Friday night. We flee the city because the city is dense. We want to get out into the country, into the mountains, somewhere else. This is because there is a heavy concentration of the human consciousness and human miscreation in the city. We feel the effects of it as density, as actual weight and fatigue upon our bodies. So we go to the hills to get recharged with the energies of God that are in the currents of the earth.

We are constantly being affected by our environment at all planes of consciousness. Pollution itself is a cause for disease. It should not be considered as something of our past karma but as something to be dealt with in our present environment. If we fail to deal with it, we'll be making karma in the present.

But whether it is the space without or the space within that we are dealing with—in other words, the environment of the city or the environment of our consciousness—change begins with the science of the spoken Word through the energy that is in the heart, which comes from the heart of God.

Jesus has given to us a number of transfiguring affirmations. These affirm God, the I AM THAT I AM, where we are. If we begin with these, then we can tackle the problems of pollution, of the ecology and of all the energies that are upon us at the national and the international level. And we can also go within and tackle the problems of our past misuses of the sacred fire.

The point of beginning is the I AM THAT I AM. Our meditation upon this name of God is with reverence and with the awareness that God is even now within our hearts. So we say:

> In the name of Jesus the Christ,
> I AM THAT I AM
> I AM the open door which no man can shut
> I AM the light which lighteth every man
> that cometh into the world

I AM the way
I AM the truth
I AM the life
I AM the resurrection
I AM the ascension in the light
I AM the fulfillment of all my needs and
     requirements of the hour
I AM abundant supply poured out upon all life
I AM perfect sight and hearing
I AM the manifest perfection of being
I AM the illimitable light of God
     made manifest everywhere
I AM the light of the Holy of Holies
I AM a son of God
I AM the light in the holy mountain of God

As I repeat these affirmations, I feel the Spirit of the living God expanding within me. I feel a cascading energy of light descending upon me like a waterfall or a wind of the Holy Spirit, and I hear the sound of this Spirit within my inner ear. It is even a physical sound. And I have found that the more these affirmations are given, the more my being and my vehicles come into a oneness, a congruency, with the temple of God.

We see that through the science of the spoken Word, healing may be instantaneous or it may be gradual. But it is always the result of our entering into a relationship of mastery with those who have mastered life before us—the ascended masters. These are the ones who will teach us the way to health and wholeness.

Where there are conditions requiring immediate attention through surgery or medication, of course we ought to be practical and avail ourselves of the opportunities that modern science affords us. But right while we are "suffering it to be so now," so to speak, we ought to be invoking the light of God to compensate for the energies that we know have been misqualified and have resulted in the present difficulty.

Our goal is to preserve the physical body, the mind and our energy here on earth so that we can prolong our opportunity to serve God. Where there are doctors and scientists who can effectively help us in doing this, we should recognize that we, working with the doctors, become partners with God to bring about wholeness. But we also ought to see about regulating our life, our self-discipline, our diet, our exercise and our meditation so that we can have greater and greater mastery of these energies of fire, air, water and earth.

Q: Mrs. Prophet, are there particular ascended masters who have a special role in healing?

A: There are indeed, Doug. Just as we have specialists in the human scene, there are specialists in heaven. There are ascended masters who have won their victory by the specific application of their life's energies to the problem of healing.

Hilarion is the master of the fifth ray. The fifth ray is the ray of science, healing, truth and the abundance of God. Hilarion has an etheric retreat over the island of Crete. He was embodied as the apostle Paul and during that incarnation was very much endowed with the scientific understanding of Christ's teaching. He was the instrument of many miracles and healings.

Then there are the Elohim of the fifth ray, Cyclopea and Virginia, whose retreat is on the etheric plane in the Altai Range, a mountain range between Russia and China. The Elohim of the fifth ray focus an intense concentration of science as well as healing.

Cyclopea is invoked specifically for the intensity of the All-Seeing Eye of God and for the opening of the third eye. The third eye is the chakra involved with healing. We are intended to use the All-Seeing Eye of God through the third eye to see the perfection of God in man, and by seeing this perfection we can create the forcefield necessary for healing.

There is one who is known as the Angel Deva of the Jade Temple, who also has an etheric retreat in China. You may wonder why these two retreats are in the vicinity of China. This has to do with forcefields and earth currents. The Chinese civilization, one of the oldest on earth, has always been marked by mastery in science and the healing arts. This influence has actually come from these temples.

The Ascended Master Jesus and Mother Mary maintain a focus of healing in the Temple of the Resurrection, which is over the Holy Land in the etheric plane.

The Holy Spirit is a major factor in healing, and by the conversion of the Holy Spirit many have had an instantaneous healing. The representative of the Holy Spirit to the evolutions of earth is called the Maha Chohan, which means "Great Lord." The one who holds this office has his retreat in the etheric plane over the island of Sri Lanka (formerly Ceylon).

The Maha Chohan is an ascended master who truly embodies a tremendous energy of love, which has been known to effect instantaneous healings right in the midst of audiences where his dictations have been given.

20

Spiritual Retreats

- *What is it like to visit an etheric retreat?*
- *How does one get to such a place?*
- *What can one do about great pain?*

Mrs. Prophet, tell us more about the healing masters and their etheric retreats.

A: These retreats are very real, even though they are on what is called the etheric plane. The etheric plane corresponds to the etheric body, or the fire body.

The etheric plane is the place where our souls abide during periods of rest between incarnations. We may also go to the etheric plane while our bodies sleep at night. The soul, in the etheric body, may take its leave of the physical body and journey to these retreats of the Brotherhood—and specifically to the healing retreats when it is healing that we are seeking.

For instance, beloved Mother Mary and Archangel Raphael have a healing retreat over Fátima, Portugal. When I say "over," I mean in the etheric plane. So you don't necessarily have to physically journey to Fátima for healing. You may make a call to the angels of Mother Mary and Archangel Raphael to take you to their retreat while you sleep at night. There you can enter into communion with the thousands upon thousands of healing angels who serve under Mother Mary and Archangel Raphael.

If you go to this temple, you will be taught how to use the science of the spoken Word and how to meditate upon the immaculate image of your being. Mother Mary holds in her heart the immaculate image for everyone on earth. You will be taken into a special room in the healing temple where meditations are given and where souls come from all over the world to work with this science. You might be taught a mantra such as the following:

Basilica at Fátima

CHRIST WHOLENESS

1.   I AM God's perfection manifest
In body, mind, and soul—
I AM God's direction flowing
To heal and keep me whole!

Refrain: O atoms, cells, electrons
Within this form of mine,

Let heaven's own perfection
   Make me now divine!

The spirals of Christ wholeness
   Enfold me by his might—
I AM the Master Presence
   Commanding, "Be all light!"

2. I AM God's perfect image:
   My form is charged by love;
Let shadows now diminish,
   Be blessed by comfort's dove!

3. O blessed Jesus, Master dear,
   Send thy ray of healing here;
Fill me with thy life above,
   Raise me in thine arms of love!

4. I AM Christ's healing Presence,
   All shining like a mercy sun—
I AM that pure perfection,
   My perfect healing won!

5. I charge and charge and charge myself
   With radiant I AM light—
I feel the flow of purity
   That now makes all things right!

This is a mantra that was given to Mark Prophet by Mother Mary. He wrote it down for those of us who may not remember the mantras we are given in the inner temples. The recitation of this mantra puts one in attunement with the consciousness of Mother Mary because these are her words dictated to the messenger.

It's really very exciting to work with the healing masters and with the healing angels. They have given us a number of decrees and mantras, which we use each Wednesday evening at our healing service and our "Watch With Me" Jesus' Vigil of the Hours. Our Wednesday evening service is dedicated especially to praying for the sick. We receive requests from all over the world asking us to pray for those who need healing. During the week these letters and requests are placed in our healing chalice. Each Wednesday evening we offer this chalice to God and we pray to God through Jesus Christ and all of the healing masters to send healing not only to those whose names are in the chalice but to all those who are praying for healing anywhere in the world. Anyone is welcome to send in the name of a loved one and we will place it in our healing chalice.

Q: Mrs. Prophet, what does one do to get oneself or a loved one to the healing temples?

A: It is important to pray to God and to Jesus and Mother Mary to take one's soul to the healing temples. Offering a simple prayer before retiring at night may accomplish this or it may not. And the reason it may not is that sometimes people's consciousness is so dense that their souls actually cannot navigate free from their own emotions or their own mental concepts about why it is not possible or why they cannot get there. Or perhaps just the general densities and effluvia of the world act as a block.

This is why those who would like to have the experience of meeting with the ascended masters on the inner planes and of attending classes held in these retreats need to begin now to give the "Heart, Head and Hand Decrees." We need to be decreeing each day so that our temples, our vehicles, are becoming lighter and lighter and we will therefore gravitate to the higher octaves of the Spirit instead of to the lower astral planes.

These astral planes can be experienced as restless nights, sleeplessness, nightmares. When you awaken in the morning, you don't feel refreshed or that you have returned from a high experience; you feel burdened with the cares of the day and the previous day, and so on.

Q: Is it possible for someone who is in a great deal of pain to benefit from these opportunities?

A: Those who are experiencing the burden of intense pain or a serious illness may find solace in the dictations of the ascended masters, which we have recorded and which are available on cassettes.

Our decree book contains many invocations and decrees for wholeness, and family and friends may diligently pursue these invocations where the one who is ill cannot do so for himself. If you have a loved one who is ill, I would suggest that you secure the "Heart, Head and Hand Decrees" and give them with your loved one.

To all those who are suffering I say, it is simply important to know that God is present now in the Father, the Son and the Holy Spirit to transfer to you the love that will produce your wholeness. Even if there has been a past sin, or karma, or misuse of energy, the decision now to become one with God is the key to your wholeness. That decision and the follow-up in properly using God's energy will insure for you, whatever the stage of your condition, a better resurrection and an eternal reunion with God here and now or in the life to come.

Doug, I'd like to offer a prayer for healing on behalf of all those who require healing. At the blanks, each one should insert the name of a friend or loved one who needs healing.

COME WE NOW BEFORE THY FLAME

In the name of the beloved mighty victorious Presence of God which I AM and by and through the magnetic power of the sacred fire vested in the threefold flame burning within my heart, beloved Lanello, the entire Spirit of the Great White Brotherhood and the World Mother, elemental life—fire, air, water and earth! I decree:

O Cyclopea, Jesus dear,
  Mother Mary so sincere,
Come we now before thy flame
  To be healed in God's own name.
Stand we in this place in time
  Invoking now thy healing chime!

Tone of golden radiance
  Tinged with brilliant healing green,
Pouring comfort through the earth,
  Perfection so serene!

Come, O love in holy action,
Give us now God-satisfaction.
By the power of holy healing
In perfection's flame now sealing!

I AM holding _____ (name or names)
  Before thy Presence here;
Shed thy love ray forth upon _____ (him, her, them),
  Release thy blessing dear!

I would like to mention that the flame of healing is a brilliant emerald green, and you should visualize it as a pulsating flame around the one for whom you are seeking God's healing love this day. We use this healing flame of brilliant green in conjunction with the violet flame. The violet flame is for the removal of the cause and core of the condition, and the healing flame is for the bringing of God's energies within the body temple into alignment once again.

21

Seven Paths to Wholeness

∞

- *What does the flame in the heart have to do with discipleship?*
- *What do the seven rays have to do with the Path?*
- *Who are the chohans of the rays?*

Mrs. Prophet, what does the flame in the heart have to do with the path of discipleship in the Aquarian age?

A: You know, Doug, there have been disciples of Christ and of Buddha for thousands of years. Even before the coming of Christ and Buddha there were followers of the essential flame of God. Discipleship, then, can best be studied in the lives of the great disciples of East and West.

I was thinking this morning of Saint John of the Cross, who wrote "The Living Flame of Love." The fulfillment of his life was the discovery of this intense love of God whereby God gives himself totally to his servant and the servant gives himself totally to God. And in this consummation of love, there is a fusion whereby God becomes man and man becomes God.

This is only possible through the threefold flame in the heart. It is only possible because God has already endowed us with sonship by placing within us that portion of the Christ, the only begotten of the Father-Mother God.

John the Beloved, who was the closest disciple of Jesus, the true mystic of the twelve, understood this joint heirship. He wrote, "Now are we the sons of God." He understood that we have been endowed with the same essential flame of the light and of the Word as Jesus.

This is our moment, our hour of initiation, to draw forth that flame through Jesus, through Saint Germain, through Gautama Buddha, through Mother Mary, through all of the sons and daughters who have found the same key to unlock the potential of God—and that key is this flame within the heart.

Discipleship is an important initiation because the disciple who places himself under the tutelage of an ascended master—let us say, Jesus—stands in line to receive not only the training and the teaching but the very God consciousness of that master. This hierarchical relationship has been known as that of the guru and the chela in the East and that of the master and the disciple in the West.

Buddha had his closest disciples. Elijah had his disciple Elisha, who received his mantle when he was taken up in a chariot of fire. In II Kings 2 we read the story of how Elisha then went forth and smote the waters of the river Jordan with that mantle.

The mantle of the master signifies his momentum. It represents his attainment, or realization of God. At a certain point the master, or teacher, passes this on to the disciple. He withdraws and the disciple then holds the key position of teacher to those who are coming after.

In this manner, the traditions of the Buddha and the Christ have been handed down to us through the ages. What I'd like to talk about in terms of discipleship are the many paths that are open to us as we pursue the way back Home.

Q: And what are these paths?

A: In order to accelerate the consciousness of God within us and to magnetize the flame of the ascension, each of us as a disciple must attain to a certain mastery on each of the seven rays.

What are the seven rays? The seven rays come out of the white light of the Holy Spirit. You might say that the Holy Spirit is the full complement of all of the rays of the Christ consciousness. As we walk toward the fullness of the expression of the Holy Spirit, we are required to discipline ourselves on one of these seven rays. These rays are noted by the spectrum of color that we see in the rainbow.

Q: Mrs. Prophet, what do the seven rays have to do with this concept of discipleship that you mention?

A: In this age of gurus and masters and teachers, it is important to realize that there are truly those who have followed the disciplines of the path of the Christ and the Buddha, mastered time and space and become one with the eternal light. These masters are called the ascended masters because they have reunited with God in the ritual of the ascension.

The ascension is merely the acceleration of the vibratory rate of the electrons and the very nuclei of the atoms of being until the vibration is so intensified that the individual actually disappears from the sight or visible spectrum of the disciples.

We are evolving on a very fine line of a spectrum. We know that there are sounds we cannot hear because they are beyond our spectrum. We know that there are manifestations we cannot see that are photographed in Kirlian photography. We sense the presence of an aura but we cannot see the aura.

Jesus was not the only son of God who ascended into the white-fire core, the central sun of being. There have been many sons and daughters of God both before and after his birth who have attained to this oneness. These sons and daughters of God are our brothers and sisters on the Path.

They are not exceptions to the rule but they are the personification of the rule, or the Logos, the Word of God itself. They have had the same resources that we have—a threefold flame of the Trinity within the heart; a Real Self, who is the anointed one, the Christ, the Buddha; and an I AM Presence, whom Moses saw in the bush that burned but was not consumed.

These masters have become authorities through their own disciplines. And some, through following one of the rays of God, have become the chohan, or lord, of that ray. They stand as the wayshowers who show their disciples the path back to the center of their own being through that ray.

The chohans, then, have come to teach us what is the true teaching of Christ for our particular ray. El Morya explains in his book *The Chela and the Path:*

> Each of the seven rays that is the fulfillment of an aspect of the Christ consciousness is ensouled by an ascended master who has graduated from the schoolrooms of earth, ascended into the Presence of the I AM THAT I AM and stands as the teacher of the way of self-mastery on a particular ray, or radiance, of the Christ mind.

The first ray is the ray of God's will, which has a frequency in the spectrum of blue. Those who serve on this ray are those who are inclined to lead, to govern, to administer, to organize and to execute. They are great devotees of the will of God, even if they may not call it the will of God. They insist upon order and system in their lives and they are very devoted to this order.

The chohan of the first ray is the one who is the teacher of disciples who serve on that ray. He is the Ascended Master El Morya. He teaches the law of the will of God through the throat chakra in the science of the spoken Word.

His retreat is in Darjeeling, India, and there he receives chelas of the will of God. Their souls journey to this retreat while their bodies sleep at night. The soul takes leave of the body in the etheric envelope and takes part in the cosmic schoolroom.

The second ray, the ray of wisdom, vibrates in the color spectrum of yellow. It is the focus of illumination, the illumined action of God. Its chohan, or lord, is Lanto. Many servants of the wisdom of God have been the teachers of mankind through the ages. Lord Lanto serves from the Royal Teton Retreat near Jackson Hole, Wyoming, which is congruent with the Grand Teton.

The second ray is the ray of those who teach, who understand and who know God through the illumined action of his wisdom and the wisdom of his law. These are the quiet souls like Saint Francis of Assisi, who is now the Ascended Master Kuthumi. Beloved Kuthumi occupied the position of chohan of this ray until January 1, 1956, when he became a World Teacher.

Lord Lanto's evolution was in ancient China, where through the wisdom schools he drew forth the light of the heart. Those who are seeking to know God by the mind of Christ and the mind of Buddha are disciples on this ray. He teaches the path of attainment through enlightenment, definition and dominion in the crown chakra.

You see, the crown chakra is the center for the mind of God even as the throat chakra is the center for the will of God. These chohans guide us in the mastery of each of the seven rays through each of the seven chakras.

The third ray is the ray of the love of God, the consummation of oneness in the Holy Spirit. Through this ray, whose spectrum is pink, come the artists, those who are the creative, sensitive and intuitive souls. These are the ones who serve mankind through love, through charity and compassion. They find their oneness with the greater Self in many creative avenues.

The lord of this ray is Paul the Venetian, who was embodied as Paolo Veronese, the great Italian artist. Art, sculpture and all forms of self-expression are taught by Paul as he receives disciples in his retreat, the Château de Liberté, in southern France.

The fourth ray extols the purity of God and his discipline. It is the white ray. Disciples of this ray come under the disciplines of the chohan Serapis Bey, whose retreat is the Ascension Temple at Luxor, Egypt.

The masters of India teach that the base chakra is the focal point for the Goddess Kundalini and the raising of the energies through the other chakras. It is Serapis Bey who teaches us this discipline.

The white flame is the way of those who would contact the blueprint, the inner design, of their handiwork. In the honor and the integrity of the soul's oneness with the law of perfection, they pursue the discipline of the mastery of their sacred labor, the work of their hands, which is the work of the Father-Mother God through them. These are the disciplined ones who are seeking ultimate reunion with God through the greatest sacrifice of the self.

This is the way of those who commune in the wholeness of the consciousness of the Divine Mother through purity of body, mind and soul. The color white, of course, embodies all of the rays; and therefore, ultimately, the disciplines of each of the seven rays bring one to this doorway and to the ascension, the soul's eternal liberation.

The fifth ray is the ray of truth and the science of God. It is the ray of healing and abundance, which vibrates in the color spectrum of green. Its chohan is Hilarion, who was embodied as the apostle Paul. His retreat is the Temple of Truth on the etheric plane over the island of Crete.

On this ray, scientists, doctors, healers, mathematicians, musicians pursue a scientific mastery of the self and of the planes of Spirit and Matter. This they do through the quest for truth in every discipline, including the healing arts. And so the fifth ray becomes the means whereby those who require the logic of the

Logos can find their way back to the Christ consciousness, back to the God-design.

Morya says:

> Hilarion is very much involved in working with atheists and agnostics. He comes to show us that true religion is the highest science and that all religion can be proven if we will accept the proof of that which manifests within as well as that which manifests without. And there is just as much empirical proof of the God within as there is empirical proof of the God without.

I think sometimes people think that the path of religion cannot be combined with the path of science, but Hilarion, the apostle Paul, shows us that, in truth, true religion and true science are one and the same vibration.

The sixth ray is the ray of the master Jesus, of peace and the ministration of God. It is the way of the selfless servant. Jesus served for two thousand years as the lord of this ray. Now as this two-thousand-year cycle is turning, Jesus serves as World Teacher and beloved Nada has become the lord of the sixth ray. She serves in the temple of Jesus, which is the Temple of the Resurrection in the etheric plane over the Holy Land.

The sixth ray has a frequency in the spectrum of purple and gold—the purple and gold as the twin flames of Christhood on this ray. It is the way of those who minister in the energies of peace to the evolutions of earth as counselors and comforters in every walk of life. Their inner vow is: "I am my brother's keeper." And their soul motto is: "He that would be great among you, let him be the servant of all."

Those who serve on the sixth ray with Jesus and Nada have a very devotional nature. Their chakra is the solar plexus, which is tied to the water element, the water body, and therefore their feeling for God is intense. But unfortunately that feeling is often translated into a fanaticism that does not admit to the expansive and progressive revelations of Jesus in this age.

The motto of beloved Nada is Jesus' own golden rule: "Do unto others as you would have them do unto you." Morya writes:

> Nada's chelas pave the way for the golden age of Aquarius under Saint Germain. The lord of the seventh ray, who is the Master of Alchemy, teaches not only the uses of the energies of freedom and the spirit of liberty but also the way of the alchemical ritual as a necessary component of soul liberation. His ritual is alive with meaning. In his retreat in Transylvania he unveils the symbology of the ritual of the atom and the formulae of the cycles for the release of God's energy in manifestation in man.

Saint Germain's retreat in North America is the Cave of Symbols at Table Mountain, Wyoming.

The seventh ray, which has a frequency in the spectrum of violet, is the ray of freedom and the forgiveness of God through the alchemy of the Holy Spirit. It is the way of the priests of the Order of Melchizedek. It is also the way of those who are one with the Great Dramatist, God himself, who has conceived of the world as a stage upon which we all play our roles.

Saint Germain is the scientist who sponsors invention, innovation, great genius and the mastery of the Matter plane through technology. But he also teaches the law of selflessness and non-attachment so that science does not become a dead materialism but a materialization of the God flame whereby we realize in Matter the fullness of the living God.

The alchemy of the seventh ray is of the Aquarian age. It is truly the way of soul freedom. Saint Germain gives us the way of self-transformation through intense invocation of the sacred fires of the Holy Spirit, that violet-flame action that is the dissolving of sin, or the records of past karma.

22

Discipleship

∞

- *What is the path of discipleship for the New Age?*
- *If we're all one, where is the place for individuality?*
- *What do the seven rays have to do with the seven chakras?*

Mrs. Prophet, can you tell us how Jesus established the path of discipleship for the New Age?

A: Jesus came as the great Guru, the great Master, the incarnation of the Word. We call him the avatar of the age, the one who was the fullness of God incarnate and who exemplified the person of the Son, although he was the fullness of Father, Son and Holy Spirit.

We speak of the Christ as the only begotten Son of God. There is a bit of confusion concerning this only begotten Son because we have confused the eternal nature of the Christ with the singular Son Jesus. Jesus the Christ gives us the understanding of Jesus the Son. Jesus became the fullness of the Christ and therefore, in the order of hierarchy, earned the title of "Son." He set this example for all of us to follow.

Beloved El Morya, Lord of the First Ray, explains in his book *The Chela and the Path* the essential nature of the Christ flame as the real identity of all sons and daughters of God and not only of Jesus. He says:

You who have discovered the flame within have at last discovered the Christ as the signet of your true being. This Christ flame is the sign, the living proof, that you are a son, a daughter of God. Let no man take thy crown.

Let no man take from thee this appellation. Behold, thou art the Christ forevermore! The Christ flame is your claim to individuality in God, to immortality—to the perpetuation of selfhood beyond the mortal frame and beyond the planes of time and space.

The Master of Galilee came to extol that flame, to set the example of a life lived in the flame. So you also have come called by God to be an example to the age, to set your mark upon the page, the mark of the life that is lived in God, of the love that is willed in Christ.

As you claim the potential of the Christ flame, as you affirm your individuality in God, know that you do so with the absolute authority of your own I AM Presence and of the Holy Spirit. For he said, "This is my body, which is broken for you."

The fragments of the light body of the eternal Logos [the Word], the same "Light which lighteth every man that cometh into the world," are throughout the creation the fullness of the living Christ whom God, because he so loved the world, gave to every son and daughter.

Understand that in the gift of life, the threefold flame, the LORD God literally gave to all of his children the flaming essence of the Only Begotten that through conformity with this essence the world might be saved from sin, disease and death.

The great flame of God abiding within us all can be understood in the sense that there is only one God, one Christ and one Holy Spirit. In time and space, God has placed a replica, a duplicate, of Father, Son and Holy Spirit as this threefold flame within the hearts of all of his sons and daughters. This flame is still only one God.

One times one times one always equals one. Though there be

a million billion sons and daughters, still the flame is only one. We all share that essential oneness. It is through this oneness that we demonstrate the law of our Christhood. It is to this Christhood that Jesus led us.

Q: Where is the place for individuality if we're all one?

A: It is in the gift of free will, which comes with the threefold flame. By this gift of free will, we choose which path of Christhood we will take. The paths are seven in number, corresponding to the seven rays that come forth out of the white light of the Holy Spirit.

If we have, for instance, a scientific nature and we would pursue the way of science, the ray for us is the fifth ray of science. Or it may be the seventh ray of alchemy and transmutation.

If we are an artist by nature and our whole life is a passion in the arts, we are not excluded from the path of Christhood simply because we are not inclined to demonstrate the law of Christhood in the same way Jesus did. Those who excel in the arts can achieve mastery on the third ray of love under the tutelage of the Ascended Master Paul the Venetian.

By the discipline of art in all of its forms, we come to a discipline in the Holy Spirit and to a total selflessness, because art itself demands the absolute sacrifice of the self for its consummation. Thus we have seen the way of love expressed by the great artists of the ages.

The seven paths of the chohans are each unique and special. Each one has its own frequency and its own way and its own discipline. All of us on earth today as children of God are finding our way back to the central sun of being over one of these rays, which come forth from that sun.

We have free will to choose our ray. And, as a matter of fact, we already chose our particular ray and discipline thousands

upon thousands of years ago when our souls first came forth from
the plane of Spirit and we began to incarnate on earth.

Many can immediately identify their position on one of
these seven rays. It's quite exciting to realize that one's calling and
the way of life one has known are truly a part of discipleship in
the Aquarian age. Through many past lives we have developed
a momentum of service and of dedication, and this dedication
is not outside of the framework of Christianity, Buddhism,
Judaism, Islam but is wholly within the Path that God has consecrated through all the world's religions.

Q: **Is each of us confined to a particular ray? Does our experience
overlap the other rays?**

A: Although we may have been evolving for so many thousands
of years in order to perfect a certain ray, many times we have
come into incarnation to work on other rays so that we would
have the full balance and the full complement.

You may find yourself, for example, very much on the first
ray as a person of authority, a leader, and one who excels in the
use of energy to draw others to a focal point of service, and yet
you may also be inclined toward science. In such a case, you
might say that you have a major on the first ray of God's will and
a minor on the fifth ray of science. And so we see the blending of
the rays creating almost an infinite expression of the personality
of the Son, the Christ.

Q: **What about the seven chakras in relation to the seven rays?**

A: God has given to us the seven chakras so that we might
experience his consciousness in different frequencies. These
frequencies correspond to the seven rays.

For instance, the heart is the place where we experience love.
So, the mastery of the third ray of love comes through the heart

chakra. We experience love through the burning in the heart for the master, and we have the intense love for the beloved.

The mastery of the fifth ray of science and healing comes through the third eye as the focalization of truth and vision and as the precipitation of God's abundance from the Macrocosm to the microcosm.

The seven chakras are a gift that God has placed within us so that we have the seven notes of the scale, the seven rays of the Holy Spirit, right within our own being. If we learn to meditate and use the science of the spoken Word, we can unlock the energies of each of these centers. And each of these centers leads us to the master of one of the seven rays (which are of the same frequency as the centers).

Q: Do the seven rays have anything to do with the seven days of the week?

A: The cycle of seven is a cycle of completion and of wholeness. The cycle of seven in the week is a way whereby God releases to us the seven rays. And so each of the days of the week is given to us so that we may master a certain one of the rays of God. And on that day we also have the testings and the initiations of the chakra corresponding to that frequency.

Q: I've heard reference in some teachings to an eighth ray. Where does that fall?

A: The eighth ray is a ray of integration. It is the perpetual flow between the Buddha and the Mother. It is a transition ray between the seven rays, which are for the mastery in the planes of Matter of the Christ consciousness, and the five secret rays, which are within the white-fire core of being.

The five secret rays represent a going within for the mastery of God, whereas the seven outer rays represent the coming without and the mastery of the environment. We go through cycles that form a pattern of the going within and the coming without, just as the Eastern teachings represent the going within and the Western teachings represent the coming without.

We see that the West is an arena for the mastery of the outer world. In this period of the turning of cycles that we are experiencing in the West, it is time to go within to the white-fire core of being. This transition of going within is accomplished through the eighth ray, whose symbol is the figure eight.

Q: That's also the sign of infinity, is it not?

A: Truly it is, and it is infinity that we attain by the mastery of time and space.

23

El Morya, Master of God's Will

∞

- *What were some of El Morya's embodiments?*
- *What is the meaning of hierarchy and what role does the Darjeeling Council play in it?*
- *Is there a spiritual world government?*

Mrs. Prophet, we've barely touched on the subject of El Morya. Can you tell us a bit more about him?

A: El Morya begins at the beginning on the first ray. He teaches that without dedication to the will of God, you cannot be disciplined on any of the other rays. And so Morya takes on those individuals who have perhaps rebelled against their inner calling and who are not really following the master of their ray because they have not yet come to grips with their own relationship to the will of God.

The most important lesson that I have learned from El Morya is that the will of God is within us. It is our inner blueprint; it is the design of the soul. To rebel against the will of God is to rebel against the Self, the True Self.

Jesus teaches us that a house divided against itself cannot stand. And so to begin the path of true chelaship we have to resolve this schism within the self. We have to realize that the will of God is good and it will not take from us our true identity, but it is the adornment of that reality.

Q: Mrs. Prophet, could you tell us something about the embodiments of El Morya?

A: El Morya, who is so beloved of his disciples, was Abraham, Hebrew patriarch and progenitor of the twelve tribes of Israel. He was Melchior, one of the three wise men who attended the birth of Jesus. In the sixth century he was embodied as Arthur, King of the Britons. Our hero of this age, if we ever had a hero, would be King Arthur. And if we were ever to go back in history, I think we would all like to be at Camelot. We know, too, that Camelot held a special significance for President Kennedy.

It is the jeweled-love quality of El Morya, who is very present with us today, that makes us hark back to this great visionary king who founded the order of the Knights of the Round Table. His knights went in quest of the Holy Grail, from which Jesus drank at the Last Supper. Legend tells us this Holy Grail was brought from the Holy Land by Joseph of Arimathea and buried in a well at Glastonbury. The focal point was thus set for the dispensation of Camelot.

The Ascended Master El Morya

In the twelfth century Morya was embodied as Thomas à Becket, Chancellor of England and Archbishop of Canterbury under Henry II. In the fifteenth century he was embodied as Sir Thomas More, the Lord Chancellor of England under Henry VIII. In his book *Utopia,* More outlined the ideal community and God-government. When he refused to take the oath repudiating the pope's authority or to uphold Henry VIII's divorce from Catherine of Aragon, he was sentenced to death.

Thomas More was canonized in 1935. Many remember him as the great heroic figure portrayed in *A Man for All Seasons*—the same Arthur come again, the same soul. Thomas More gave a prayer that to me is most precious in that it shows his devotion to God:

> Give me, good Lord, a longing to be with Thee: not for the avoiding of the calamities of this wicked world, nor so much for the avoiding of the pains of Purgatory, nor the pains of Hell neither, nor so much for the attaining of the joys of Heaven in respect of mine own commodity, as even for a very love of Thee.

Thomas More longed to be with God just for the sake of loving him and not for any other compensation. He asked God to purify this longing, "even for a very love of Thee."

Q: What were some of El Morya's later embodiments?

A: El Morya is probably one of the greatest saints of the Church in his devotion to Jesus Christ. Yet he was also embodied as Akbar the Great, who founded the Mogul Empire in India and was the greatest of all its rulers. His policies were considered to be among the most enlightened of his time. He was a superb organizer and administrator of conquered territories. He introduced many reforms, put an end to extortion, increased trade and showed tolerance toward the many religious faiths of India.

In the embodiments of El Morya we see the soul of a great devotee of God weaving in and out of the paths of East and West. And we take special note that in each of his incarnations he is perfecting the diamond of the will of God within his soul—through God-government, through the vision of community that he wrote about in his *Utopia* as Thomas More, through his supreme devotion to the will of God in his incarnations as Thomas à Becket and Thomas More. Even attending the birth of Christ in his embodiment as Melchior was the fulfillment of his longing to serve that will.

He was also known and loved as the Irish poet Thomas Moore. Among his many ballads, the best remembered is "Believe Me, If All Those Endearing Young Charms." The tenderness of the works of Thomas Moore shows the heart of one devoted to the will of God, the intense love that must be the other side of the fiery devotion and authority of the first-ray man or woman. We find that those who have the greatest power of God as rulers also have in their souls the gift of poetry and the flow of love as the sweet balance to their immense power.

El Morya's final embodiment was in India in the latter part of the nineteenth century. He was born a Rajput prince. Known as El Morya Khan, he worked closely with Kuthumi and Djwal Kul in attempting to acquaint the West with the reality of the invisible world and the teachings of the Law and hierarchy through the Theosophical movement. He was known as the Master M., while Kuthumi was known as the Master K. H., or Koot Hoomi.

Since his ascension in about 1898, El Morya has worked tirelessly with Saint Germain in the cause of world and individual freedom. To that end he has given many dictations and many lectures on the true teachings of the Christ and what they mean for us in this age. In his book *The Chela and the Path,* he writes:

> Until men recognize the darkness, they do not reach for the light. Thus the grossness of materialism and of a mechanistic civilization continues unchallenged. To challenge, men must have a sword; and the sword is the sacred Word of truth to this age.
>
> The Darjeeling Council is a unit of hierarchy. I am its chief. Numbered among those who deliberate in our chambers are Saint Germain, Mary the Mother, Jesus the Christ, the Master Kuthumi, Chananda, the Great Divine Director,

Lord Maitreya and the Ascended Master Godfre.

Assisted by many unascended chelas, we serve the cause of the will of God among humanity, in the governments of the nations, in the economic councils, in the social strata, in the institutions of learning and, above all, in the diamond hearts of the devotees.

El Morya is explaining here the interaction of hierarchy. Hierarchy is simply the succession of masters and their disciples that exists and has always existed in the scheme of things as souls have made their way Godward.

In this hierarchy there are ascended masters, those who have become one with God through the acceleration of consciousness that Jesus demonstrated. And then there are their disciples who yet remain in embodiment, people like you and me, who are called chelas. In Hindi, *chela* means "servant" or "disciple." We, as the disciples of the masters, interact with the masters to work for the cause of light and freedom on earth.

The Darjeeling Council chambers are located in the Temple of God's Will over Darjeeling, India. Chelas may journey there out of the body in the etheric sheath, or the etheric vehicle.

While we sleep, our souls take leave and we do go to the

retreats of the Brotherhood that are most fitted to our soul evolution. We may have recollections when we awaken in the morning of being among these great teachers, our elder brothers and sisters on the Path who are showing us the way.

El Morya, who is greatly concerned about the condition of government and freedom on earth, came forth to train Mark Prophet as his messenger. Then he appeared to me in Boston and called me to be a messenger also. He writes:

> Those who see the crumbling of the old order look for the new. The path of chelaship [or discipleship] is the way of transition. For those who would arrive at the station of the new cycle, we provide answers and a formula. And there is no turning back. In those in whom selfishness has not marred the vision of the new day, there is the burning desire to be free and to make that freedom available to all.
>
> Such was the purpose of the Darjeeling Council in the founding of The Summit Lighthouse in Washington, D.C., in 1958. With humble beginnings yet with the torch of our trust passed from God and anchored in the heart of a band of devotees, we built our organization—an outer arm of the Great White Brotherhood, a forum for the will of God, a focus for the purity of its fiery core.

The Great White Brotherhood is the order of ascended masters that has existed for thousands upon thousands of years, and it is the association of ascended masters and their embodied chelas. The term *white* refers to the white light of the aura in all of those who are its members. It is the crystallization of the Christ consciousness, the halo of the saints. It is not in any way a reference to race. Whether black or white, Eastern or Western, Chinese or Indian, all can be—and all who have "made their calling and election sure" indeed are—a part of the Great White Brotherhood. Morya writes:

Mark Prophet—and later his twin flame, Elizabeth—
was trained by me to be a messenger for that hierarchy of
adepts composed of all who have graduated from earth's
schoolroom with honor. These are they who have mastered
the laws of their own karma and by the pursuit of the Bud-
dhic light have been thrust from the wheel of rebirth. These
are the ascended ones whose souls have been lifted into the
glory of the life universal and triumphant. By their striving
on the way, by their excellence in self-discipline and by the
grace of Christ, they are the overcomers.

Q: Does El Morya have anything to say about the way government
is being handled today?

A: El Morya will work with and inspire all who are concerned with
government. Of course he believes in government of the people, by
the people and for the people, but he tells us that those who have the
right to rule are those who have exalted the threefold flame in the
heart. Those who have the greatest amount of attainment in the
Christ consciousness are those who have the authority of the Christ.

It is for the coming of the reign of the Prince of Peace that
El Morya is preparing us. This reign he explains as the advent of
the Second Coming of Jesus Christ, which is the kindling of our
own self-awareness in that Christ and our oneness in service with
Jesus. And, therefore, the reign of the Prince of Peace is the reign
through the rule of those who have the light in the heart. No
matter what their religion or following—they may be Buddhists,
they may be Jews, they may be Muslims—it is their dedication to
the light and the flame of God that gives them the ability to rule
others who are working toward that same discipline.

Q: The ideal that you describe seems far removed from the reality
that we know, Mrs. Prophet. Are there practical steps that can get
us from here to there?

A: The first step is always the establishing of the self within the altar of being, within the consciousness of God. Without God we can do nothing. As Jesus taught us: "I of mine own self can do nothing; it is the Father in me who doeth the work." This work of God through us is the only way we can deliver our nation and every nation into the hand of God.

El Morya has written *A White Paper from the Darjeeling Council Table* in which he discusses his views on politics—right- and left-wing. His opening statement is one that I have cherished ever since he wrote it:

> The orphans of the Spirit are our concern—those who, without the thread of contact with Deity, remain wedded to an unwholesome environment, those to whom the real purpose of life is never revealed; for the crystallization of their intellectual concepts and the hardness of their hearts, rooted in selfishness, do not open the cosmic doorway to our domain.

Morya and the Darjeeling Council provide us with the opportunity for conscious cooperation with the hosts of heaven so that we might lead our nation, our life, our community into God-dominion, into the true dominion of the sons and daughters of God. Doug, this is what the coming revolution in higher consciousness is all about.

Q: It sounds like they've got something in mind for all of us, right?

A: That's right, and it is direct participation in higher consciousness that will truly revolutionize America and every nation!

24

God-Government

- *What is the ascended master ideal for government?*
- *What do the masters have to say about the right wing and the left wing?*
- *Do the masters influence our leaders?*

Mrs. Prophet, you've spoken somewhat about El Morya's ideals for government. Could you tell us a bit more?

A: The closeness of the American people to El Morya is nowhere more evident than in their intense concern for government. And from the very beginning, government has been intended for the participation of all people.

In his *White Paper from the Darjeeling Council Table,* El Morya analyzes what our attitude should be toward government, because government and its correct functioning is the direct manifestation of our dedication to the will of God. Government is the will of the people, of the governed, implemented by their representatives. Without this we cannot proceed on the path of true religion or true science. El Morya says:

> So many are the mysteries of life, so many are the powers of love. Yet the dust seems to be more the choice [of some] than the destiny God ordained. Now there is a remnant, and the remnant is one of hope; and these are responsive hearts, but the great cosmic net must reach into

the deep and find them out.

We must draw many to the higher pilaster. We must amplify the filaments of light in the body-bulbs of those who are the true seed of God. We must protect and direct. Yet the veil of obscurity is very, very heavy.

While man's concern for his ecology mounts, what shall I say is happening to the soul within? The moral standard, recognition of the plane of Spirit, listening to the music of the stars and the spheres, creating that tie of cosmic identity that is the forte of the will of God—these are the strong banners we raise.

Remember that El Morya is our own personal guru, the ascended master who founded The Summit Lighthouse. He says:

Now we compliment those who have assisted in the expansion of the light beams from The Summit Lighthouse: those who perceive our reality standing behind the printed word, those who understand that the messengers and staff are glad servants, a veil of flesh through which we indicate strands of the holy pattern.

Turning his attention to the world scene, Morya writes:

Noting the widening schisms, the deliberately maneuvered divisions being created through the dichotomies of mind and spirit in the total world order today, it is my desire to speak from our level concerning our viewpoint and our intent. Those who would set nation against nation, those who would set people against people, those who would point the accusing finger of one religion at another, by so doing create that fracture in consciousness that is a destructive negative spiral.

May I, then, set forth so that all may hear me once and for all, the policy of The Summit Lighthouse, sponsored by the Great White Brotherhood. As the brother of humble service who assisted in the pangs of birth, may I now order the promulgation of our statement of policy and see that this shall reflect our thoughts both now and in the future.

It is well known that there are in the world millions who are labeled "left wing." There are other millions labeled "right wing." There are others who choose, in some degree of human pride I might add, the position of the middle of the road. May I say that we do not espouse any of these causes, and may I tell you why.

To me, this was the most refreshing aspect of El Morya's consciousness when I first encountered him. I found that I could be free to support the will of God anywhere in the political spectrum. I didn't have to be right wing, left wing, middle of the road. I could see the will of God and be a chela of this guru and yet be directly involved with government in America and in every nation. So Morya is the great liberator of my soul from partisan politics. And being a political science major, I found this to be a wonderful solution to a difficult problem. He writes:

> The magnitude of Cosmic Christ service is such that we cannot identify ourselves or our movement with one confined to a secular slice of opportunism. Those who desire to sell many copies of their magazine espouse controversial subjects, knowing that half of the people in the world will probably subscribe to their view. They play the percentages, and to them life is a wheel of roulette.
>
> From our level we can scarcely engage in such conduct. We choose, then, not to favor any of these positions but rather to recognize the whole spectrum from right to left, including the middle of the road, as the valley of reality where truth may appear mingled with error.
>
> Ours is not to create division, and The Summit Lighthouse, our organization, reflects those goals that are sound and strengthening to the human spirit. May I say in all cosmic honor that there are virtuous causes across the whole range of human endeavor, but there are many that are unvirtuous, unrighteous, deceptive and wrongly motivated.

We cannot identify with any, for our purpose is not to be popular but to be truthful and to embrace those spiritual causes that will enable the soul itself to expand its life.

I have not denied that the poor, as Jesus said, are with you always. I have not denied man's right to fulfill those social needs which to some have become a way of spiritual service. Likewise, we clearly see that among the traditions of men there are many of virtue, albeit sometimes sagging, that ought to be upheld; but where shall we position the timbers? We cannot identify with the right or the left, and we cannot identify with the middle of the road.

We see that the position of the ascended masters is not to ratify any human position, not to tell us that we are right, but to tell us to be wed to truth rather than personalities or platforms, because these always represent a mingling of truth and error.

What we must strive to do is to isolate truth and then champion it wherever it is found. And since all men and women have a creative potential to bring forth an element of God, we should test what is brought forth by the standard of the will of God, which we all have within us, and as God gives us the wisdom and the gift of vision to see and to know that will.

Q: How do we do that, Mrs. Prophet?

A: By the consecration of our day and our life to that will—calling to God, kneeling in intense prayer before we go to sleep at night, asking God to realign our consciousness. Every night we should dedicate the next day to God. Then, while we sleep God will purify our souls, purify our motives, give us solutions to problems. We can tune in to the cosmic mind, which is just like a fantastic cosmic computer. It releases to us through the night all that we need to deal with the challenges of the coming day.

Our leaders and representatives especially should realize that they have a supreme duty to meditate upon the will of God. They must not be tied to their own personal preferences or bound by political commitments. They need to be bound solely by and to the will of God, which will surely come forth and inspire consciousness if they open themselves to it.

Q: Do the masters influence our leaders?

A: El Morya has chuckled when he has told us of the many leaders he has worked through, perhaps leaders that we would not particularly vote for. But he says, "Whoever is in office we must work with." He writes in his *White Paper*:

> Spiritual knowledge is the highest knowledge and takes into account the total compass of the brotherhood of man. For example, when we make a pronouncement that seems to sanction one [cause] or the other—and as I have said before, the garment of righteousness must run the whole spectrum—we find ourselves being labeled and our outer voice of cosmic reason, The Summit Lighthouse, being labeled also.
>
> The choice we make, then, is to render the greatest service to all men and women upon the planet wherever they appear on the social scale, from the poorest to the wealthiest, from the weakest to the strongest, from the most unspiritual to the most spiritual, from the foolish to the wise. We must serve them all.

When El Morya says "we," he's talking about the Darjeeling Council and all of the ascended masters. He says:

> Unless we do, we have fallen short of our divine office. When human reform is needed, let us be about our Father's business; but let us put the brakes on those unfortunate situations that literally tear from man the vital energies of his life, leaving him a profitless servant.

Q: Have the masters had a great involvement with the development of this country?

A: The masters, through Saint Germain, have sponsored America to be a pilot nation for the republican form of government, for representative government according to the inner path of initiation. Those who have the greatest attainment in the Christ consciousness are intended to rise to the position of being statesmen and great examples of virtue to the people.

They are not intended to be simply political figures but examples of the great virtues of religious leaders of the past and those such as Socrates and Plato and the great philosophers and scientists. They are intended to have integrity—the determination to be wed to a cause with nobility, love, purity, and so forth.

This is what we need in America and in every nation today. And, of course, the ascended masters do sponsor every nation as the leaders of the nations are responsive to their vibrations.

Q: Then would you say that the resemblance between the republican form of government and hierarchy, as you describe it, is no coincidence?

A: It is not a coincidence. But you know, El Morya has said it really doesn't matter what the form of government. Any form of government can work when the basic principle of the integrity of the soul and the soul's relationship to God is maintained, and when the ruler or governing body—be it the single enlightened despot or a committee or a larger group or the people themselves —considers its supreme obligation to be the safeguarding of the individual's right to become one with God.

25

Mystery Schools

- *What is the real meaning of Camelot?*
- *What did the thirteen original colonies of America symbolize?*
- *What were the mystery schools?*

Mrs. Prophet, would you tell us how El Morya's ideas of government evolve?

A: El Morya has chosen the will of God from the very beginning of his evolution, as we all make a choice by the gift of free will. And so he became chohan of the first ray, the ray of God's will (and God-government), by the expansion of that flame within his being and entire sphere of consciousness. One goes back to Lemuria, to Atlantis, to other worlds to find the origin of the evolution of individual genius. But more recently we find El Morya as the center of Camelot, the once and future mystery school.

Camelot represents the ideal of God-government, but it also represents the original twelve apostles and the master in the center of the disciples, who are the knights and ladies of the court. There is the round table, the table of initiation. There is the quest for the Holy Grail. Indeed, Camelot can be seen as the community of the Holy Spirit and as a continuation of the mission of the community of disciples of Jesus as well as of the sangha of the Buddha.

The Buddha teaches us of the three refuges—the refuge of the teacher, who is the Buddha; of the doctrine, which is the dharma, or the law; and finally, the refuge of the community, the sangha. We understand that discipleship in the New Age and our oneness with the masters of the seven rays depends upon these three elements.

And so we must have a teacher, and we find that teacher in the Real Self within as well as in the chohans of the seven rays of the Christ. We must have a teaching, and we find that teaching through all of the sons and daughters of God who have ever lived on earth to show us the way. Finally, we must have a community, which is like the mystical body of God within the Church. It is that group of souls who are pursuing the path of initiation with the ascended masters.

The ascended masters themselves are a part of that community. So we find a cooperation between those who are in heaven and those who are on earth. And we understand that Camelot, as a mystery school, was the opportunity for a cooperative endeavor based upon the central teacher, the Christ. The quest for the Grail, which symbolizes the cup of the teaching and the essence of the Blood of Christ and of Communion itself, was for the assimilation of the Body and Blood of Christ—the essence of Spirit and Matter. This is the foundation of the ritual of Communion.

It was El Morya's dream to bring forth such a community. As King Arthur, he worked with Merlin, an embodiment of Saint Germain. These initiates of the Great White Brotherhood formed a nucleus for the future mystery school that was to come in the thirteen original colonies—the thirteen symbolizing once again the number of Christ and his apostles.

America was intended to be the place where those who were pursuing the light of God could come and found that new order of the ages based on the four freedoms—the *Novus Ordo Seclo-rum,* which we find inscribed on the one dollar bill, symbolized in the Great Pyramid. And we have spoken of the Great Pyramid as representing the four planes of Matter and the mastery of the four vehicles of consciousness.

What all of this has to do with the will of God and God-government is expressed in Proverbs: "He that is slow to anger is better than the mighty; and he that ruleth his spirit than he that taketh a city." The chohans of the seven rays teach us that we must master the energy within in order to master the energy without. And they teach us how to take dominion within the environment of the self so that we may take dominion over the environment that is without.

And so the discipline of Camelot, which was to be the discipline of all of the nations, was to provide a platform through freedom of religion, freedom of the press, freedom of speech and freedom of assembly for the individual soul's fusion with her* own Christ-potential. It was to provide a platform for that collective mastery that people can accomplish together through government.

Q: Mrs. Prophet, what do you mean when you refer to Camelot as a mystery school?

A: The ancient mysteries of the Great White Brotherhood have been passed from teacher to disciple throughout the ages. We read of Crotona and Pythagoras and the disciplines in the way of life that became a geometry of the soul as well as the foundation for modern geometry. We see Socrates and Plato. We see Christ and his apostles. We see the Dalai Lama and the great Hindu teachers in the Himalayan fastnesses, each with their little nucleus

---

*Whether housed in a male or female body, the soul is the feminine principle and Spirit is the masculine principle of the Godhead. The soul, then, is addressed by the pronouns *she* and *her.*

of disciples. And in all of this there is a passing of a tradition from the elders of the race, from the ascended masters themselves, to their embodied representatives, to their disciples.

This concept of the mystery school has been at the heart of those orders within all of the world's great religions that have preferred a more intense relationship with God. You have the Sufis of Islam, you have the Gnostics and the Essenes of early Christianity, and you have those who take the path of the priest or nun—those who tie themselves to holy orders because they are enamored of the mysteries of God for the very love of God himself.

I see Camelot, then, as a school of the ancient mysteries, where Merlin came as a representative of the Brotherhood to teach Arthur, Launcelot, Guinevere and all of the knights and ladies of the flame about the flame of life, the inner meaning of life on earth and the path that leads to the ascension by soul liberation.

Q: Mrs. Prophet, what place does the science of the spoken Word have in Morya's plan for the establishment of a spiritual order for the world?

A: Being the chohan of the first ray, El Morya teaches us the mastery of the throat chakra, which corresponds in frequency to the blue ray. He teaches us to draw the energies of the heart and to release these through the power of the Word, the Word that was made flesh, the Word that God speaks through us when we give our invocations, our mantras and our decrees.

El Morya teaches us that the authority of the Word is the authority that we must express in self-government. Through our use of the Word and of the mantra, Morya assists us to transmute, or change, the injustices we find in the social order and to invoke the light to build the new temple and the new order of the ages.

Q: How far are we supposed to go in using these powers—that is, should we pray for the overthrow of leaders we disapprove of?

A: We should call to God for the full power of his All-Seeing Eye to enable us to have the faculty of discrimination, or the gift of discernment of spirits. We need the truth of God to expose right and wrong, truth and error, good and evil. And then we must use our right to vote and every means available to us in our representative form of government to remove those individuals who espouse causes that are not centered in the light of God and to elect those into office who have both the ability and the dedication to the will of God.

Q: How do we distinguish truth from error in public policy?

A: We can meditate upon the heart as the source and seat of consciousness and pray to be illumined. We must also be up to date and fully informed as to the facts, the issues, the record of our representatives. And we must make our invocations to God for his will to be made known to us and to be upon our leaders. Then we can only do what is obvious—take the nearest right step that is humanly available to us and ask God to day by day reform our consciousness and reform and purify our understanding of what is right through government and through individual self-mastery.

Q: What's the goal of all this? I mean, does Morya envision a single world order?

A: We should call to God for the full blueprint of God-government. Morya is concerned that the individual genius of each nation, each state, each group be fulfilled through a consciousness of community, a working together, a caring for one another. With the present evolution of mankind being as it is, El Morya and the Darjeeling Council consider that a single world order for the earth is something that the people are not yet prepared for.

They have not yet learned self-government within the individual or within their local nation-states. And so Morya is concerned lest in our concepts of world government the sense of karma and of dharma and of working out the process of individuality in God-government be lost.

Q: Does that mean that the present system is recommended?

A: The present system that we have in the United States under our Constitution is recommended by the Darjeeling Council for our present level of evolution. And wherever a republican form of government with a constitution with checks and balances such as we have can be adopted, El Morya considers that this is the most advantageous for the individual development of the Christ consciousness.

26

The Master of the Wisdom Ray

∞

- *Who is the Ascended Master Lanto?*
- *What does he teach?*
- *How can we study at the Royal Teton Retreat?*

Mrs. Prophet, who is Lord Lanto?

A: Lord Lanto, chohan of the second ray, is an ascended master of high attainment whose evolution is of the mystery schools of China. He teaches now in the Royal Teton Retreat in North America, which is congruent with the Grand Teton. There he initiates souls who are pursuing the path of the wisdom teachings of Confucius, Lao Tzu, the Buddha, Jesus Christ and Mary.

Q: What does Lord Lanto teach?

A: Lord Lanto teaches us to meditate upon the threefold flame within the heart and specifically upon the central plume of that trinity—the yellow flame of wisdom. He teaches us in our meditation to draw this flame out of the heart and to raise it to the point of the crown chakra, which is the center for illumination, for the enlightenment of the Buddha and the Christ.

He asks us to visualize in our meditation the white light in the heart as a great sphere symbolizing and actualizing our cosmic consciousness. This place in the heart is our seat of authority and our seat of consciousness; it is also the seat of meditation.

As we close our eyes and breathe deeply and relax the body, we enter into the chamber of the heart that is known as the secret chamber of the heart. Here we commune with the ascended masters, with our own I AM Presence and our own Christ Self.

"Going within" in meditation, which Lanto teaches, is actually going into the inner temple of the soul. Within this temple we can hear the soundless sound and commune with our elder brothers and sisters who have gone before us on the path of initiation and who are one with the white light through the ascension.

Lanto teaches us the opening of the crown chakra through the mastery of the heart center. It is always the balance of love, wisdom and power that is the key to Christhood and to Buddhahood. Lanto teaches the way of this mastery through the yellow ray. He has given to us a beautiful prayer that we give in the name of Almighty God:

LANTO'S PRAYER

In the name of Almighty God
I stand forth to challenge the night,
To raise up the light,
To focus the consciousness of Gautama Buddha!
And I AM the thousand-petaled lotus flame!
And I come to bear it in his name!
I stand in life this hour
And I stand with the scepter of Christ-power
To challenge the darkness,
To bring forth the light,
To ensoul from starry heights
The consciousness of angels, masters,
    Elohim, sun-centers
And of all of life
That is the I AM Presence of each one!
I claim the victory in God's name.
I claim the light of solar flame.

I claim the light! I AM the light!
I AM victory! I AM victory! I AM victory!
For the Divine Mother and the Divine Manchild
And for the raising-up of the crown of life
And the twelve starry focal points
That rejoice to see the salvation of our God
Right within my crown,
Right within the center of the Sun
Of Alpha—It is done!

This is the prayer of the mystic who communes with the flame of wisdom through the Trinity of Father, Son and Holy Spirit.

Q: How can someone in the West profit by this?

A: We find that wisdom is an active flame and that we require wisdom to daily be about our Father's business. *Wisdom* simply means "wise dominion." It means using the laws of God wisely to take dominion in our lives. We need wisdom to run our affairs, our households, our businesses, to rear our children and to see that the education in our schools for our children prepares them for the initiations of life that come to all of us because earth itself is a mystery school.

Q: Are all of us taught at the Royal Teton?

A: We have the opportunity to call to the God flame within, the I AM THAT I AM, that our souls might be transported to this key retreat in North America where we can study under the ascended masters and the chohans of the rays. Anchored in the Royal Teton is the wisdom flame, and this wisdom is intended to be used by the people of North America in every endeavor for the enlightenment of all peoples.

We can meditate on this flame and also on the flame of precipitation, science, abundance and supply. The flame of precipitation is a brilliant Chinese green tinged with yellow. As we meditate upon this green flame, we can draw forth from the heart center, or the white-fire core of being, those energies and resources that we need to master our environment.

Until recently the American way of life has been the symbol of a genius of a people who were able to master their environment. But today we have increasing problems in our ecology and in the use of God's energy. If we will meditate upon the heart and upon the masters of the Royal Teton Retreat, we can be tutored in the way of the mastery of our culture and our environment and once again be prepared to give to all nations the genius of our collective meditation upon the God flame.

Q: Mrs. Prophet, what happens at the Royal Teton?

A: The Royal Teton Retreat was described by Godfré Ray King in *Unveiled Mysteries,* which he wrote in the early 1930s. Godfré Ray King was a chela of the Ascended Master Saint Germain, who also uses the Royal Teton Retreat for the training of his chelas.

There are many chambers within the Royal Teton Retreat and there is a large amphitheater. This retreat can accommodate thousands upon thousands of souls. It is a hub of activity of lightbearers in embodiment, of those who are serving in the etheric retreats preparing for reincarnation, and of the ascended masters. We meditate on this retreat through the music "Song to the Evening Star" from *Tannhäuser* by Wagner.

The Ascended Master Confucius is the present hierarch of the Royal Teton Retreat. He anchors there the momentum of his great service to the people of China. He brings the strains of the East and even the momentum of Zen Buddhism and the way of the Tao to North America, where students of light are communing with the inner flame and finding the thread of contact with hierarchy through the Eastern disciplines. The Lords of Karma, who are the great overseers of mankind, also convene at

Teton Range, Wyoming

the Royal Teton, and the mighty Elohim of God have a focus of the seven chakras there.

Godfré Ray King described the great council hall, which he personally visited with his master, Saint Germain. He noted that in the center of the arched ceiling is a large disc of gold. A seven-pointed star formed entirely of dazzling yellow diamonds fills the center of the disc and emits a brilliant golden light. Surrounding this focus of the Central Sun are two twelve-inch rings, the inner ring rose pink and the outer a deep violet. Seven smaller discs also surround the Central Sun, focusing the seven rays of the Elohim, which contact and invigorate the seven chakras in man.

The currents that the Elohim direct through these focuses also benefit the elemental kingdom and plant life on earth. The tremendous currents released by the Elohim are stepped down by the ascended masters and made available to mankind and the elementals. Focused in the wall at the far end of this great council hall is a large eye, representative of the All-Seeing Eye of God watching over America.

And so the Royal Teton Retreat is like the heartbeat of America. And if you would like to study at this retreat in your finer body, write to us for an application to join the Keepers of the Flame Fraternity and to receive the Keepers of the Flame Lessons. These lessons describe in detail the necessary meditations and uses of the science of the spoken Word as well as the technique for consciously leaving the body and journeying at will to the retreats of the Great White Brotherhood.

Q: **What are some of the applications of the teachings of the Royal Teton, Mrs. Prophet?**

A: The teachings given forth by the ascended masters to their chelas in this retreat are a practical application of the law of the great masters of East and West. This practical application is seen in the mastery of time and space, which has been the pursuit of America over the last two hundred years.

We can see that the consciousness of our people is very much aligned with this aspect of God consciousness. And we can see how different the American people are from peoples in other nations, who respond to other retreats of the Great White Brotherhood where other aspects of God's flame as genius are ensouled. This is what gives nations and peoples their individuality.

The American way of life is brought to a spiritualization through the mastery of the flame of the Mother in Matter. It becomes practical as the right form of education at all levels of learning, clearing the brain and the consciousness to be a focal point for the mind of God. Clearly, then, studying at the Royal Teton will enable us to obey the injunction of Saint Paul: "Let that mind be in you, which was also in Christ Jesus."

27

The Master of the Flame of Love

∞

- *Who is Paul the Venetian?*
- *What is the relationship between love and art?*
- *What effect does modern art have on consciousness?*

Mrs. Prophet, can you tell us who Paul the Venetian is?

A: Paul the Venetian is the chohan, or lord, of the third ray. He is an ascended master whose final incarnation was lived as Paolo Veronese, the great Italian artist of the Venetian school. He lived in the sixteenth century and many of his great works, which hang in London, Paris, Madrid, Washington and New York, are of religious scenes. He portrayed episodes in the life of Christ in such works as *The Marriage at Cana, The Presentation in the Temple, The Via Dolorosa, Christ and the Centurion,* and *The Resurrection.*

One painting, entitled *The Holy Trinity,* he completed after his ascension and it hangs in his retreat, the Château de Liberté, in southern France. The retreats of the ascended masters are on the etheric plane but they are often congruent with a physical focus. The physical focus of beloved Paul's retreat is a château that is maintained by a private French family.

The Holy Trinity embodies the essence of the inscription beneath it: "Perfect love casteth out fear." This painting is viewed by souls who come as students of the master. Paul has portrayed the heavenly Father in a majestic figure, and the Son in the likeness of Jesus, and the Holy Spirit as an immense white dove with a nine-foot wing span.

The ascended master known as the Goddess of Liberty is the Mother of the flame of liberty and the sponsor of Paul the Venetian. The Statue of Liberty (a gift of France to America) is the focus of her flame in New York Harbor. The flame of liberty that burns both in the heart of France and in the heart of America inspired the movement for independence in the French Revolution and the American Revolution. It is this flame of liberty, shared by the people of France and America, that binds us in our common devotion to freedom.

The threefold flame of liberty is identical to the threefold flame in the heart—in fact, it is simply another name for it. And that liberty is the freedom of the soul to choose to be God incarnate. The threefold flame of liberty is the perfect fusion of the elements of Father, Son and Holy Spirit. And upon this foundation Paul teaches his disciples the meaning of love as a discipline of the qualities of the Trinity in each of us.

He bids us welcome to his retreat as our souls journey at night while our bodies sleep. He welcomes us to one or more of the many workshops in his retreat where we can perfect our art, our sculpture and the very design of the soul on the path of initiation. He takes us individually to a room where there is a canvas and he asks us to meditate upon our own Christ consciousness and to bring forth our own self-image of the Christ. It's a self-portrait of the Real Self.

Some of us have gone there hundreds of years ago and we come again in this embodiment and view the painting that we painted long ago of our conception of the Christ within. Through evolution and a greater oneness with God, we have improved that awareness and so we ask Paul if he might not allow us to repaint the painting. And this is the idea of discipline—Paul knows his disciples will return, constantly perfecting the image of the Christ within in preparation for the path of the ascension.

Q: Mrs. Prophet, can you tell us about the relationship between love and art?

A: Art is the expression of the love of the soul and it is intended to portray the footsteps on the path of initiation—the stations of the cross, the waymarks of our overcoming of our trials and our tribulations. Love, the cohesive power of the universe, is the foundation of life and is in every cell, and therefore love is a geometry of being. And that geometry brought forth is intended to be exalted in art.

Paul teaches his students that meditation upon art is for the awakening of the power of God within and that all art should lead to this. And of course he points out the discrepancy between modern art and this basic goal.

He teaches that many of the modern artists today are not tuning in to the delicate vibrations of his retreat and the great master artists but instead are tuning in to the subconscious, the collective unconscious and what is known as the astral plane. And from out of this astral plane the artists are bringing forth not the love and the discipline of the soul but great dissonance and inharmony, which is not productive of the true culture of the Holy Spirit.

Q: What is the effect of imperfect forms on the consciousness of those who see them?

A: The ancient proverb goes, "As a man thinketh in his heart, so is he." The masters understand the creative science of vision, the science of the immaculate concept: as we see, we become. If our children meditate upon imperfection, discord, dissonance, they will outpicture this in their consciousness. In ancient Greece and Rome it was the way of life to have pregnant women meditate upon beautiful statues so that they could mold in their consciousness the perfect form and transfer this to their offspring.

This is a very real science. What we see, we do become. And so Paul teaches us that we must guard the consciousness of little children and surround them with paintings and art that are conducive to the harmony of their souls.

Q: Mrs. Prophet, what does Paul the Venetian teach on love?

A: Paul gives us the essence of love that is the Holy Spirit, love that is a self-sacrifice and a surrender to the will of God. It's amazing, but the more we understand of God's love, the more we realize it involves the total giving of the self to that God in manifestation. And in order to totally give ourselves, we must discipline our energies and our way of life. Therefore there is no love —as the true compassion of the Christ for us, for humanity— without the discipline of the self.

Paul uses the symbol of a rose unfolding within the heart to represent the unfolding of the consciousness of love. He teaches that love is a pink flame, an intense fire that consumes all hatred

of the Christ and manifestations of anti-Christ, which are anti the Real Self.

He gives us an awareness that love is simply the perpetual flowing of the crystal stream of God's consciousness. And this flowing of the stream is both the giving and the receiving of the beloved and the soul, who is reaching up for that union with God.

Paul gives us a beautiful mantra that was dictated to the Messenger Mark Prophet for our meditation on love. This is the way it goes:

LOVE ME

1.   I AM so willing to be filled
        With the love of God;
    I AM calling to be thrilled
        With the love of God;
    I AM longing so for grace
        From the heart of God;
    Yearning just to see his face
        By the love of God.

Refrain: As a rose unfolding fair
    Wafts her fragrance on the air,
    I pour forth to God devotion,
    One now with the cosmic ocean.

2.   I AM hoping so to be,
        Made by love divine.
    I AM longing Christ to be,
        Wholly only thine.
    I AM so peaceful in thy love,
        Feel at home with God above.
    I AM at one with all mankind—
        The cords of love God's children bind.
    I AM fore'er one living soul
        With angels, man and God as goal.

3. I AM locked in God's great love,
 His mighty arms of power;
Cradled now by heaven above,
 Protected every hour.
I AM alight with happiness,
 Wholly filled with God-success,
For I AM love of righteousness.
 I love thee, love thee, love thee,
My own God Presence bright;
 Love me, love me, love me,
Protect me by thy might.
 Remain within and round me
Till I become thy light!

Paul the Venetian teaches us that we can pursue art and love and beauty as the discipline for our ascension, the acceleration of our soul into the white-fire core of being.

28

The Master of the Ascension Temple

- *Who is the Ascended Master Serapis Bey?*
- *What is the ascension in the light?*
- *What are the requirements for the ascension?*

Mrs. Prophet, who is Serapis Bey?

A: Serapis Bey is one of my favorite ascended masters. He is the hierarch of the Ascension Temple at Luxor, Egypt, and is known as the great disciplinarian. He is the beloved master who disciplines us in the initiations for the ascension.

Q: We've talked a little about the ascension. Now, what exactly is the ascension, Mrs. Prophet?

A: The ascension is our acceleration of the consciousness of God within us and our return to the white-fire core of being. Christians call it going to heaven and Buddhists call it entering parinirvana, the great soul liberation. It is indeed liberation. It is our freedom from the rounds of rebirth and our freedom from our own karma.

Q: What's the connection between Serapis Bey and the ascension?

A: Serapis Bey is a son of God who came to earth with many sons and daughters of God, led by the one who is referred to in the Book of Daniel as the Ancient of Days. The Ancient of Days is Sanat Kumara, one of the Seven Holy Kumaras, who are masters of the seven rays on the planet Venus. Serapis Bey was embodied on Atlantis as a high priest in the Ascension Temple. Prior to the sinking of Atlantis, he was directed to take the focus of the ascension flame to Luxor, Egypt, and to establish there the temple that is now in the etheric plane.

Serapis Bey's teaching is a practical initiation on the path of purity so that we can understand how we may earn our ascension in this life on any one of the seven rays of the Christ. Serapis says: "The future is what you make it, even as the present is what you made it. If you do not like it, God has provided a way for you to change it, and the way is through the acceptance of the currents of the ascension flame."

I really think that the awareness that we can return to God in this life is something many do not have. Others have a misconception of it; they think that by a simple declaration of faith or confession of the name Jesus Christ they will automatically be received into the courts of heaven. Unfortunately this is not so, for the Great Law requires that we balance every jot and tittle of the law—and this law is the law of karma. Hence, God has provided for us the way of reincarnation whereby the soul takes embodiment again and again so that she can finally prove the law of love and reunite with the living God.

Serapis teaches that the path of the ascension is the path of love. He says it is love and the dream of love fulfilled. So we know that it is the way of love that leads to the way of purity.

The ascension flame corresponds to the base-of-the-spine chakra. The white chakra is the focal point of the energy of Mother, which the Hindus refer to as the Goddess Kundalini.

Whatever way we pursue the flame of Mother, it is the raising up of this energy to the crown of life and to the third eye via the caduceus action that gives us the mastery over sin, disease and death and our ultimate overcoming. In the East, Ramakrishna regarded Jesus the Christ as the great yogi, the Son of God. And truly he was because he mastered the energies of the chakras.

I remember coming out of a Christian church when I was just a teenager and feeling the presence of the Holy Spirit descend upon me. I suddenly had the very intense awareness, "Why, I have to ascend in this life!"

I knew that God was telling me that my soul must return to him, never to go out again. It was then that I began pursuing the path of the ascension as it is taught in East and West. And the end of my search was the discovery of the master Serapis Bey, chohan of the fourth ray of the ascension, and his retreat at Luxor.

In this retreat on the Nile River, there is the focus of the ascension flame. Candidates for the ascension from all over the world and from every religion are invited to come to this retreat in their etheric bodies while they sleep at night. The training that Serapis gives is a training of the highest discipline of the white light of Alpha and Omega in each one of the seven centers of God's being.

You may think that the ascension is something of the past or

that it was only for Jesus the Christ or Mother Mary, but in fact there are many modern saints who have earned their ascension. One such saint is Pope John XXIII; another, Saint Thérèse of Lisieux. Mother Cabrini made her ascension and so did Mary Baker Eddy.

Those who have ascended have come from every continent and through every religion, and all have achieved that ascension through the disciplines of love. As Serapis Bey says, "The disciplines for the initiations of the ascension into higher consciousness can be borne only by love—by the heart and the soul so filled with love for God, the great Guru, that it will endure unto the end, the end of the cycles of human consciousness." That human consciousness that Serapis Bey is talking about is a qualification of the energy of God with the imperfection of the human mind and its limitation.

Serapis teaches us that we have the dispensation today whereby we need balance only 51 percent of our karma in order to pass through the initiation of the ascension. We can balance the remaining 49 percent after the ascension from inner planes.

Formerly it was required that we balance 100 percent of our karma prior to the ascension. That meant that every erg of energy, every jot and tittle of the Law—all energy that God had given to us since our first incarnation in Matter—had to be balanced and requalified with light. Every fear and doubt, every hatred, every wrong deed from every lifetime had to be balanced through the flame of the Holy Spirit.

Now, in the Aquarian age, we have the dispensation of the great mercy of the Law whereby 51 percent is an adequate manifestation. And so by the grace and the gift of the Holy Spirit and of the Lord Jesus Christ, we are able to reenter that state of union and from that point balance every remaining debt to life.

Q: Are there any other requirements for the ascension, Mrs. Prophet?

A: Yes, Doug. A most important requirement is the fulfillment of one's inner divine plan, or the soul blueprint. We all came forth from God with a special mission, a special purpose on earth—to be a scientist, to be an artist, to be a minister, to be a saint. Whatever it is, we must fulfill that calling and many times it requires a number of incarnations to do so.

Many souls on earth today who are advanced in the way and the calling of the Christ have already fulfilled a great portion of that inner blueprint, and so they are seeking the path of the great reunion. This reunion with God was taught by beloved Yogananda and his masters, Sri Yukteswar and Lahiri Mahasaya, Babaji and Mataji.

Among other requirements for the ascension are the balancing of the threefold flame and the alignment of the four lower bodies—the etheric, mental, emotional and physical bodies—so that they can be pure chalices for the flame of the Holy Spirit.

Q: What demands does Serapis Bey make on his disciples?

A: Serapis Bey asks the supreme question of all of us: "How much do you love—how great is your love? Is your love great enough to make the sacrifice for the overcoming, for the Path, for the cause of the Great White Brotherhood in order that others among mankind might also receive the teachings, the Law and the understanding of the fulfillment of the promise of love?"

He says, "Faced with this question, the individual must either retreat into his old ways of the self-centered existence or come forth from that cocoon of selfishness and fly with the wings of the Spirit, the wings of love that are the certain victory."

29

The Healing Master

∞

- *Who is the Ascended Master Hilarion?*
- *What does he have to do with the apostle Paul?*
- *What is the real meaning of "conversion"?*

Mrs. Prophet, who is Hilarion?

A: Hilarion is none other than the apostle Paul, now the Ascended Master Hilarion. He did not ascend at the conclusion of his life as the apostle. In his final incarnation he was Saint Hilarion. Hilarion lived between 290 and 371 and was the founder of Christian monasticism in Palestine. He was a renowned healer who spent twenty years of his life as a hermit in the desert. Throngs of people would come to him for healing, yet he desired to be only the humble, unobtrusive servant of God.

Q: Where is Hilarion's retreat?

A: Hilarion's retreat is focused in the etheric plane over the island of Crete in Greece. There he serves with the ascended lady master who is known in Greek mythology as the goddess Pallas Athena. Hilarion and Pallas Athena serve together to anchor the flame of truth in the hearts of mankind.

That flame of truth was anchored on Atlantis. Just a short time before the sinking of the Atlantean continent almost twelve thousand years ago, Hilarion was bidden by God to transport the focus of that flame and the artifacts of the Temple of Truth to what is now Greece.

The focus of truth that Hilarion established became the focal point for the oracles of Delphi. These were the messengers of truth who served under the direction of Pallas Athena as priestesses in the temple. Eventually there was an invasion of the Delphic Order by certain black magicians who perverted the truth. The Great White Brotherhood then withdrew this dispensation from embodied mankind. It was one of the last episodes in the direct interaction of the ascended masters with unascended mankind.

Q: What does the apostle Paul have to do with truth?

A: You will remember the conversion of Saul on the road to Damascus when Jesus appeared to him in a great light and said, "Saul, Saul, why persecutest thou me?" Saul fell to the ground and Jesus told him to go into the city and it would be told to him what he should do. When Saul rose he was blinded and did not see, eat or drink anything for three days. This blinding of Saul and his subsequent renaming as Paul was the act of conversion.

Jesus has taught us, "Except ye be converted and become as little children, ye shall not enter into the kingdom of heaven." This conversion, Doug, is a scientific process. Hilarion has explained it in a dictation: It is the arcing of that ray of light from the heart of Jesus to one's own that is so powerful "that it reverses the downward spiral of death and disintegration, causes the involuting of that spiral in the upward, commanding presence of life, of the ascension and of immortality."

Conversion, then, is the moment of the swing of identity back onto the road of God, the displacement of error by the reestablishment of the flame of truth within one's being. When truth comes unto us suddenly as it did unto Saul, who was a sinner and who had persecuted the Christians, it causes our sin to precipitate out upon the body.

Hence, Saul was blinded by his own misqualification of God's energy; the presence of Jesus brought the light as well as the judgment of his misdeeds. When Saul was raised up by Jesus and by that flame of truth, he became Paul, a great preacher of the Word and truly the one who established throughout the Holy Land and Asia Minor the foundation of Christianity.

In a dictation that Hilarion gave through me, he said: "First he humbled me on that road to Damascus, the humbling that I sorely needed that I might bow to my own Christ flame, which he revealed to me as he also gave to me the key of meditation upon that flame that I might walk in his footsteps on the fifth ray of science and healing and the apostleship and the preaching of the Word."

The byword of those who serve with the Ascended Master Hilarion on the fifth ray of science is "And ye shall know the truth, and the truth shall make you free."

Q: What does Hilarion teach?

A: Hilarion teaches his disciples how to use the flame of living truth to master oneself and one's daily life in a practical application of the law that Christ taught. As you know, the apostle was a fiery preacher of righteousness and he had the gift of the Spirit and the gift of conversion. He teaches us today of this process of conversion, which is so necessary because it is the return of the soul to God, the reentering of the path of initiation.

Hilarion says that in the moment of conversion there is the infiring of the name of God, your own new name. It is the solar pattern of your solar evolution. He teaches us meditation on the name I AM THAT I AM that we might also contact the inner name and the blueprint of the soul. Contacting this, we then have the key to the release of the energy of the science of being.

Q: How is one converted, Mrs. Prophet?

A: Hilarion says, "Resist not the call or the conversion or the coming of the master. . . . Do you wait for him to appear to you as in a vision, to flatter you with the presence of angels and trumpets and harps and an entire retinue of God-free beings? You may wait long, you may wait hard. For I say, unto some it is required to provide the welling up from within of that love that says, 'O LORD, I would be converted! Convert me this day! Let me be reborn in thee that I might go forth to work the works of my God!'"

Q: Where is the place of will in conversion?

A: Conversion implies a will—a will forged and won within your heart, the very center of your identity. It is a will that magnetizes a member of the ascended hosts who will respond to the call of your heart for the teacher. That one will then come and invest you with that magnet, that flame, that fiery coil, that momentum that is able to reverse the course of death and destruction.

Q: It doesn't appear that Saul was seeking conversion. How do you explain his conversion?

A: Jesus came to Saul to remind him of their inner association and of their long service together thousands and thousands of years before that particular moment. And therefore he said, "Why are you persecuting me?" His inference was: When we have been one in Christ for so long, how have you gone out of the way? Saul had actually sought the Christ in previous incarnations but in that life he had disregarded the inner call of his soul for God.

Q: Why do agnostics deny God, Mrs. Prophet?

A: To a great extent, the denial of God by the agnostic is due to the soul's great disappointment in having been part of the various religions of the world and having been given false promises of heaven and salvation by the wolves in sheep's clothing.

For when these souls have passed from the screen of life, they have not been ushered into the courts of heaven but have been greeted by angels of record and by Jesus and the Lords of Karma, who have explained to them that they have not met the full requirements of the Law and therefore must incarnate once again. These souls have then become angry against their teachers and when they incarnate again they become agnostics because their disappointment in their teachers has caused them to become disillusioned with God.

Q: Mrs. Prophet, may we assume that atheists and agnostics are devout souls?

A: The ones I have known have been very devoted to a particular discipline, often the discipline of science. But they have not understood that science and religion are one. They have not understood that the God that is energy—that is the I AM THAT I AM, that is in the nucleus of the atom, which they would explore—is the same God who appeared in his Son Jesus Christ to Saul, who was himself a scientist and one trained in the law.

I have found that when agnostics understand the path of initiation they become the greatest devotees. And this is why Hilarion, master of the fifth ray of science, is so concerned with working with atheists and agnostics. He understands that the real truth of the path of Christhood has been withheld from them.

Q: Do the disciples of truth have a special mantra?

A: Indeed they do, Doug, and here it is:

LIVING TRUTH

O God of Truth, I AM in all,
For understanding now I call;
To see thee in thy fullness, LORD,
Behold, is living truth adored.

I AM aware by reason pure
That only God can make secure
The lifetime's search for heaven's Law
That enters, filling hearts with awe.

Come now and help me truth enshrine;
All understanding now is mine
Whene'er I open wide the door
No man can shut forevermore.

O blazing light of living truth,
Thou fountainhead of lasting youth,
Come pour thy radiance through my mind
Until in peace at last I find

That God's own Spirit manifest
Is ever and alone the best
And holds each man in right secure
To understand the Law as pure;

That God's own Law is truth alone,
For every error does atone,
And lifts all to the pure estate
Where Silent Watchers watch and wait

To vest ascended master youth
With blest Hilarion's ray of truth.
Pallas Athena, thy truth be
Our scepter of authority!

30

The Ascended Lady Master Nada

∞

- *Who is the Ascended Lady Master Nada?*
- *What does she have to say about the family?*
- *And what does she teach about the Law?*

Mrs. Prophet, who is Nada?

A: Nada is an ascended lady master who is the chohan of the sixth ray. She is a feminine being of great light and love who once served in the temples of Atlantis. She made her ascension about twenty-seven hundred years ago.

While in embodiment on Atlantis, Nada served in the Temple of Love, whose etheric counterpart is above New Bedford, Massachusetts. This retreat is designed after the pattern of a rose, each petal being a room. In the center of the Rose Temple is the flame of divine love, which the brothers and sisters of the third ray expand to implement healing throughout man's four lower bodies.

Lady Master Nada also serves with Jesus in the Temple of the Resurrection over the Holy Land. Her service on the sixth ray, which is the ray of devotion and service, teaches us to implement the law as a practical service to God in humanity.

In another incarnation Nada was embodied as a lawyer on Atlantis. She teaches us to defend the law. And she calls to the women of the world to become the ones who defend that law for their families and their communities, not only in the legal profession but in the day-to-day encounters with life.

She teaches cosmic law and she wants us, as mothers, to defend the Christ-potential of our husbands, our children and the members of our community. Defending that law and defending the soul's right to become one with that law is practicing the teachings of Jesus Christ and Gautama Buddha.

In her final incarnation Nada was the youngest of a large family of brothers and sisters, all of whom were talented except herself, or so she thought. While she was a child she was visited by the archeia Charity. Charity came to her and taught her how to draw the love from her heart and to radiate that love into nature, into the elemental builders of form, and to commune with all life for the expansion of the God flame.

She was also tutored at inner levels by the master Serapis Bey, who assigned her to a branch of the Ascension Temple. There she was taught how to assist her brothers and sisters by meditating upon their divine plan. The outcome of her discipline was that she remained unknown in that incarnation whereas every one of her brothers and sisters became famous in their fields of endeavor because of her selfless love and discipline.

By her selfless service, Nada achieved her eternal victory. She stands with the ascended masters today to teach us the way of service as the means to the balancing of our karma and our return to the flame.

Q: **Mrs. Prophet, can you tell us more about what Nada teaches her disciples?**

A: She teaches us the path of service, Doug—both through the family and through holy orders. The purple and gold of the sixth ray, the twin flames of Alpha and Omega, are best expressed in mutuality, in cooperation with one another.

She speaks of the family as the basic unit in life. She tells us that when mankind destroy the family, they destroy the nucleus for the individualization of the God flame. And when individualization is lost, identity is lost.

The family is the cradle for the bringing forth of the Christ in father, in mother and in the offspring. She says that every household needs a head and that is the father; every household needs a heart and that is the mother. And then the hands of the household become the children, who are extensions of the heart and head as they go out into the community and as they bring forth a new generation, a new energy in school, in education, in service, in involvement with the community. Nada teaches us, then, that we must keep the balance of the sacred Trinity as Joseph, Mary and Jesus did—and that through the family we can fulfill our dharma.

Q: **What about those who don't have families, Mrs. Prophet?**

A: Having a family is only one way to fulfill one's dharma. We can also fulfill our dharma by merging with our own God Presence for a greater service to life. As those who have consecrated their lives to God throughout the ages have recognized, life is not simply for pleasure or the things of this world but for the giving of self in love.

America is founded on the principle of service. We have all kinds of service organizations. We have volunteers helping people in all strata of society. We have our churches, which nurture in people a sense of responsibility toward one another.

Nada teaches the motto: "I am my brother's keeper." When we make this our way of life, we are gaining our mastery on the sixth ray. And as you know, Jesus was the chohan of that ray for the two-thousand-year cycle of Pisces. Only recently did Nada become the chohan, after serving the flame of love for many hundreds of years.

Q: What else does Nada have to say about the Law?

A: The Law is the very foundation of service. She says that any law that does not stand in fulfillment of the law of God cannot stand; it is there, waiting to be challenged.

Nada says that any individual son or daughter of God who perceives injustice and incongruity in any man-made law, who in the name of the Christ will challenge that law, who will take to the Lords of Karma and draw to the people's attention the existence of injustice, will have immediate action from the Lords of Karma and from the individual Christ Self.

Q: How relevant is this teaching on the Law to today's society, Mrs. Prophet?

A: I think it's extremely relevant. Take, for example, the violation not only of human rights but of divine rights happening right now in Russia, in China, in many of the countries of Africa.

When there are laws that are depriving the individual of his freedom to freely commune with God and to offer that communion for the benefit of the world community, we must challenge those laws. And we must challenge those who uphold laws that are not the fulfillment of the law of God.

It is important for Americans to realize today that we are appointed to be the guardians of freedom not only in America but in every nation. And our failure to fulfill this calling is our failure to realize our dharma, or our duty, to fulfill the inner blueprint.

So our service on the sixth ray must include fervent prayer to Almighty God, made in the name of Jesus Christ, and also to the ascended hosts of light that these laws that are unjust and tyrannical be broken and that those who are perpetuating these laws be challenged. We must call for the truth to expose error and for the lie to be broken.

I have seen the answer to prayer come forth miraculously

when individuals had the courage to stand on truth. But when our leaders tell us that it is counterproductive for us to champion the rights of man, we are forced to retreat without seeing the salvation of our God that can be wrought through prayer.

If Americans would realize how great is the power of prayer, they would know that those who are not on the side of light must retreat at the coming of the Faithful and True and the armies of the LORD, who do come in answer to our prayer and to our use of the science of the spoken Word.

Q: **Mrs. Prophet, how far should we go in this challenge?**

A: I am not recommending civil disobedience or violent revolution. I am recommending fervent prayer whereby we stand before the altar of God and we say:

> In the name of Jesus Christ, I challenge all tyranny and injustice in this and every nation! And I call forth the living God to work through the ascended hosts and his emissaries on earth to secure freedom for all peoples, beginning at home and then extending to every nation on earth.

Calls like this need to be made many times a day whenever we have a free moment. We must realize that God needs our call and that "the effectual fervent prayer of a righteous man availeth much." This is the teaching of Jesus Christ. It is also the teaching of the Ascended Lady Master Nada.

31

The Master Saint Germain

- *What does Saint Germain have to say about freedom?*
- *How does he feel about the world situation?*
- *What is the greatest threat to freedom?*

Mrs. Prophet, you've mentioned Saint Germain. Could you tell us more about him?

A: Saint Germain is the ascended master who is the chohan of the seventh ray of freedom. He is more than an ascended master to me—he is the very spirit of freedom in the heart of America. You may recall that I have spoken of him as the master of the Aquarian age. He is the master of the Aquarian age just as Jesus was the master of the Piscean age.

Saint Germain comes to teach us the way of freedom. He asks the question: "What does it really mean to choose freedom?" And he answers it: "It means to free the electrons in your body and consciousness to flow with freedom's fire. It means to allow the electron to choose the path of freedom and not to subject that electron to the bondage of a limited consciousness, a limited matrix. It means to free your own self-awareness so that you can be aware of the self as having the potential of the Infinite."

I have spoken about the moment when I first contacted Saint Germain in this life—the moment when I saw his portrait

Saint Germain by Charles Sindelar

by Charles Sindelar in a book of my mother's. At that moment, I remembered my calling.

I know that I am not unique in that millions of Americans today feel the tie of their heart flame to our beloved Saint Germain, our Uncle Sam. He was embodied as the prophet Samuel, hence the name. Saint Germain overshadowed the early American patriots in the framing of the Constitution and in the designing of our flag. He even anointed our first president, George Washington.

We have seen Saint Germain in his incarnations as Saint Joseph, Christopher Columbus, Francis Bacon and as Merlin at the court of Camelot. In the eighteenth century, as the Count Saint Germain, the Wonderman of Europe, he tried to save and unite Europe. When this attempt failed, he turned his attention toward the United States to form a more perfect union.

Saint Germain is concerned about freedom and its preservation in every nation. He speaks out about the selling away of America—the giving away of her funds and technology. The American people should not have to bear the burden of the support of all nations. Saint Germain especially deplores the selling of military secrets, arms and weapons to those who turn around and use these against the sons and daughters of God in every nation.

Q: Mrs. Prophet, what does Saint Germain see as the biggest foe to freedom?

A: Saint Germain has taught us that it is our own selfishness and self-indulgence that will cause us to lose our freedom. He inspires us to make greater sacrifices for freedom, to not indulge ourselves so much in luxuries but to realize that the calling and destiny of the American people is to guard freedom and to be the watchmen on the wall of freedom for the world.

This involves sacrifice, but Saint Germain says that if we allow America to be the last remaining republic and the last place where full freedom is accorded the individual, we will not stand. Therefore he is for the defense of freedom in every nation and he holds us accountable for allowing the deaths of millions of people, as we have previously supported the totalitarian regimes that have taken over their nations.

Saint Germain is determined that we should defend Taiwan as an island of people of light and that it should not become a football between East and West. He is also concerned that children in America receive the right education and the right understanding of our nation and its peculiar genius.

Rather than advocating the blending of all nations into a one-world type of government, Saint Germain teaches us that the individual genius of every nation must be preserved as a crucible for individual self-government and that the types of self-government that people evolve must be unique to their own souls' evolution.

Our form of government is not necessarily the best for every nation, nor should we try to have some sort of a world-elite body ruling peoples who ought to be ruling themselves and who ought to be taught the way of self-government.

Saint Germain sees World Communism as the greatest threat

to individual freedom, especially the freedom of the soul to walk the path of initiation with the Christ and the Buddha. Where that freedom is denied, the purpose for life and for living is lost and then the very purpose for the perpetuation of earth itself is lost.

Every soul on earth is intended to be free to attain reunion with God. Where that freedom is denied, those who deny it must be challenged. Saint Germain is fervent about this because the people of the world today are in embodiment to inaugurate a new age—two thousand years when the flame of freedom in science, education, art and culture must be extolled.

So we as a people and as a government cannot compromise. We cannot sit at the table with the enemies of freedom and proceed to give away entire territories and nations and actually seal the fate of millions of souls in the hands of those who are the tyrants.

These tyrants exist in both the East and the West. Saint Germain says that we need to watch our representatives in government, we need to watch those who are not actually continuing the purposes for which America was founded and that we realize it is more than material freedom that must be guarded: it is spiritual freedom.

Those policies that seem correct in the way of socialism may not seem correct when we understand that the purpose of America is to champion the free enterprise system. That system gives the maximum opportunity for the individual to develop the Christ-potential within himself. As soon as the government or large corporations are doing for the individual what he can do for himself, he is being deprived of his freedom—his freedom to create.

Saint Germain teaches that without the freedom to create there is no freedom. The opportunity to create is the basic endowment we have with the gift of free will. When you have a government that provides everything the individual needs so that he does not have to exercise the muscles of the mind or of the soul or even move himself, then the energies of sloth, self-centeredness and the pleasure cult set in. The danger of the pleasure cult in America today is greater than ever.

Saint Germain has given a fiery mantra to his devotees, which I would like to give now for lovers of freedom:

THE FLAME OF FREEDOM SPEAKS
by Saint Germain

The flame of freedom speaks—the flame of freedom within each heart. The flame of freedom saith unto all: Come apart now and be a separate and chosen people, elect unto God—men who have chosen their election well, who have determined to cast their lot in with the immortals. These are they who have set their teeth with determination, who have said:

> I will never give up
> I will never turn back
> I will never submit
> I will bear the flame of freedom unto my victory
> I will bear this flame in honor
> I will sustain the glory of life within my nation
> I will sustain the glory of life within my being
> I will win my ascension
> I will forsake all idols and
> I will forsake the idol of my outer self
> I will have the glory of my immaculate
>   divinely conceived Self manifesting within me
> I AM freedom and
> I AM determined to be freedom
> I AM the flame of freedom and
> I AM determined to bear it to all
> I AM God's freedom and he is indeed free
> I AM freed by his power and his power is supreme
> I AM fulfilling the purposes of God's kingdom

Q: What can the individual do in defense of freedom right now?

A: Right now you can say: "In the name of Jesus Christ, I call to Almighty God to defend freedom in the heart of every American and every citizen of every nation! And I call to the heart of the blessed Ascended Master Saint Germain, to the heart of Mary the Mother, and I call for legions of angels and the hosts of heaven to intervene in the destiny of every nation on earth. I invoke the flame of freedom as the violet flame. I call it forth now! Let it come from my own I AM God Presence! And let it descend into the chalice of my heart to be released this day and to clear the way for the coming of the hosts of the LORD."

It is important for people of every religion to realize that this form of impassioned plea to the Almighty is a fiat that is made in the name of the Christ and one's own Christ Self. You can make fiats while you are driving your car, cooking dinner, doing your ironing or taking a shower. Whenever you have a moment, whenever you hear a news report of some dire calamity, immediately make a call in the name of the I AM THAT I AM to one of the ascended masters, to Almighty God himself, and know the infallible law of the cosmos that declares: The call compels the answer!

32

Brother Afra

∞

- *What is race?*
- *Where does the black race fit in the Great White Brotherhood?*
- *Who is the Ascended Master Afra?*

Mrs. Prophet, some of our black brothers and sisters are wondering where they fit in the Great White Brotherhood.

A: Doug, our black brothers and sisters are very much a part of the Great White Brotherhood. The black race was originally part of what was known as the blue race and the violet race, a high civilization that existed on the continent of Africa at the time of Lemuria. The first ascended master to rise from the black race was the Ascended Master Afra. Afra is a soul of great light who evolved on the continent of Africa. The Ascended Master Kuthumi told us about this brother in a conference that Mark and I held in Ghana, West Africa, in 1972.

Kuthumi explained that this one was such a humble servant of God and so one with the flame of love that he asked to be called simply "a brother"—or *frater* in Latin. And so "a frater" became the word *Afra*. And from his name, the name of the continent was taken. This great soul of light stands as the sponsor of the people of Africa today in their movement toward freedom and soul liberation.

Q: Has beloved Afra ever given a dictation, Mrs. Prophet?

A: Yes. He has given several dictations. In September 1976 I held a conference at the University of Ghana in Accra. It was a conference on Ghana's destiny in the Holy Spirit, and at that conference beloved Afra gave a dictation. It was such a wonderful experience for me to see so many of our brothers and sisters who are part of these teachings in Ghana receive that message. Afra said:

> I am your brother—not your lord, not your master, but I am your brother on the Path. I have shared your passion for freedom. I have shared with you the hours of crisis when you beheld injustice, when you sought the LORD and prayed to him for justice and the LORD gave to you the divine plan for this nation and for this continent.
>
> I have lived in your hearts these hundreds and hundreds of years as you have toiled under the burden of oppression from within and without. And although many have considered the outer oppression the greater, we who are among those who have graduated from this continent consider that the only true slavery is the slavery from within—the slavery of the carnal mind and its selfishness, its failure to sacrifice upon the altar as Abraham and Isaac sacrificed.
>
> So, the failure to sacrifice the beasts of the carnal mind: this is slavery.
>
> Now then, it is because some have been willing to make the sacrifice of selfishness that the outer slavery has also been broken, and it is the evolution of the people themselves toward the light of God that has given this new opportunity in this age to this continent.

I've always felt as though I had a second home in Ghana, so wonderful is the warmth of the people and the fervor of their hearts for freedom. They understand the science of the spoken Word because it is a part of their race consciousness, which goes way back to the golden-age civilization that they knew at the time of Lemuria.

Q: Mrs. Prophet, what is race?

A: In the truest sense of the word, there is no such thing as the black race or the white race. Really no one is black or white, but all of the races that we find on earth have come forth from the heart of God under the seven rays—and these seven rays, as we know, are paths of initiation.

Those who are of the so-called white race came forth for the mastery of the yellow, the pink and the white flames—hence, the various mixtures and tone qualities of their skin. These evolutions were intended to place upon the altar of God the gift of their self-mastery in the way of wisdom, love and purity.

The members of what is called the black race have come forth on the blue ray and the violet ray. In the ancient civilization on the continent of Africa, their skin actually had a blue or a violet hue. These colors are related to Alpha and Omega, the beginning and the ending.

And it is easy to see that those of the yellow race and the tradition of the wisdom of China—the people of the land of Chin—are on the yellow ray of wisdom. Individual nations also have their calling, or dharma.

We find, however, that down through the centuries, man has wandered from his high estate since his departure from Eden, and the pure colors of the rainbow of God are no longer reflected either in the skin tone or in the aura. Division has set in—and the divide-and-conquer tactics of the fallen ones. Instead of the races embracing one another as brother and sister, there is division: one race enslaves another race and the great unity of all children of God and their oneness in the flame is destroyed.

Beloved Kuthumi, who was embodied as Saint Francis, wrote a decree for brotherhood. I would like to offer it now as our gift of love for the healing of the scars and the wounds that have been caused by racial strife in this nation and every nation.

DECREE FOR BROTHERHOOD

In the name of the beloved mighty victorious Presence of God, I AM in me, Holy Christ Selves of all earth's evolutions, beloved Jesus the Christ and Kuthumi, beloved Lanello, the entire Spirit of the Great White Brotherhood and the World Mother, elemental life—fire, air, water and earth! I decree:

> Out of the One,
> Thou, God, hast spun
> All of the races of men.
> By thy great Law
> Do thou now draw
> All to their God Source again.
>
> Take away hate;
> By love abate
> All mankind's vicious intent.
> Show thy great pow'r
> Every hour
> Of love and compassion God sent.
>
> I AM, I AM, I AM
> Divine love sending forth
> The wonderful feeling of true divine healing,
> Unguents of light now sealing
> All of the schisms of men.
>
> Stop all division!
> By God-precision
> Love is the hallowed law-key.
> Ultimate peace,
> Make all war cease,
> Let the children of men now go free!
>
> Stop mankind's friction,
> All their predictions
> Tearing bless'd heart from heart.
> By God-direction
> Produce now perfection
> In thy great family—one heart.

33

Children of Afra

- *What are the perils of nationhood?*
- *What is the key to winning one's freedom?*
- *What is the real cause of racial strife?*

Mrs. Prophet, I'm sure our black brothers and sisters would like to hear more about what Afra had to say to all of the African people in the dictation he gave in Ghana.

A: Yes, beloved Afra gave a magnificent dictation. In it, he said:

> Let the children of Afra look within and find the inner key to the God consciousness in this age. Let them be imitators of Christ and not imitators of the carnal minds of the other nations. So as the Christ has come forth in every nation, that Christ may be imitated here. So is power in him and in him alone. The knowledge of the peril of nationhood that I bring to you this day concerns the failure of the people to be obedient to the laws of God and to make the necessary sacrifices so that the whole can be won—forged and won.
>
> The great danger, then, the great peril to Ghana and to every nation is the danger of chaos and confusion that is born of selfishness, where there is no path, no way or truth or life as taught by the avatars, no desire for initiation in God, no realization that life is for testing, life is for the exercise of free will, life is for the balancing of karma, the

fulfillment of dharma, and the return of the soul unto the altar of the Ancient of Days in the ritual of the ascension.

The peril of nationhood is the peril of the absence of vision, for without vision the people perish. And the people lose their vision proportionately as they increase in self-indulgence, in selfishness, in the cults of success, ambition and pride.

This is a disease that begins in the leaders, that is transferred to the people, that is then increased in them and returned to the leaders until the nation is at odds...and there is nothing but the spying on one another and the attempts at the coup to remove the statesmen and those who are in the position of leadership.

There is envy, there is jealousy, there is graft, there is greed, there is bribery. These are the perils of nationhood—when a people who have been deprived of their resources and of their energies, who have been enslaved to others for so many centuries, become drunk now with the wealth of their nation, become drunk with power and the desire to rule over one another. Have they so early forgotten that once all were common subjects of other masters? Have they forgotten that they are brethren?

O this people! If you could see me as I walk the streets of Accra and of Ghana and of these nations, you would see me as the prophets of Israel of old! And I rend my garments for the sins of the people, for their failure to see that if they fail in this age to forge this union, then Afra will go down like the other powers and civilizations of this world have gone down—ever since the sinking of Lemuria and Atlantis, the days of Rome and Greece and ancient China and all of those civilizations who have come to naught because they have worshiped the god of Baal.

Let it be seen, then, that the hour for the coming of the victory on this continent is nigh. If you fail to accept the torch of liberty, if you fail to take with you the science of the spoken Word, if you fail to sacrifice the lesser self, then you will go the way of all the rest.

The people of Afra have the supreme opportunity to learn from every civilization and every history.... When civilization as materialization reaches its peak, there are only two courses that are open: either material decline and decay because of indulgence or spiritual transcendence where (by the alchemy of the Holy Spirit) all that has been attained in Matter becomes the foundation of the pyramid whereby this attainment is transferred in Spirit and the people experience the new birth in Spirit and in Christ.

The Ascended Master Afra

In this very hour, this moment of the peaking of material attainment has come for many nations in East and West. In this moment the idling of the energies of God in the nexus of the cross of white fire is for these peoples to choose this day the Word of the LORD and the message of the prophets in every age, to choose to spiritualize consciousness. My friends, the choice is: To be or not to be!

Q: Mrs. Prophet, what significance does this message have for the sons and daughters of Afra in the United States?

A: It shows their cultural heritage. Here in America today, freedom must also be won by the choice to be. Saint Germain has said, "He who chooses not to be becomes the slave of him who chooses to be."

We see this in our everyday life, even within the races. Those who are the strong, who have a strong identity, are those who rule.

The challenge of life is to choose to be in God the master of oneself. When one is the master of oneself, he cannot be the slave of any.

It is my desire that the sons and daughters of Afra in America take the teachings of the ascended masters and the science of the spoken Word and use these for the liberation of the tremendous love and light that God has given to them.

Q: Mrs. Prophet, what causes racial strife?

A: I firmly believe that racial strife is caused by the divide-and-conquer tactics of those known as the fallen ones. Morya made an interesting comment about this in his *White Paper.* He said, "I do not believe that manipulators do not exist in the world. I know that they exist, and that they exist to the total degradation of man." Jesus said the same thing when he explained the mystery of the tares among the wheat: "The good seed are the children of the kingdom; but the tares are the children of the wicked one. The enemy that sowed them is the devil."

We find that the fallen ones are those who, by choice, by free will, have taken what is known as the left-handed path. They appear in every race and in every nation. The ascended masters call them the spoilers because wherever you have light, wherever you have true religion, wherever you have joy, they come in to spoil that pure and holy innocent vibration of the good seed. The fallen ones have used race to divide the children of God on earth, and I think that it's about time it be exposed!

A civilization of great light, a veritable golden age, once existed on the continent of Africa. It was through the divide-and-conquer tactics of the fallen ones that this civilization was infiltrated. Mark and I explain this in *Climb the Highest Mountain:*

> To accomplish the breakdown of order, it is necessary
> to invert every other quality of God in man and in society:
> love must be turned into hatred; peace into war; truth into

error; faith into doubt, fear and suspicion; and the sweet wine of Holy Communion into the bitter fruit of psychic intercourse. These perversions are systematically enforced through infiltrating God-government, education, science and religion, the family, the church and the community with the warped concepts of warped minds. The authors of these perversions of the God flame have one goal in mind: the destruction of man and society through the dethroning of the Real Image. [The Real Image is the Christ in us all.]

By employing distraction and confusion as alternate weapons, the very few have turned the many upon this planetary home away from the main issues of life and the central order of the universe. The masterminds who brought down the children of Africa and an ancient civilization of great light that once flourished on what has come to be known as "the dark continent" did so through the perversion of its sacred rituals and art forms. By injecting distortions of the divine art into the consciousness of the people, they were able to capture their minds and emotions and to divert their attention from the Presence, causing their energies to flow into matrices of dense desire.

As time went on, the people lost the wisdom of their ancestors, worshiping those they should have emulated. The accounts of sacred powers wielded by their forebears became folklore; all forgot that long ago they, too, had been entrusted with the secrets of the universe. Thus the history of a people who perished for want of vision is written in akasha—a dramatic portrayal of the cultural sinking of a continent.

What we are witnessing today, Doug, is the return of light and of the Mother flame to the continent of Afra, and we are seeing the children of Afra responding to the fires of freedom. May they choose to be the Christed ones and manifest the victory for all.

34

Buddha and Christ

∞

- *What is it like to be in love with the Buddha?*
- *What does it mean to become the Buddha?*
- *How can the Buddha meditate on Mother Mary?*

Mrs. Prophet, would you tell us about your love for the Buddha?

A: Doug, I have a secret. And the secret is that I am in love with the Buddha because the Buddha is in love with the Mother. When I was meditating upon the Buddha one day, I found that his adoration was upon the bliss of the Cosmic Virgin, and I saw that through his communion with the Mother he was also one with her blessed Son, Jesus Christ.

I thought upon Buddha's coming. Lord Gautama meditated under the Bo tree and discovered the Four Noble Truths and the Eightfold Path about the time that Ezekiel was preaching to Judah and Israel. Then I thought of Jesus' statement "Before Abraham was, I AM," and I realized that the presence of the blessed Son of God enabled Lord Buddha to meditate upon that Christ and upon his Mother. I realized that he attained enlightenment because of his oneness with the Mother and the Son. There is no Son without the Mother and a mother cannot be called Mother save she give birth to the eternal Christ.

So my love of the Buddha is the love of the Mother for the Father, God the Father. It is also my love for the disciple, because

Gautama Buddha is indeed a disciple of Jesus Christ. This is not an anachronism. We can all come into the knowledge of Christ through the flame in the heart. It was Gautama Buddha who opened that flame—the threefold flame of love, wisdom and power; Brahma, Vishnu and Shiva; Father, Son and Holy Spirit—for sons and daughters of God who were following in the way of the East.

Gautama came in an hour when Hinduism was at its worst state of decadence. The priesthood was involved in favoritism and guarding the great secrets, the real mysteries of God, from the people, thus keeping the masses in ignorance. The caste system had become a means of imprisonment of the soul instead of a means of liberation through dharma. And so there arose Gautama Buddha. Born as Prince Siddhartha, he left palace, power, wife and son to gain that enlightenment whereby he could give back to the people that which the interlopers had taken from them.

Jesus did exactly the same thing through the same power— the power of the eternal Christ. Jesus came in an hour when Judaism was entrenched with the activities of the Sadducees, the Pharisees and the Sanhedrin. He came to give back to the people their understanding.

In his prayer to the Father spoken on the way to Gethsemane Jesus said, "I have declared unto them thy name." He came to teach us the name of God, as did Moses: the name I AM THAT I AM. Guru Nanak came to give the people the name of God, Sat Nam.

This immense understanding—that in the name of God is the key—is the same understanding that the Mother gives to her children today. As we understand all of the ascended masters to be one with the central flame of life, we can rejoice in their coming and we can find in each ascended master the one flame of God, which leads us to the presence of life within ourselves.

Q: What does it mean to become the Buddha?

A: To become the Buddha means to realize the great love of the Buddha where you are—the love of Buddha for Mary, for Jesus and for all sons and daughters of God. One can feel this intense love of the Buddha as one's attention rests upon his peace and his flame.

Q: What is it like to commune with the Buddha, as you must have done while writing about the Buddha?

A: It is as Saint John of the Cross described it and as the many mystics of the Church have described it: it is being in love with God. It is feeling that God is the beloved and the one who loves us so intensely. We find union, we find wholeness, we find bliss, not because we desire to depart from this world but because in that oneness with God we can minister to our family—to husband, to wife, to friend, to children, to pilgrim on the way.

We can love the God within each other with that same intensity of devotion because we have gone to the mount of transfiguration with Jesus, we have gone to Horeb's height with Moses, we have gone to Carmel with Elijah. And we have found that intense love of this union of the flame of man with the flame of God. This is the consummation. Until we have found this, we do not enjoy the richness in our relationships with one another.

I have often found that some people do not have a real capacity to love, but their love is a human sympathy or an emotionalism or a sensuality. So I have asked God, "Why do they not have the capacity to love?" And he has answered me, "Because they have not known my love and therefore they cannot give love to one another."

Q: Mrs. Prophet, could you explain how the Buddha can be meditating on Mother Mary?

A: Mother Mary is one who represents the feminine nature of God. Our God is Father; our God is Mother. Mary is one who communed with Mother to the point of fulfilling within her being the Christ, bringing forth the Christ by the Holy Ghost. Mary is simply a code name for Ma-ray, which means "Mother ray." Hindus sometimes refer to the Divine Mother as "Ma." This syllable brings down the energy of the feminine principle.

Just as Buddha meditates on Jesus, he meditates on Mary because Mary has become one with the universal Mother, the universal God. All feminine beings who have realized that oneness become the object of the Buddha's veneration.

Mother Mary comes to us in her great love for all of the sons and daughters of God, whom she can claim as her own because she has merged with the flame of God as Mother. One day as I was in meditation upon Mother Mary, so grateful for the understanding of her being, she said to me, "I want to give you a rosary for my sons and daughters for the Aquarian age." Then she began to recite the Hail Mary for me as follows:

> Hail, Mary, full of grace
> the Lord is with thee.
> Blessed art thou among women
> and blessed is the fruit
> of thy womb, Jesus.
> Holy Mary, Mother of God,
> Pray for us, sons and daughters of God,
> Now and at the hour of our victory
> Over sin, disease and death.

She explained to me that we should no longer pray to her as sinners as in the traditional rosary, because we would be sinners as long as we held that concept of ourselves. She said: "You are joint heirs with Christ. You are sons and daughters of God. I want you to pray for my intercession now. There is no death.

Jesus proved that death is unreal. Therefore, call to me that I might reinforce within you the light of Christ in the hour of your own victory over sin, disease and death."

Students who come to Summit University find on our altar a statue of the Buddha, a statue of Mother Mary, a magnificent painting of the Lord Jesus Christ and a painting of Saint Germain, the master of the Aquarian age. Thus the blending of our spirits in East and West has produced a meditation upon the Mother, the Christ and the Buddha.

35

Reincarnation

∞

- *Did Jesus teach the doctrine of reincarnation?*
- *Why is reincarnation so seldom taught in the West?*
- *What is the real meaning of vicarious atonement?*

Mrs. Prophet, would you tell us how you came to believe in reincarnation?

A: You know, Doug, I don't even remember starting to believe in reincarnation because when I was a little girl, probably at the age of two or three, I had a series of recollections of being in Egypt on a large river and playing there as a little child. And these recollections (which were really a part of my self-awareness) would continue to come back to me and I would ask my mother about them. I knew nothing about Egypt—nothing about its geography.

And so I can remember my first lesson on reincarnation coming from my mother when I was about five. She said, "You are seeing yourself in that place because you have lived there before in a previous life." Then she explained to me that the only thing that had ever made sense to her about life and the seeming injustice of people being born with infirmities or children dying very young was this concept of reincarnation—that the soul, in reality, does not begin at birth and does not die at death but continues its evolution.

Q: This is primarily an Eastern idea, isn't it?

A: Not really. We find it in our own scriptures in the West but people don't have the ear to hear, as Jesus said.

Q: Did Jesus teach reincarnation?

A: Jesus taught reincarnation, and it's also in the Old Testament. For example, the last words of the Old Testament in the Book of Malachi read: "Behold, I will send you Elijah the prophet before the coming of the great and dreadful day of the LORD. And he shall turn the heart of the fathers to the children, and the heart of the children to their fathers, lest I come and smite the earth with a curse." Here is God speaking through Malachi, a famous prophet quoted by presidents, and actually saying that Elijah is going to come again.

If that were not enough, we find Jesus making the same statement. In the eleventh chapter of the Book of Matthew Jesus says, "Among them that are born of women there hath not risen a greater than John the Baptist: notwithstanding he that is least in the kingdom of heaven is greater than he." And then he says, "And if ye will receive it, this is Elias, which was for to come," meaning his coming was prophesied. And so Jesus is saying, "He came. He was beheaded. They did with him what they would. And so they will do to me."

What we see in both the Old and New Testaments is that the statements concerning the coming again of Elijah are so naturally mentioned that one has to accept the fact that they are being spoken within the context of an already established understanding. Malachi had the understanding of the coming again of the soul and therefore God could speak to him of the coming again of the prophet. The same with Jesus—he could give his disciples this instruction because they had a prior understanding of reincarnation.

Q: I gather, then, that there is a difference between what was taught to the disciples and what was taught to the world at large?

A: Not necessarily. I'm quite certain that the Essene community had the understanding of the doctrine of reincarnation. And I think that inasmuch as in the East there was common understanding of reincarnation in Hinduism and Buddhism, people were aware of it in Jesus' time. I think that is what the Bible substantiates.

Q: What is the significance of reincarnation for all of us in regard to how we live our lives?

A: I can't really understand how people can make any sense out of religion—unless they are simply coming from some kind of an intellectual perception of the teachings of Christ—without the understanding of reincarnation. The continuity of existence and of being has always been a great reality to me.

We know of a number of psychiatrists who have used hypnosis to regress patients to early childhood. And some patients have gone beyond early childhood and have recounted where they left off in their last life, going on to describe that life and then previous lives.

Now, the ascended masters teach us that we should not submit ourselves to hypnosis, and I would certainly never employ hypnosis to prove the doctrine of reincarnation. But it is very interesting to see that within the subconscious memory of man is the record of previous existence.

This enables us to understand what the ascended masters have taught us—that we carry with us the cause, effect, record and memory of our past and that this influences everything we are today. In fact, the masters teach us that we are what we are because of what we have been before. And that was Buddha's teaching to his disciples.

Q: If reincarnation is so important to believing in a just God, why is it not taught in the West?

A: I think it's a matter of control. The Church has attempted to control the people by fear, saying: "You know, if you don't do what I tell you to do, you're going to go to hell." I think the early Church Fathers feared that if people understood reincarnation, they wouldn't go to church but would just kind of wave a hand at the father and say, "Well, I'll go in my next life."

So it has always been a question of ecclesiastical control: if the people know too much, they will have too much power and too much independence. And this is what disturbs those who try to hold the secrets of the kingdom and to control people by that knowledge.

Q: Then you don't feel that the idea of reincarnation takes away from the sense of personal responsibility?

A: On the contrary, it completely affirms the responsibility of the individual because it reinforces the statement of the Law: Every man shall bear his own burden, and not one jot or tittle of the Law will pass till all be fulfilled. Whatsoever a man soweth, that shall he also reap.

Newton's law states the law of karma in scientific terms. It states that for every action there is an equal and opposite reaction. What is in our consciousness today is the reaction of a cause that we set in motion perhaps yesterday, perhaps ten years ago, perhaps a hundred years ago in a previous lifetime. So, energy is God, and energy in us that we qualify and send forth returns to us.

Now, the grace of God is this: We do not have the fullness of opportunity in a given lifetime to balance what we have put upon life—some call it sin, the Hindus call it karma. If we murder someone and then murder ourselves, it's over. According to Christian theology, we should go to hell unless perhaps we had asked for forgiveness just before we died. The cosmos doesn't work that way. It gives opportunity for the soul to evolve again and again.

As Revelation says: "He that killeth with the sword must be killed with the sword." In order to experience the reaction to his deed, man must come again to confront the one whom he murdered, to confront the energy—not as punishment but as a lesson in the laboratory of earth's schoolroom.

What effect does the energy of hatred that manifests as murder produce? It must be an equally violent action in return. Thus the soul is chastised by her own action and learns that it is wrong to commit such a crime.

Q: **Then, is there any place for vicarious atonement?**

A: Indeed there is, because Christ Jesus came in the person of the Saviour of the world. He died for our sins in the sense that he bore the weight of our karma of many, many lifetimes—he actually bore the entire accumulation of the weight of world karma, or world sin. He bore it in his body, therefore mitigating the descent of our karma for a certain dispensation.

This dispensation is known as the Piscean dispensation—a two-thousand-year cycle whereby our souls were given a new opportunity to come to grips with the Law and the teaching of the Christ and our own inner God flame in order to build up a consciousness, a forcefield of light whereby we would have the capacity to stand and meet our own energies and past sowings face to face. This is why we have now come upon a time at the conclusion of this two-thousand-year period when the earth is in such darkness. We are having to face our own karma.

The purpose of the coming of Jesus Christ was that through him we might learn to walk in his footsteps and do the works that he did, which he promised we would do if we believed on him—

on the Christ within Jesus. At this point in our soul's evolution
we are expected to begin to bear the sins of the world through the
baptism of the sacred fire of the Holy Ghost. That baptism is a
cleansing action of sacred fire, which itself is the transmutation of
karma, or sin. So the baptism by sacred fire is altogether necessary
in order for us to balance our karma of thousands of years.

We have to realize that forgiveness of sin is the setting aside
of karma until the soul matures to that place where she can face
what it is that has burdened her. It is like going to a psychiatrist
and digging up the records of one's childhood and being able to
come to grips with those records. It takes a tremendous amount
of energy to do this and most people are not willing to go
through it. They are not willing to face their past. They are not
willing to take responsibility for past actions.

It is very convenient to say, "It is not possible for me in any
way to attain virtue because I am a sinner. Christ died for me; he
did the whole thing." But we must remember that Jesus gave us
the command "Be ye therefore perfect, even as your Father which
is in heaven is perfect." Jesus gave us the command to perfection.
He gave us the teaching and the law whereby we could attain it.

The acceptance of the law of reincarnation forces the soul to
come to grips with her own past sowings. But what does Paul say
to the Galatians? "Be not deceived. God is not mocked; for whatsoever a man soweth, that shall he also reap."

36

The Law of Karmic Return

∞

- *What happens to people who refuse to balance their karma?*

- *What have Church scholars said about reincarnation?*

- *How important is the notion of reincarnation?*

Mrs. Prophet, what happens to those who will not take responsibility for balancing their own karma? And what about those who withhold the teaching of karma and reincarnation from the people?

A: Jesus said, "Woe unto you, lawyers! For ye have taken away the key of knowledge: ye entered not in yourselves, and them that were entering in ye hindered."

Jesus was speaking of those who take the letter of the Law and split that letter and destroy the key of knowledge of God, which is in the great mystery that is revealed by the Holy Spirit. The understanding of the continuity of the soul's evolution is absolutely basic to true Christianity.

Q: Then, do people not go to heaven or hell when they die?

A: It is not so much heaven and hell that I am concerned with but those in the pulpits of every nation who are preaching that there is no return of the soul, there is no opportunity. What this means is that there are individuals who have defied God, who are unwilling to atone for that sin, to reincarnate and undo the wrong they have done—in other words, to balance their karma and serve life and to set themselves and that life free.

They want someone else to do it for them and so they take the teaching of Jesus Christ as the World Saviour, they take his tremendous demonstration of love for us and they turn it into an escapism whereby they can totally escape from the law of karma. This is the great tragedy—that the real teaching and the real meat of Christ's teaching is taken from his children today.

Q: What happened to that teaching, Mrs. Prophet?

A: As I said before, Jesus taught that John the Baptist was Elias come again. There's no way we can rationalize that Jesus was not teaching the doctrine of reincarnation. But if we need further proof, we can read Matthew 16, where Jesus says to his disciples, "Whom do men say that I the Son of man am?" And his disciples answer, "Some say that thou art John the Baptist; some, Elias; and others, Jeremias or one of the prophets."

The point here is that the disciples are telling him that others are speculating on who he might have been in a previous incarnation. Jesus never rebukes them, never says to them, "This is of the devil. It is wrong for you to speak of this." But he goes right on with his question because he is not interested in speculation on who he was in his last life.

He wants to know if they have identified the eternal nature of the Christ, so he says, "But whom say ye that I am?" And this is when Simon Peter gives his famous answer, "Thou art the Christ, the Son of the living God." Jesus blesses him and says, "Flesh and blood hath not revealed it unto thee, but my Father which is in heaven."

And so Jesus demonstrates to his disciples that the Christ is his eternal nature and that it is by the identity of the Christ that he desires to be remembered, not by his previous incarnations. Thus he teaches us all where we should place the emphasis.

We're not particularly interested in knowing who we were in our past lives. But the doctrine of reincarnation enables us to face the fact that what we are today is the totality of what we have been before. Without that understanding we cannot evolve to the place where we can reunite with the I AM THAT I AM.

Q: Mrs. Prophet, have any of the Church scholars taught reincarnation in the period since Jesus left us?

A: Well, as a matter of fact, Origen of Alexandria, one of the most influential members of the early Church—as influential as Augustine—actually taught the preexistence of the soul and the doctrine of reincarnation. His writings have been almost completely destroyed because he was condemned and his theories were anathematized.

But, in fact, he set forth not his own logic but the understanding of the Christian mysteries prevailing among the group of souls who had retained the message that Jesus gave. John speaks of this when he says that there are so many things which Jesus did that the world "could not contain the books that should be written."

Nevertheless, Theodora and Justinian determined in the year 543 that certain of Origen's teachings should be anathematized. And therefore the doctrine of reincarnation has fallen into what we might call the subconscious body of knowledge of the Church.

It's interesting to note that Theodora was a prostitute before she became empress and the wife of Justinian. In contemplation of the doctrine of reincarnation, she could not face the consequences of what a future life might be because of her previous sins. She would rather make permanent the doctrine that she could be saved through the Christ than bear her own burden, which the law states we must all do. And so we see that it was rebellion against the inner law that Christ taught that caused so much controversy to rise up against Origen.

Q: **Mrs. Prophet, how important is it that a person come to believe in reincarnation?**

A: Saint Germain, who is the master of the Aquarian cycle, teaches us in one of his dictations how important it is. He says that it is the keystone in the arch of being. Without the understanding of reembodiment, as he calls it, we cannot really understand our soul's path of evolution. He says:

> It would be most beneficial if the human monad would refrain from prejudgment in matters of cosmic doctrine and even better if he could universally accept the reality of reembodiment. For it is in the acceptance of this fact of life that he will truly discern the wisdom of the ages and more easily understand his reason for being.
>
> It is most difficult for people in any age, observing in the life span of a comparatively few short years a series of events relative to the personal self, to be able to judge the world in which they live and the society from which they have derived both bane and blessing, and then to be able to perceive matters pertaining to the Spirit and properly assess them.
>
> By correctly understanding and accepting his own reembodiment, the individual develops a cosmic sense of the continuity of self—past, present and future—and is better equipped to see behind the surface effects of today's circumstances the underlying personal causes that stretch back across the dust of centuries. Simply because men lack conscious memory of a previous existence does not deny the validity of this truth. Many have experienced the sudden feeling of having done before that which they are doing

for the first time in this life.

Many have noted with interest the incidence of genius (that some call a "gift" or "talent") in art, music and science, or other aptitudes that appear at an early age, indicating the soul's resumption of the broken thread of identity. Modern physicians take note of the distinct personality of babies on the day of their birth. And all over the world fascinating stories have been documented concerning people's recall of vivid scenes and experiences from a past life.

Q: In the book *Quietly Comes the Buddha,* Gautama Buddha says, "Consider that you yourself have sown the wind and that if you would enter into the fiery core of being, you must first reap the whirlwind." What does that mean, Mrs. Prophet?

A: To "sow the wind and reap the whirlwind" simply describes the law of cause and effect. In order for that law to be fulfilled, the individual soul must reincarnate because one cannot receive the full impact of all he does in a given lifetime.

So Gautama is talking about the fact that we must face our karma first, *before* we come to the judgment, before we come to the trial by the sacred fire, before we are to be weighed in the great balance of life. God allows us to balance our karma and he gives us extensive opportunity until, ultimately, when that span of opportunity has been fulfilled, there comes the final judgment, which is written about in the Book of Revelation.

Q: It seems, Mrs. Prophet, that most people in the world are actually getting behind in the game rather than getting ahead. Is there any hope for them?

A: The problem is that people in the West are not actively balancing their karma because they do not consider it a necessity. The children of God have unwittingly derived their philosophy from the fallen ones, who say: "Eat, drink and be merry, for tomorrow you die." These fallen ones are actually teaching the doctrine of the death of the soul. And the children of God have nowhere to turn because their leaders teach them: "It doesn't matter what you do, you can never pay your debt. You can only lean on Christ, who died for your sins."

And so, with round after round of this false doctrine, embodiment after embodiment, comes the utter disappointment that the soul cannot yet be received in the resurrection by the Lord Christ because she has not settled her accounts. Therefore the Lords of Karma direct the soul once again to return to the scene of her crime, if you will, to stand, face and conquer all that has transpired in the past.

Q: So then, you would attribute the general spiral of decay in the world to people's failure to take responsibility for their previous lives?

A: Not only previous lives, but the present life! Not only do people not come to grips with the distant past but they can scarcely take responsibility for what they did yesterday. People are walking out on responsibility everywhere and this is what is behind the moral decay of civilization.

Q: Mrs. Prophet, don't you preach a rather hard doctrine?

A: It is the Law. And if we betray the Law, we betray our own souls. We will all keep reincarnating until we are willing to balance our karma.

37

"As Ye Sow, So Shall Ye Reap"

∞

- *Is the law of karma inexorable?*
- *Was Jesus a special creation of God unlike other men?*
- *What part does karma play in the final judgment?*

Mrs. Prophet, tell us more about karma and reincarnation.

A: You know, Doug, since I've always had the awareness of a prior existence, I have never had to prove to myself the concept of reincarnation logically or doctrinally or scripturally. Only after I realized that it was such a hard saying for so many people did I come to the idea that perhaps I might find corroboration for what God was teaching me. And truly I have been taught of God and not by doctrinal disputes, and I am not trying to engage in doctrinal dispute.

I happened to notice one day that in the ninth chapter of John concerning the man who was born blind, the disciples ask Jesus, "Who did sin, this man or his parents, that he was born blind?" That question is very astute; it shows that the disciples understood the law of karma and reincarnation. They knew that the consequence of sin outpictured upon the body would be some form of sickness or infirmity. They understood the interrelationship of karma within the family and therefore realized that the blind man's parents could have sinned or that he himself could have sinned.

It is so obvious: if it were the man who had sinned, he would have sinned before that incarnation because the passage clearly states he was blind from his birth.

Jesus does not rebuke their question. He answers it, "Neither hath this man sinned, nor his parents, but that the works of God should be made manifest in him." This is another teaching. It shows us that some volunteer to come into life with infirmity for the glory of God, not because they have karma of a prior existence. This is the way of the bodhisattvas of the East, who come to bear the karma of mankind.

So Jesus is teaching his disciples that this man volunteered to be born blind so that at this moment and this hour he could be brought before him to be healed so that God might be glorified. Nevertheless, the concept of karma is unmistakably present as a part of the disciples' common awareness with their master.

Q: But, Mrs. Prophet, what about the statement in Hebrews, "It is appointed unto men once to die, but after this the judgment"?

A: Here again is the problem of doctrinal dispute, which I really do not wish to enter. Christians always cite this as the final proof that there's no such thing as reincarnation—but look, what are we talking about? We already know that Jesus has overcome death and, as Paul said, that we do not die but only sleep.

The verse is not talking about the cessation of life in the body temple, which we call death. It is talking about the death that is most important, the same death that Jesus exemplified upon the cross. To go through the initiation of the crucifixion means the complete death of the lesser self. The author of Hebrews is teaching us that there is one death of the carnal mind, and after we have put to death the carnal mind, then God brings us to the final judgment. But until this death is experienced, we will keep on reincarnating because we are not ready for the judgment.

Q: Mrs. Prophet, is the law of karma absolutely inexorable?

A: The other day I was reading a paperback book entitled *The Lost Books of the Bible and the Forgotten Books of Eden.* This is a compilation of scriptures that were written by members of the early Church but were rejected when our Bible was put together, somewhat arbitrarily. Some say they are a collection of legends, but they contain much authentic material that corroborates the scripture we have today.

In *The Forgotten Books of Eden* there is a conversation that takes place between the LORD God and Adam and Eve after Adam and Eve have been dismissed from the Garden for their disobedience.

Adam and Eve Driven Out of Eden by Gustave Doré

They are very penitent and they fast and pray to God night and day. They say: "God, please let us return! We only sinned for an hour and now we have to pay this terrible price for our sin."

This appeal comes from Adam and Eve again and again. And again and again God says the same thing: You have been disobedient to my Law. You must wait 5,500 years for the coming of my Son. I will send my Son and he will be a redemption to you and through him you will attain the resurrection.

The obvious implication here is that if Adam and Eve are going to be around 5,500 years from now, they will have to reincarnate. God tells them that they will have to continue outside the Garden and toil by the sweat of the brow until the coming of his Son. He does not say "succeeding generations" or "your children's children's children" will benefit from this but he addresses Adam and Eve directly. To me the implication is clear.

Q: Mrs. Prophet, was Jesus, then, a special creation of God unlike all other men?

A: If he were, then we would all be lost, because unless Jesus is like us we cannot follow him in the regeneration or in the resurrection, we cannot do the works that he did, and the point of his coming is lost. It is in the imitation of the Christ, the following in his footsteps, that we attain immortality.

Jesus feared that a personality cult would grow up around him whereby he would be worshiped instead of emulated. He came as the fulfillment of the Law, not as its exception. And therefore I believe that he lived before and walked the path of righteousness as a very enlightened soul—nevertheless one who had to evolve through time and space, through earth's schoolroom, in preparation for that final incarnation when he would fully exemplify the Christ, the only begotten Son of God. This he did so that we might go and do likewise.

Saint Germain teaches us that this life in this cycle may very well be for many children of God that final incarnation when they can walk hand in hand with Jesus and the other ascended masters. Now they can prove their resurrection and their ascension in the light by the same law and the same science that Jesus demonstrated. This to me is the great joy of living.

Q: But, Mrs. Prophet, there were many miraculous occurrences associated with the life of Jesus. Doesn't that make him unique?

A: It certainly makes him unique in the sense that there are so many disobedient, rebellious ones on earth who are not fulfilling the law of the Christ and of the prophets. In a world where people are taught to believe that they are sinners and where they fulfill the law of sin and mortality, the son of God who is obedient to the law of life everlasting is indeed the exception. But that does not mean that we cannot all be the exception to a way of life that is not the way of God.

Q: Mrs. Prophet, what part does karma play in the final judgment?

A: Jesus himself taught that "every idle word that men shall speak, they shall give account thereof in the day of judgment. For by thy words thou shalt be justified, and by thy words thou shalt be condemned." We read in the Book of Revelation that in the final judgment "the dead were judged according to their works." And it repeats: "They were judged every man according to their works."

Now, if the judgment of whether the soul is to inherit eternal life comes by a man's word and his works, then where does the literal interpretation of vicarious atonement come in? How can Jesus save our souls and guarantee us eternal life when we confess his name if the judgment is not according to that confession but rather according to our words and works, as it is written in the Book of Life?

Q: Can the soul die, Mrs. Prophet?

A: The Book of Revelation speaks of the "second death." The second death is the death of the soul. It is written in scripture, "The soul that sinneth, it shall die." This shows the possibility that the soul who does not choose to glorify God, to bend the knee before the Christ and to walk in the way of Christ (or of the eternal flame of that Christ as it appears in the Buddha, in the Mother, and so forth) may face the second death in the last judgment. The last judgment takes place at the Court of the Sacred Fire before the Four and Twenty Elders, who sit before the great white throne—the throne that is the forcefield of Almighty God.

There is the possibility, then, that the soul who rebels against God may be canceled out as an energy field, as a consciousness. And the energy of God and the Christ within, as well as the I AM Presence, would then be returned to the consciousness of the universal Christ and the universal God.

Q: Does the Spirit die?

A: The Spirit can never die. The *Bhagavad-Gita* says, "Never the Spirit was born; the Spirit shall cease to be never." The Spirit is the point of origin, the I AM THAT I AM, but the soul represents the consciousness evolving in time and space. That identity, which reincarnates again and again, which makes karma and balances karma and is destined to ascend back to the Spirit of God, can be lost. This is the teaching of the scriptures of East and West.

38

The Power of the Word

- *What is the origin of the science of the spoken Word?*
- *What is the significance of the name of the LORD?*
- *What does the word* Elohim *mean?*

Mrs. Prophet, tell us about the relationship between the Word and the Christ.

A: If we could all read akasha, the records of all that has ever transpired on earth, we would look back to the years of Lemuria and Atlantis and to civilizations unrecorded and we would find priests and priestesses at the altar intoning the Word, which they also understood to be the Logos, the eternal Christos.

The word *Christ* is derived from the Greek *Christos,* meaning "anointed." Jesus was anointed with the Holy Spirit. And so that Christ, who has manifested in us and through us from the foundations of the world, is the one who comes to anoint us by the Word, as the Word and as the communicator of the Word.

I could begin with any of the world's great teachers. I could begin at any point in time and space, whether with Krishna or Confucius or Lao Tzu or Buddha or Muhammad. And I could begin with the Word, whom John proclaimed: "The Word was made flesh and dwelt among us.... In the beginning was the Word, and the Word was with God, and the Word was God."

It is not a coincidence that the word *Christ* has been used synonymously with *logos,* meaning "word." *Word* with a capital *W* tells us the function of our own Real Self as the communicator of Reality.

Q: Could you share with us your experiences with the Word? How did you discover the science of the spoken Word?

A: I think it all began when I was a little child and then continued later when I was in high school and college. I had three key experiences in which God revealed his Word to me. These experiences were frightening experiences because I came so close to the sacred fire that is God. As we read in scripture, "Our God is a consuming fire."

In each instance I was in a moment of communing with God and calling upon God, a moment of great need. I cried out to him and I asked him to respond and to deliver unto me the answer to my call. Out of my desiring and my contact with the LORD's Spirit, I called for a manifestation and within the hour the manifestation occurred.

On the third occasion it was just a simple, mundane request. I was in the middle of the United States and I needed to get to the East Coast quickly. It was an emergency and I said, "God, you get me there!" No sooner had I walked out of my dorm than a man was standing there saying, "Does anyone want to go to New Jersey?" And I said, "I do!" and he was ready to take off.

I had never seen him before and all the girls in the dorm said, "You're crazy! What are you doing going with a man you've never seen before?" I said, "I'm going." I was home in record time— about twenty hours—but I was frightened because God's manifestation in answer to my call had been so clear.

It wasn't that I didn't know God was an ever-present, loving being in my life. But I was beginning to see that there was a force, there was a power, there was an energy and there was a science—

that somehow when the fire welled up within me creating a fountain that would reach God, God would arc back and the matrix that I had set forth would instantly be fulfilled.

I knew that I was standing in the presence of a tremendous power and I began to think what that power would do when mankind discovered it. So I began to search and search for the science that I knew existed. And we've read the words of Joel:

> And it shall come to pass afterward that I will pour out my spirit upon all flesh; and your sons and your daughters shall prophesy, your old men shall dream dreams, your young men shall see visions. . . . And it shall come to pass that whosoever shall call on the name of the LORD shall be delivered.

I sensed, and I think many of us are sensing, that we live in an age of the turning of cycles. The two-thousand-year age of Pisces is merging into the age of Aquarius. There are new energies and we are having visions and dreaming dreams and we are feeling the LORD's presence. The charismatic movement is sweeping the churches while many people are leaving the churches because they do not find the LORD's Spirit there. They are seeking within the heart and the temple of being the Reality they know exists.

We have a right to seek. We have a right to know God. We have a right to claim our inheritance. But we must keep humble before this awesome presence even as we are humble before the nuclear reactor when we know there is that atomic energy, that nuclear fission and that energy released. We have respect for science. Whether it is material or spiritual science, all science involves energy and the equation of energy.

Q: **What significance does the name of God have in the science of the spoken Word?**

A: I believe that God is energy and that the energy of God is locked inside of us. I believe that all of the great teachers of East and West have taught us that the way to unlock that energy is through the science of the spoken Word.

I also believe that the name of God is a key. In scripture, reference is made to the name of the LORD again and again, but the name is concealed or not used. The only place that I could find in all of scripture where the LORD reveals his name and says "this is my name" is in Exodus 3 when Moses experiences the phenomenon of God as a fire.

God as fire has always intrigued me because it is sacred fire, and fire is something that transcends planes of consciousness. I've discovered that the great leaders of all time in all of the world's major religions have at one time or another experienced God as a living flame, a tangible flame.

The LORD God spoke to Moses out of the flame that burned in the bush, and yet the bush was not consumed. Can you imagine a fire speaking to you?

Moses was a very humble soul. He was a shepherd tending the flocks of his father-in-law and he was commissioned by God to go back to Egypt to bring the people of Israel out of Egypt— an enormous task. Their culture, their way of life had become totally involved with the Egyptians. He had to convince them that he represented God and that God had sent him.

So he speaks to the flame and asks, "What is your name and

who shall I say sent me?" And God speaks back to Moses and says, "I AM THAT I AM.... This is my name for ever, and this is my memorial unto all generations."

I AM THAT I AM is more than a name—it is a power. It is a statement of Being. Whose being? God's being. Where? Where else can God be but within the temple of the heart, within the temple of man, his manifestation.

Where do we look for God when we look for him? Do we look for him in the wind and in the stars and in the sun or in the center of the earth? Or do we look for him in the highest of his creation, his sons and his daughters?

We can only translate God by going from the known to the unknown by the process of induction. To find him we have to find a point of contact. Our point of contact is consciousness. We can speak the name I AM THAT I AM and we can declare being and consciousness. We can also say, "God is where I AM," and by the power of his Word, he can also speak his name where I AM.

Searching and searching again concerning this name, I found that there had been a settling of darkness causing people to forget God. But it is recorded in Genesis that with the coming of the son of Seth, "Then began men to call upon the name of the LORD."

Q: I have heard you use the term *Elohim* when referring to God. What does this mean?

A: *Elohim* is a Hebrew term for God. It is used about two thousand times in the Old Testament, translated as "God" in English. In Genesis we read that God (or Elohim) said: "Let us make man in our image, after our likeness."

This is very interesting because *Elohim* is a plural noun. It suggests a unity in plurality. This plurality created man "after our likeness... male and female." We experience, then, the polarity of the masculine and feminine action of the universe, the active and the passive, the Alpha and Omega who figure in the Book of Revelation.

And so, the declaration of being and the affirmation of God's being is in his heavenly hosts, in his emissaries, in his archangels and angels and seraphim and cherubim and all of the key figures who move in and out of the Old and New Testaments—walking and talking with Abraham, with Lot, coming to the prophets, speaking to them, coming to Mary in the figure of Gabriel, coming in the figure of Archangel Michael, coming as the two men in white apparel.

When we start looking, we find in the Bible all sorts of visitations whereby we suddenly realize that God in all of his wondrous manifestations as the heavenly hosts, as that which we call the mystical body of Christ, is actually a unity in plurality. This never detracts from the fact that God is one God: "Hear, O Israel: The LORD our God is one LORD." It doesn't detract from the fact that God is a trinity of Father, Son and Holy Ghost.

There is a great mathematics of God. There is only one God and one "only begotten Son," and yet one times one times one always equals one. For the purposes of time and space, we find that the great Spirit of God is individualized over and over and over again. Take away time and space and I dare say we would not figure ourselves separately but we would all know one another as one Spirit, as many rays emanating from the one Source.

39

The Incarnation of the Word

- *How do we know we're supposed to be like Christ?*
- *Is the age of miracles past?*
- *What is the meaning of the washing of water by the Word?*

Mrs. Prophet, how do we know that Jesus intended us to be like him and to prove the same laws he proved?

A: Jesus said, "He that believeth on me, the works that I do shall he do also; and greater works than these shall he do because I go unto my Father." To me the promise is unmistakable, and yet it is considered blasphemy for anyone on earth today to make himself equal with Christ, let alone greater than Christ.

It is my understanding that Jesus came to set the example for the incarnation of the Word. I believe that if we accept him as the Word, he releases and ignites the flame within us and we individually experience the Second Coming. We are born again—because he is one with the Father and because we now experience that same Word, that same anointing that he knew. As we walk with him hand in hand, the fire of our heart, the fire of his heart, can work his works. And by his grace and only by his grace, we together can do those greater things.

Q: But how do we actually perform the works that Jesus did?

A: By the action of the Word. It is written that Jesus cast out spirits with his word. He had tremendous power in his word and he derived that power from the Father and the Son and the Holy Spirit. He drew it forth from his heart center.

Catholics have long referred to the Sacred Heart of Jesus and the Immaculate Heart of Mary. The heart is the heart chakra. It is known by all who meditate to be the center of that burning love of God that the disciples knew when they met their Lord on the road to Emmaus and said, "Did our hearts not burn within us?"

In the secret chamber of the heart there is an altar, and our own Real Self presides at that altar as the priest, the minister, the rabbi. In our soul we can kneel before that altar. We can find the cathedral of the heart as the place of the Holy of holies.

The Word of God is power. The Book of Hebrews describes Christ as "upholding all things by the word of his power." Jesus walked on the water by the science of the spoken Word. He stilled the tempests. He said, "Peace, be still!" and the waters were stilled.

I don't think that we should consider that the age of miracles is past but that the age of miracles is fulfilled in science. We should consider that Jesus was the greatest nuclear physicist, the greatest alchemist that we have known in our recorded history. He mastered all energies, all flow of life forces. He mastered time and space. He ascended into that white cloud, the white-fire core of the atom of his own Self. Hence, we call him an ascended master and we call all who have done the same ascended masters; for many sons and daughters have proved that oneness with God and mastered time and space, both before and after the advent of Jesus.

It is written in Genesis, "Enoch walked with God: and he was not, for God took him." I believe that this is another record of one who ascended through the mastery of time and space. Elijah was caught up into a chariot of fire. We also have the assumption of Mary the Mother and even the ascension of John the Revelator—all of this by the power of the Word.

Q: What did Paul mean when he spoke of the washing of water by the Word?

A: Paul said that Christ "loved the Church and gave himself for it that he might sanctify and cleanse it with the washing of water by the Word." The washing of water by the Word is an amazing concept if you meditate upon it in your own heart, sitting under your own vine and fig tree, under your own source of communion with God.

First of all, the Church always figures as the Bride of Christ. We are told that we are the temple of the living God and therefore we can consider ourselves to be the Church. Christ loves us because we are really the Church. Organizations, temples made with hands, doctrine and dogma—these are not the Church. The Church is only alive when its members are living, kindled flames. The Church is a white cube. It's the philosophers' stone. The Church is consciousness.

To me, the washing of water by the Word means an alchemical action whereby the waters of our consciousness are cleansed as we invoke the Word and as we, through the Word, invoke the sacred fire. That sacred fire is a baptism that we are all waiting for.

Remember the words of John the Baptist: "One cometh after me whose shoes I am not worthy to unlatch. He shall baptize you with the Holy Ghost and with fire." We find the reference to fire over and over again. It is a sacred fire, a cleansing fire. It is the fire in the core of the atom. It is energy. That energy is God.

God didn't walk into the office of Edison or anyone else. He let man meditate upon the lightning for thousands of years until someone decided to capture the energy, harness it and use it. Could it be that he expects us to do the same, to experiment with that fire that is God and in a spiritual way harness it and do those greater works that Christ promised?

It is written of the two witnesses in the Book of Revelation that "fire proceedeth out of their mouth and devoureth their enemies." Not out of their hands, their head, their stomach or their feet, but out of their mouth. It's a clue to me, as I have a hypothesis that I am about to prove. To me it means that the fire that proceeds out of their mouth is an action of the sacred fire and of the Word, which they have mastered.

Isaiah said of the LORD, "He hath made my mouth like a sharp sword." And we read of the Faithful and True in the Book of Revelation, whose name is "The Word of God" and whose outstanding feature is that "out of his mouth goeth a sharp

sword, that with it he should smite the nations." What is this sword? If you look at the word itself, you see that it has *s* and then *word—sword.* Maybe it's an abbreviation for "sacred word."

It comes out of the throat center, which the Hindus long ago acknowledged as the power center. For thousands of years the use of mantras and the intoning of the Word, the name of God, has been the basic form of meditation of yogis.

Q: Did the science of the spoken Word originate, then, in India?

A: It may have actually come to us from Lemuria. James Churchward wrote a number of books on the lost continent of Mu (Lemuria). He found tablets in a monastery in India that the priests had guarded for thousands and thousands of years and that had been brought to them from beyond their shores. The priests knew the interpretation of these clay tablets. Churchward became a student in this monastery and he was the only one, as far as he knew, who was given the key to these tablets. So he deciphered them and he has four or five books of his decipherings.

The tablets give a description of Lemuria, of the temples. There are stones that have been found in Mexico that have the same hieroglyphs. They speak of four cosmic forces, just as we have in our scripture the four beasts on the four sides of the Ancient of Days. They also speak of the science of the spoken Word. Perhaps the thousands of years of mantra is a tradition that came to India from that very place.

However, this science, after all of our investigations, after all of our consideration of scriptures, cannot be proven until we try it. Only as we use the Word can we experience it in our own laboratory. To me, a laboratory, and a cathedral or a church, are one and the same. They're the place where we go to meet our God and to commune with him and to discover the secrets of our soul's evolution and of the cosmos itself.

40

The Aura

∞

- *What is the human aura?*
- *What can it tell us about ourselves?*
- *Does the aura ever lie?*

Mrs. Prophet, you have a book on the human aura, a subject that many people are thinking about lately. I am wondering if you could tell us just what is the aura?

A: The book *The Human Aura* by Kuthumi and Djwal Kul is a series of letters dictated through Mark Prophet to his students throughout the world. It goes into the aura in an exceptional way. We are all interested in knowing about the aura because at sublevels of awareness we all perceive one another's aura. We're all reading each other and that reading is being translated to our conscious mind.

When we have a sense of danger about a certain individual or an immediate affinity with someone or we sense that someone has a certain personality, we are contacting the aura. It's an energy field. It's a blueprint, and it exists before birth and after death.

Scientists have conducted studies on this energy field and have postulated that this nonphysical matrix, this electromagnetic blueprint, or "life field," exists around every living thing on the planet—not just around people but around animals and plants. It has also been shown to exist around inorganic matter.

Scientists call it an L-field.

Researchers have also discovered an energy field originating in the mind, which they call a "thoughtfield" (T-field). This in turn controls the L-field, or the life field. They say that the thought field exists independently of the physical brain, and both the T-field and the L-field are influenced by greater electromagnetic fields of the universe.

When we start thinking about this and the flow of life, we begin to reconsider our entire world view, even our concepts of theology and science, and we begin to realize that there is a continuity of being that we have been divorced from by the way we view the universe in the West.

Q: Is the aura what is photographed in Kirlian photography?

A: Personally, when I see the aura I see much more than what is being photographed, but certainly Kirlian photography substantiates a nonphysical energy that we have not figured on scientifically before.

There's no question that the great avatars have taught of the aura. Jesus said: "The light of the body is the eye. If therefore thine eye be single, thy whole body shall be full of light. But if thine eye be evil, thy whole body shall be full of darkness. If therefore the light that is in thee be darkness, how great is that darkness!"

That statement denotes a mystical teaching. It cannot be understood from the context of the words themselves but only in the light of energy and its qualification. In the concept of the eye being single, Jesus is talking about our attention. Where our attention rests, so will be the light of the body. If the eye is single, or single-minded—on God, on good, on developing the highest potential of being—then the body is full of light. But if the eye is evil, that is, if the eye descends out of that single-mindedness into the duality of a dual vision, which is seeing constantly the relativity of good and evil, then the body is full of darkness.

This shows that we have an energy field. That energy field can be full of light or it can be qualified as darkness. I have seen some people whose auras were literally surrounded by a black energy. And I have seen others whose auras were filled with light. Their eyes reflected that light as well as their joy, their laughter, their communion with the bubbling brook of the Holy Spirit, if you will.

I have noticed that the people who have a black energy around them also have chakras that emanate a darkness. When such people are in a state of anger, the blackness becomes charged with a crimsonlike lightning, which emanates from the mouth if they are verbalizing their anger or from the solar plexus if they are feeling that anger but not expressing it. The aura records moment by moment by moment the feelings and the thoughts of an individual.

The conclusion of Jesus is: "If therefore the light that is in thee be darkness, how great is that darkness!" But how can light be darkness when they are opposites? The answer is that light is another name for energy, and energy is another name for God. The aura, then, is a receptacle that we have been given to contain God's light, God's energy, the very essence of God himself.

Through the thoughts of our hearts, we may put a forcefield on the aura, creating greater light or creating darkness. The aura is the greatest proof that man has the gift of free will and that we have a certain portion of God's energy allotted to us daily. This energy registers as the aura, and we can choose whether we are going to make that aura dark or light.

We are living in what would be considered by some standards on other systems of worlds quite a primitive era in that most people do not readily perceive the aura with the eyes and therefore do not readily see what people are in actuality. We do not have the aura to bear witness, so we grope blindly, trusting people we shouldn't trust and not realizing that even the coming of illness or death registers on the aura before it occurs.

This great science of the aura that we are now discovering can lift us out of the era of the blind leaders of the blind where people follow whoever smiles at them and says nice words. People cannot conceal what they are in the aura. The aura is a giant mirror of the soul and of the consciousness.

Q: Does the aura ever lie?

A: The aura is like a garment, and it is possible for people to completely conceal very dark modes of consciousness by putting over the aura a patine of great light and the manifestation of light. Kuthumi describes this in *The Human Aura.*

He says that at various moments when individuals are off guard and they suddenly become enraged or irritated or challenged, the aura will turn inside out and these dark manifestations hidden neatly between the folds of the garment will come to the surface. We see this happening again and again as people's hidden selves come to the surface for judgment.

Part of this is an activity of the soul itself. The soul is not content to be dwelling within a personality that is deceitful, because the soul's basic orientation is to move toward oneness with the

The Ascended Master Kuthumi

Spirit of the living God. And therefore the soul arranges circumstances whereby we are exposed or we betray ourselves.

This is why many times criminals who commit the perfect crime will make an obvious mistake. At subconscious levels the soul really wants to be caught, wants to be discovered and wants to be brought to judgment so it can begin to atone for its sin—or, in Hindu terms, to balance its karma. We can hide certain emanations of our consciousness for a time but not permanently because the law of God forces them to the surface for cleansing.

Q: Does the knowledge of the aura have any practical uses?

A: I think the practical uses of the aura have to do with garnering an energy field of light. The aura is a receptacle, an outer garment that we wear. In other words, our identity does not stop with our skin. And sometimes when people are in a certain frame of consciousness or very relaxed, they can look over at a friend and see an energy wavelength around the body. It is a forcefield right next to the body that has to do with the protective emanation of the soul.

Now, that is only the beginning. There are forcefields beyond forcefields that go out from that immediate energy field, and these forcefields are interconnecting receptacles. We have the option by our free will to invoke the light of God and to fill the aura with more and more energy of the sacred fire and therefore to contain within these receptacles a greater concentration of what is called God's consciousness, or the God consciousness, or cosmic consciousness.

Interpenetrating and working with the aura are the seven chakras. These focuses of the sacred fire are points of God-awareness that can be developed by meditation and by the science of the spoken Word. The key chakra, as we have said, is the heart itself and the threefold flame within the heart.

Meditating upon the heart and the threefold flame and using the violet-flame invocations, one begins to establish a momentum that builds day by day until the momentum is so great that it becomes as great as that of Jesus. We know that the woman who had the issue of blood for twelve years needed merely to touch the hem of his garment to be healed.

But the touching of the hem of his garment was not simply a physical touching. The woman touched his aura, and by touching the aura and placing her attention upon it, she became a siphon. She was empty; he was full. His aura immediately was transferred to hers and made her whole.

And Jesus said, "I perceive that virtue is gone out of me. Who touched me?" He knew who touched him, but he made the statement so that we could realize that healing occurs through a transfer of energy. He wanted us to know that if we would follow him all the way, as he is the great example of our overcoming, we must also fill our auras and our chakras with light so that when people come in contact with us we will have a reservoir of energy that can be used. Having the aura filled with light is being ready to extend the cup of cold water in Christ's name.

41

Reading the Aura

∞

- *Is our aura our contact with other dimensions?*
- *What does it take to read the aura?*
- *What is the meaning of color in the aura?*

Mrs. Prophet, we've been talking about the aura. Can you tell us more about it?

A: The aura is an example of the interdependence of all life, because it is through the aura and the seven chakras that emanations of love, feelings of joy and buoyancy flow and are received and transmitted. Through the aura we all interact with life. We interact with distant galaxies and distant stars, and we have the capacity to give and receive energy.

The concrete forcefield of man, the physical body, is the focal point on which all of this hangs. The physical body, the mental body, the emotional body and the memory body all interpenetrate as four interconnecting sheaths. These sheaths are surrounded by the L-field and T-field we were discussing earlier.

The fact that researchers have postulated the preexistence of those energy fields makes us grapple with questions of theology because we are discovering more and more of man as we discover more of the aura. What is the source of the aura?

We can conclude that our Creator has placed a portion of

himself within us, beginning with the threefold flame in the heart. We know that the aura is actually a garment we wear. It is a transmitting and receiving station. It is highly susceptible to the mass consciousness, to emanations from beyond our planet, and even to beings who are beyond our level of consciousness. I often think of the plane in which we live as a thin line in time and space, with a vast cosmos above and below.

This cosmos consists of frequencies that our five senses are not equipped to deal with. Considering this, we can realize that if the aura itself extends beyond this thin black line, then it can be used as an extension of the self into other dimensions—for instance, as a space probe or a time probe or as an energy that actually enables us, while we are tied to this physical frame, to explore many planes of consciousness.

Q: Is it the aura that accounts for such things as ESP?

A: Certainly the extrasensory perceptions, perceptions beyond the five senses (and scientists tell us we may have hundreds of senses), must come to us through the emanation of the aura. Many people realize that as our moods change, so our forcefield changes. We know how we feel when we have had a good night's sleep. The aura is recharged. It is charged with prana and with the emanations of the stars and of the earth currents, and we awake with a certain charge of energy. We also know how we feel when we are depleted.

These are not merely physical conditions. These conditions are based on how much of the energy of God's consciousness we take in and retain. People notice that in prayer or meditation they increase self-awareness and increase the manifestation of the aura and of the chakras.

We notice that children can deplete the aura very quickly when they have a prolonged period of crying or a tantrum or become angry because their needs are not immediately met. At the conclusion, they usually drop off to sleep. They are exhausted because they have expended the energy content of the aura.

We find that certain types of music deplete our auras, while other types of music give us a sense of buoyancy and joy and of contacting realms of light, where we feel imbued by the consciousness of angels and ascended beings.

The aura is constantly being played upon; and the reading of the aura, as Kuthumi discusses in his book, is a profound science because there are so many levels and layers of the aura to be reckoned with. Truly it takes a level of adeptship that most people who claim a psychic clairvoyance actually do not have. This is why Jesus said, "Judge righteous judgment." An accurate analysis of the aura cannot be made from the surface, just as a doctor cannot produce an analysis of the health of the body by simply looking at the surface.

We may see manifestations in the aura that have to do with the type of environment the individual lives in, the pressures and tensions of life that he is under or the amount of karma that he is carrying that day. But that surface reading may tell us nothing of the deep soul yearnings and of an intense manifestation of light that comes from other lifetimes and incarnations.

It is important to realize that the aura is continually changing, like the blip on a tape-recording machine that registers the levels of one's voice. The aura is a pulsating manifestation. It changes color and actually reflects the colors of frequencies that can be interpreted by the one who reads the aura as qualities of light or of darkness.

Q: What are those colors, Mrs. Prophet?

A: Each color represents a certain band of frequencies in the electromagnetic spectrum. Color is more than color; it is actually vibration. For instance, when we love with purity without desiring to possess, control or manipulate loved ones, there is a pure stream of pink energy that comes forth from the heart and fills the aura.

This is why we say when people are in love that life is "rosy" and that people see through rose-colored glasses. Their auras are so imbued with the pink energy and the pink spectrum that they can only behold life in that love energy. Therefore they are not critical or analytical, but they are buoyed up by their own sense of the presence of God as love.

When love becomes impure because of lust and darkness and carnal manipulation and a misuse of that sacred energy of life, the auras of people become charged with a vibration—hence a color—that is not the pure pink of that rosy-cheeked babe that represents the fullness of our concept of love. The pink will take on perhaps a crimson color of passion or a dark gray and black tone and quality—the deathlike grip of the attempt to control individuals, whether one's children or whomever one is sharing a relationship with.

But because most people are not capable of reading the aura, they are often misled by the words, the sweet words that someone may be speaking, rather than seeing beyond to the motive of the heart and the motive of desire within the subconscious. Because people do not read the aura, they must rely on an inner sense, almost a sixth sense.

Pilate was not able to read the aura of Jesus or he would never have turned him over to the Sanhedrin. He had to rely on the dream of his wife to determine that "this is a good man—leave him alone!" How impoverished we are that we think we have to rely on dreams, astrology, et cetera, when the aura is giving us, as though it were shouting from the housetops, every reading we need.

What can we do in the absence of our ability to read the aura? We can tune in to the soul, because the soul will always tell us the truth if we maintain contact with this center of God consciousness. The soul knows—and will tell us by giving us that immediate first impression about someone—whether a person is right or wrong or rightly or wrongly motivated.

When we listen to the soul speaking within us as an inner voice, we can avoid costly mistakes in business and financial situations as well as in our love life and in our interactions with people. It is important to trust our first impression of someone, because subsequent to it, the individual will become familiar and we will start to incorporate his or her ways, actions and aura into our own. There will no longer be that sharp impact of the initial contact.

So the aura is our best defense, but we need to be still. As Jesus said, "Be still, and know that I am God." We must be still and know that the I AM within us is the God who will direct us and care for us until we can expand our soul faculties to make full use of the aura, which is our gift from God.

Q: Mrs. Prophet, is there a distinction between that intuitive feeling we get about each other and reading the aura?

A: Yes, there is a great distinction, Doug. The intuitive feeling acts independently of the ability to read the aura and is a substitute for it. It is just another safety valve that we have—something that we can have without the development of aura reading and aura probing. It is a necessary faculty of self-protection that is built into the human psyche.

The reading of the aura demands years of study, but the very first principle that Kuthumi teaches us is the purification of the faculty of vision. This has to do with the clearing of the third-eye center, the *Ajna,* at the brow so that we can begin to see as God sees, which is God's basic desire for us.

42

The Aura of a Saint

∞

- *What is special about the aura of a saint?*
- *Is purity too much to expect in today's world?*
- *Why is the light of the saints so often rejected by their fellowman?*

Mrs. Prophet, what is the difference between the aura of the saints and the aura of most of us?

A: I think it can be summed up in the simple statement of Jesus: "Blessed are the pure in heart, for they shall see God." Not only shall they see God but they shall be God. For the pure in heart—by purity of desire, motive, speech, conduct and works—continually qualify with light the stream of energy that flows through the heart. And that pure light fills the aura.

So, seeing God is possible because there is something within us that we can equate with God and thereby we can identify God. That "something" is his light. God's light is his greatest gift to us. It is like water: it will take on the color, the vibration, the density that we put upon it. We can change water from a liquid to ice or vapor.

God's light is our immediate resource, and it is continually flowing like liquid, like moving fire. It is what manifests in the aura and determines the personality of the individual. The difference between a saint and an ordinary person is that the saint has chosen day by day, hour by hour to amplify the light of God as good works.

Jesus said, "Let your light so shine before men that they may see your good works and glorify your Father which is in heaven." Wherever we go we have the opportunity to let our light—our aura—shine. We can consecrate the garment of our being, our aura, to be worn by the Holy Spirit. Hence, our good works become the activity of the Holy Spirit.

There are many saints walking around on earth today who do not know that they are saints and who are not recognized by others as saints because many people truly walk in darkness, having not the vision of God. And many in the pulpits teach that it is not by good works that we enter in but only by grace. In other words, there is nothing we ourselves can do whereby we can inherit the consciousness of God, the gift of the Holy Spirit.

Yet we have this direct order from Jesus to qualify the aura with light, to let the aura shine, to let it be amplified so that men may see our good works. If good works are not necessary, then why should we let men see them that they might glorify God? It is through our good works that men recognize God and therefore increase their faith.

So the difference between the saint and the non-saint is the difference between the individual who has elected to be God and the one who considers it blasphemy to elect to be God and therefore does nothing.

Q: Isn't this kind of purity too much to ask in today's world?

A: I don't think so at all, because the soul's natural inclination is toward purity. I think we all have a desire to be the best kind of person we know how to be. Even when things come out of us that aren't so nice, it is because the basic desire of the soul is to be whole. And in order to be whole, the soul has to rid herself of the absence of wholeness, which may be the darkness that lies at subconscious levels.

People want to achieve, want to do well, want to be successful. Although many are motivated by greed, beneath that motivation there is often a kernel of light (God within the individual) that has a desire to unfold a higher level of consciousness. When we realize how much of himself God has placed within us, what a useful tool the aura is and how close it can bring us to cosmic beings, ascended masters and our own Christ Self, we will want to begin immediately to strengthen and expand the aura.

I think people want oneness with God, but they have been confused as to what God really is, what heaven really is, and what the conditions are for getting from where we are today to where God is. People have an innate understanding of God as peace, as freedom, as love and as the flow of life, but they are programmed to believe in sin and death and to see themselves as sinners. So they act out their little parts and they feel completely helpless to do anything to increase the God consciousness on earth.

Kuthumi, who was embodied as Saint Francis of Assisi, frees us from this misconception. He teaches that those who truly understand the meaning of God, Christ and life see that there is no difference between the divine nature in Jesus and the divine nature in them-

Courtesy of the Nicholas Roerich Museum, New York

St. Francis by Nicholas Roerich

selves. There is no partiality in heaven. All can equate with the image of the beloved Son.

Who is that beloved Son? That beloved Son is the Christ, the Second Person of the Trinity of Father, Son and Holy Spirit. Who are we? We are sons and daughters of God, but all of us have that potential of the Trinity in the threefold flame within the heart.

Yes, there is only one Son, the eternal Christ, who incarnated in Jesus. But all sons and daughters of God have the same opportunity to have the fullness of that Son dwell in them if they will equate with that opportunity and realize that it is not exclusive to one son but an opportunity for all.

In the threefold flame that God has placed in our hearts, we have the gift of God the Father, God the Son and God the Holy Spirit. There is only one God—only one Father, only one Son and only one Holy Spirit. But we must realize that this one flame of life can manifest infinitely and still remain as one.

Therefore, there is not any doctrinal division; there is only a need for the acceleration of consciousness to the place where we can all realize that we share the inheritance of this Sonship in the flame in the heart. Beginning from that point, we can expand the flame as Jesus did and our auras can become a veritable beacon of light and salvation to the world.

Q: Would you say that finding God and magnifying the light in the aura are the same thing?

A: Finding God is certainly a means to magnifying the light in the aura, and magnifying the light in the aura certainly enables us to find God. It is the principle of hallowing time and space—that is, sanctifying the body temple where we are, sanctifying life where we are so that more and more of the energy of infinity is compressed into globules of time and space until our consciousness is perpetually transcending itself. Right within this physical matrix we can experience planes of consciousness beyond and beyond and beyond.

Q: Why is the light of the saints so often rejected by their fellowmen?

A: I think that the light, as it increases in the aura, is so intense that it activates pockets of darkness in others. It can activate hatred and even demons and discarnates in those who profess to have the only way as far as religion is concerned. Individuals who are possessed of demons of false doctrine become annoyed when they are in the presence of those who are expanding the light of the aura and actually increasing the presence of Christ on earth.

That hatred of Christ, the Lamb who is "slain from the foundation of the world," is the anti-Christ manifestation that is present in those who have not elected to purify the heart, the motive, the desire and consequently the aura.

Q: Mrs. Prophet, why are there people of such light and darkness on earth when all people are created equal?

A: Jesus stated it in another of his mysteries that is still not understood: "For whosoever hath, to him shall be given and he shall have more abundance; but whosoever hath not, from him shall be taken away even that he hath."

Jesus was talking about light—light in the aura, light in the chakras and light in the heart. Those who have light become a great magnet magnetizing more and more and more of God until they shine like the shining of Jesus' face in his transfiguration. Those who have not the light, those who have misqualified light with darkness, find that even the light that they had is taken from them because they have no magnet of God within them to retain that light.

So it seems that the light ones get lighter and the dark ones get darker, even as they say the rich get richer and the poor get poorer. This is a law of the universe because each one has to elect to be the fullness of the abundance of God's light. This we can do for one important reason: because God already dwells within us.

Q: Mrs. Prophet, what would happen if everybody on the planet were conscientiously trying to magnify the light in his aura?

A: It would be tremendous! God said he would spare Sodom if he could find ten righteous men in the city, but ten couldn't be found. Ten righteous men are ten individuals expanding the light of the aura.

If everyone on the planet were doing this today, we would not have the problems we have, because all problems—world problems, political and economic problems—are the result of the caving in of the aura and individuals not taking a moment in the day to give the decree to expand the light, to consume darkness and to make a thrust of cosmic consciousness here in time and space.

43

Angels and Your Aura

∞

- *How does daily experience affect the aura?*
- *Do angels influence our auras?*
- *How is the aura contaminated?*

Mrs. Prophet, how does our daily experience affect our auras?

A: Kuthumi gives us an interesting explanation of this. Truly, when I read his writings I am most impressed by the profound understanding he has of the psychology of man, and indeed he is a psychologist among ascended masters.

Kuthumi speaks of the transmittal of the data of our experience world to the subconscious. He explains that this transmittal is automatic; it functions by the law of each man's being. Out of the storehouse of memory we have an instantaneous recall of events, persons and places of an entire lifetime, which is almost a magical feat.

He explains the process as one that involves the individual's own Christ mind and the one who assists that Christ mind, the recording angel. Jesus spoke of the recording angel when he gave his teaching on not offending little children. He said, "For I say unto you that their angels do always behold the face of my Father which is in heaven."

Jesus' words give us the understanding that the recording angel is always aware of God and yet always aware of man. This angel stands at that midpoint of the Mediator with our own Christ Self and is responsible for assisting in the recording of our every thought, word, deed and feeling, even though it is an automatic, computerlike process. The recording angel assists us in sorting, classifying and transferring data from the world in which we live to the subconscious mind, which assimilates that data.

The subconscious mind is reflected in the aura, and the aura itself reflects the total being—the tip of the iceberg as well as the iceberg that is below the water. God has assigned to us this recording angel, and not only the recording angel but many others among the angelic hosts are available to man in the hour of need.

Q: Mrs. Prophet, what role do angels play in determining the nature of our auras?

A: Angels are the creations of God who are sent to minister unto the sons and daughters of God. Angels act as "angles" of God's consciousness. An angle of God's consciousness is a mathematical formula, a geometric forcefield that allows for the transfer of energy from a higher frequency to a lesser frequency, just as we have transformers for the distribution of electricity.

Angels serve to amplify the feelings of God. Yes, God has feelings. God has desire. What is God's desire? God has one desire and that is to be God. In order to be God, he has created his entire cosmos and the supreme creation, man and woman made in his image and likeness. In order for God to be the fullness of himself, he has also created angelic beings, who, by cosmic law, must come in answer to the call of man and woman, his own sons and daughters.

And therefore Jesus said in Gethsemane, "Thinkest thou that I cannot now pray to my Father, and he shall presently give me more than twelve legions of angels?" Jesus knew that if he called upon the angelic hosts they would deliver him from his plight.

Yet he desired not to be delivered because he was fulfilling the initiation of the crucifixion as an example for all of us to follow.

The point here is that we can, in the name of Jesus Christ, in the name of the Christ within us all, call to the Father to send us angelic hosts to deliver us from personal problems, world conditions, financial matters, grief over the problems our children are facing or pornography in the cities. Whatever the condition, we can call to God in the name of the Christ, and by cosmic law these angelic hosts will answer.

The connection with the aura is that they come, as it were, "trailing clouds of glory." They come with their auras filled with the light of God because they are electrodes and storehouses of energy. And when they come to us in answer to our call, they fill our auras with their light.

It is like a transfusion from the Great Central Sun. Angels have access to so much more of God's energy than we do, and when we call them, we receive this enormous quantity of light. It is this light that transmutes the darkness.

When there is grief, they bring joy. When there is fear and darkness, they bring love. When there is envy and jealousy, they bring the light of truth. So the angelic hosts conduct the feelings of God, the gentle qualities of mercy and justice. The angelic hosts are our greatest friends. They keep the way of the Tree of Life as the great seraphim and cherubim.

There are many offices and hierarchies of angels, including the seven beloved archangels, who are headed by Archangel Michael and his legions of blue-flame angels. These are the defenders of the faith and they protect the Holy Church. They protect the teaching of Christ and, above all, they protect us from harm. So it is important to develop the habit of invoking the angelic hosts. You can simply say:

> Dear God, send me your angels today. Send them to me, I pray. I call for the light of the angelic hosts to protect me and fill me with healing, with understanding. I call for the angelic hosts and legions from the Great Central Sun to heal the wounds of the nations and to bring balance to our government and our education. I pray to you, dear God, to send your angelic hosts to intercede for our youth that they might come into the Christ consciousness and the understanding of the Buddha.

Q: Mrs. Prophet, if there are so many angels about, how does the aura become contaminated?

A: By its susceptibility. The aura is made of a "plastic" substance. It's almost as if the aura were a chameleon. It takes on the colorations of its environment and is susceptible to the subconscious of the individual. If the free will of the individual gives consent, the aura will reflect the darkness of the mass mind and the individual's own latent darkness rather than light.

When we watch a horror movie, we contaminate our aura with horror vibrations. We enter fully into the fear. The solar plexus begins to churn. We find that our body chemistry changes. Even our heartbeat can change; the pulse will change. This is because by free will the arc of the attention is centered on a vibration of horror that then fills the aura.

We can choose to entertain angels or we can choose to entertain the darkness and demons that are in opposition to the angelic hosts. It is truly a question of free will.

Q: Mrs. Prophet, why is it that people don't have more contact with angels?

A: Because of ignorance, for the most part. People do not realize that the angelic hosts and the ascended masters cannot enter into the world in which we live, into time and space, unless we give the call. And this involves the law of octaves: God will not interfere in our lives unless we call to him.

This is why Jesus taught us to pray the Our Father. We must pray in order for God to contact us. God has given us the opportunity to prove whether or not we will come into alignment with his being.

God said, "Heaven is my throne and earth is my footstool." In this footstool kingdom man is given complete dominion and complete authority. He is a lawmaker; he does what he will and he bears the consequences. Earth is a laboratory that God has created for us to learn right and wrong and to return to him by free will in the ritual of the ascension. Therefore, by cosmic law, the angelic hosts are not allowed to intercede or to enter our life unless we call to them.

In the book *The Human Aura*, Kuthumi writes about his incarnation as Saint Francis. He says that the brothers recognized the angelic hosts as God's appointed messengers and looked to them for assistance. They did not expect God himself to intercede in the everyday situations that required some special ministration from heaven. They understood that God would send angelic legions in his name—with the seal of his authority and power—to do his bidding.

Kuthumi laments that some men, through the puffiness of

human pride, will speak only to God directly. They thereby ignore those whom God has sent, including the ascended masters and those upon the planet whom God has ordained to convey the message of truth to humanity.

Here is the point: God has ordained his angelic ministrants to minister unto us and they will come in full force in answer to our call. I know many devotees who would not go a day without calling to Archangel Michael and his legions for the protection of our children, our homes, our lives, our cities, our nations.

I have seen the intervention of Archangel Michael in the most miraculous way. I have seen cases of car accidents where the driver got out to see what happened and found no injury to either car. The only explanation is that the impact was broken by an energy field that was not physical. Physically there was a crash, but a nonphysical matrix—an auric emanation of a powerful being, an archangel—actually prevented damage to the vehicles as well as loss of life to those who were driving.

We see such tragedy on our highways today and tragedy on the battlefield of life. So much of this could be averted by the recognition that we are created to interact with the angelic hosts and that they are indeed the servants of God and man.

44

Strengthening the Aura

- *How can we strengthen the aura?*
- *How do we invoke the tube of light?*
- *How can Archangel Michael protect us?*

Mrs. Prophet, since the aura is so susceptible, how can we strengthen it?

A: In *The Human Aura,* the master Kuthumi teaches a threefold exercise that we can give to strengthen the sheath of the aura so that we can maintain the consciousness of Christ, of God, of Buddha, of Mother.

For this exercise, you can sit in a lotus posture or in a chair with your hands and feet uncrossed. Your spine should be erect and your eyes closed. You begin by visualizing the threefold flame expanding from within your heart.

The threefold flame is the energy of the Father, Son and Holy Spirit—of power, wisdom and love. Its three plumes are blue, yellow and pink. In our studies with the ascended masters, we always begin with the flame in the heart because it is the point of our own reality; it is the spark of life and our seat of consciousness.

Once you have visualized the threefold flame, the next step is to seal yourself and your consciousness in a globe of white fire. Visualize a sphere of white light around the threefold flame within the heart. See this globe of white fire expand and see yourself inside an imaginary sphere, or world.

When you are set in this visualization and your meditation is firmly upon the flame in the heart, proceed to recite Kuthumi's "I AM Light" mantra with humility and devotion:

I AM LIGHT

> I AM light, glowing light,
> Radiating light, intensified light.
> God consumes my darkness,
> Transmuting it into light.
>
> This day I AM a focus of the Central Sun.
> Flowing through me is a crystal river,
> A living fountain of light
> That can never be qualified
> By human thought and feeling.
> I AM an outpost of the divine.
> Such darkness as has used me is swallowed up
> By the mighty river of light which I AM.
>
> I AM, I AM, I AM light;
> I live, I live, I live in light.
> I AM light's fullest dimension;
> I AM light's purest intention.
> I AM light, light, light
> Flooding the world everywhere I move,
> Blessing, strengthening, and conveying
> The purpose of the kingdom of heaven.

Kuthumi says, "As you visualize the cosmic white-fire radiance around yourself, you should not be concerned with the errors in thought that have intruded themselves through the years upon your consciousness. Do not allow yourself to concentrate upon any negative quality or condition. Do not let your attention rest upon your supposed imperfections, but see instead what the light can do for you. See how even your physical form can change and how there can be a strengthening of body, mind and spirit."

Q: Mrs. Prophet, are the exercises for strengthening the aura limited to the mantra that you've just given us?

A: This mantra is complete and basic. Kuthumi gives us this simple mantra so that we will practice it and use it again and again. Out of this worded matrix, we actually build within our aura a forcefield that is a geometric matrix, like a geodesic dome.

Some people don't realize that a mantra or prayer is actually a forcefield of energy that is reinforced each time it is given. This is why the Our Father and the Hail Mary are so powerful—because they have been given by devotees again and again for centuries.

Kuthumi's "I AM Light" mantra is also given in his retreat in Kashmir. Kuthumi, the master of the Golden Robe, trains students who are on the ray of wisdom in the art of meditation and the science of the Word so that they may become master psychologists of their own psyche, or soul.

We can give Kuthumi's mantra for the development of a tremendous momentum of white light and the wisdom of God. It brings us to the realization that God can and does dwell within us. When we draw nigh to him, he draws nigh to us. When we give mantras to God, not only does God draw nigh but the angelic hosts also gather for the strengthening of the aura.

Saint Germain teaches us to invoke the violet flame. The simple mantra that we have from Saint Germain—"I AM a being of violet fire! I AM the purity God desires!"—is one that we can use again and again as we go about our service. Each time we give it the Holy Spirit fills us with the intense violet light, which transmutes the records of imperfection.

The violet light polishes and strengthens the aura. Hence, the use of the violet flame, along with Kuthumi's mantra, helps us to keep our auras in tune with God so that we can be receiving stations for the thoughts of the mind of God, the feelings of his angels and the direction that he gives us for our daily lives.

Kuthumi recommends that we invoke the tube of light. The tube of light is a cylinder of God's energy, which he places around us, just like the wall of fire that he placed around the city of Jerusalem. It is a wall of light protecting our comings and our goings. The Ascended Master El Morya, friend and co-worker of Kuthumi, has given to us a tube of light decree in his "Heart, Head and Hand" series. It goes like this:

TUBE OF LIGHT

> Beloved I AM Presence bright,
> Round me seal your tube of light
> From ascended master flame
> Called forth now in God's own name.
> Let it keep my temple free
> From all discord sent to me.
>
> I AM calling forth violet fire
> To blaze and transmute all desire,
> Keeping on in freedom's name
> Till I AM one with the violet flame.

Kuthumi strongly urges us to use his threefold exercise and to insulate ourselves against the intrusion of foreign vibrations by invoking the tube of light and the violet flame. He also encourages interaction with the angelic hosts. If we are determined to bring God into manifestation in our auras, we should call daily to Archangel Michael for his transfer of light, protection, energy and God's will.

Archangel Michael is familiar to all of us as the one who defeats the dragon of the human consciousness and preserves the Divine Mother, who gives birth to the Divine Manchild in us all.

Devotees throughout the world give Archangel Michael's mantra with a tremendous sense of victory and the awareness of his presence as he comes with thousands upon thousands of his legions of angels. This is the mantra:

LORD MICHAEL

In the name of the beloved mighty victorious Presence of God, I AM in me, my very own beloved Holy Christ Self, Holy Christ Selves of all mankind, beloved Archangel Michael, beloved Lanello, the entire Spirit of the Great White Brotherhood and the World Mother, elemental life —fire, air, water and earth! I decree:

1.   Lord Michael, Lord Michael,
         I call unto thee—
     Wield thy sword of blue flame
     And now cut me free!

Refrain: Blaze God-power, protection
             Now into my world,
         Thy banner of faith
             Above me unfurl!
         Transcendent blue lightning
             Now flash through my soul,
         I AM by God's mercy
             Made radiant and whole!

2.   Lord Michael, Lord Michael,
         I love thee, I do—
     With all thy great faith
         My being imbue!

3.   Lord Michael, Lord Michael
         And legions of blue—
     Come seal me, now keep me
         Faithful and true!

Coda: I AM with thy blue flame
             Now full-charged and blest,
        I AM now in Michael's
             Blue-flame armor dressed!

I can remember the day when I welcomed home from Vietnam a student of the ascended masters. He told me how he had given this call to Archangel Michael many times a day and how he had been spared when surrounded by artillery fire. Many were killed on his right and on his left but he still stood. On another occasion he was in a helicopter crash where all were killed save him. And I thought in my heart that this mantra indeed fulfills the protection promised in Psalm 91:

> He shall cover thee with his feathers, and under his wings shalt thou trust: his truth shall be thy shield and buckler.
>
> Thou shalt not be afraid for the terror by night, nor for the arrow that flieth by day, nor for the pestilence that walketh in darkness, nor for the destruction that wasteth at noonday.
>
> A thousand shall fall at thy side and ten thousand at thy right hand; but it shall not come nigh thee.

When this man told me his story of Archangel Michael's protection and intercession, I thought, Would to God that every mother of every son lost in Vietnam might have her son home today because this science of the spoken Word was known. The intercession of the LORD's hosts is so available in answer to our call.

This is why it is my deep desire to convey to all people God's teaching on the invocation of the light and the coming of the angelic hosts to deliver us. For God has promised to deliver us through these emissaries in this age.

45

Intensifying the Aura

∞

- *What does consciousness have to do with the aura?*
- *What does it mean to hallow space?*
- *What are the seven churches of Revelation?*

Mrs. Prophet, what is the link between our consciousness and our aura?

A: Consciousness is our connection with our source, and its flexibility is our greatest asset. The aura is the counterpart of consciousness. It is the effect of consciousness. It is both the manifestation and the vehicle of consciousness.

I think that one of the most precious teachings I ever received from Mark Prophet is the concept of hallowing space. It is similar to the concept of intensifying the aura. We all believe that God is, and that God is everywhere. But the concept that God is more in the cathedral than in the brothel is something we can appreciate yet perhaps not understand scientifically. It has to do with this concept of hallowing space, or intensifying the aura.

Saint Germain touches on the intensification of the aura in his book *Saint Germain On Alchemy.* He teaches us to create a "cloud," which is based on the same principle. As we create a "cloud of infinite energy" according to Saint Germain's instructions, we are multiplying the x-factor of God's consciousness right within our aura. Hence, we achieve in the space that is our identity, that is our immediate environment, a hallowing effect whereby life becomes sacred and even the perfumed fragrances that emanate from the auras of the saints can be experienced.

How do we hallow space? How do we intensify the aura? It has to do with consciousness, filling the consciousness with that which is God—God as energy, God as life. It all goes back to the heart and the meditation upon the flame within the heart.

The threefold flame of the Trinity within the heart is a multiplier of consciousness. Not only is it the focalization of Father, Son and Holy Spirit, but it is a multiplier because it is the sacred fire. Meditation upon the threefold flame, then, intensifies the aura much as the physical flame causes water to boil by accelerating the movement of the atoms and molecules.

And so the action of multiplying God's consciousness within us comes by our meditation upon the flame. As we adore and love this essence of God, his very gift of life itself within our heart, we find that this love increases the fire, just as increasing the fuel and oxygen will fan a physical flame.

Therefore devotion is an important part of the intensification of the aura. It is the path of bhakti yoga followed in the East. Through devotion we become one with the flame. It is the oneness of the lover and the beloved. The love so intensifies that there is a union that creates this release of energy, hence the intensification of the aura.

Another path that enables us to intensify the aura and accelerate consciousness is the path known as jnana yoga, the study of the wisdom of God. By this study we appreciate the mind of God, we become in tune with that mind, and we begin to develop that mind which was in Christ Jesus, in Buddha Gautama.

Through Kuthumi's teachings on the aura, we can take the principles taught and lived by Jesus Christ and the avatars of the East and make them our own. As we hallow space, we draw by the magnet of the flame within our heart more and more of the awareness of God. God is, but as we increase our awareness of him through devotion and sacred study, more of God lives in us consciously. And when we are consciously aware of God, we increase consciousness. When we increase consciousness, we thereby intensify the aura.

I remember one day when I was in India in 1970. I was in a crowded marketplace, enthralled with observing the people in all states of development of life. I was fascinated with the ancient culture and the naturalness of the devotion of the yogis in the midst of the scene.

I noticed a man walking across the marketplace. I saw him coming from afar—tall, intent, with piercing eyes. And El Morya showed me through my third eye the extension of the aura of that man. It was very large, and he seemed almost oblivious to all in his surroundings as he was traversing the square, so focused was he upon that flame within.

It presented such a contrast to those involved in selling their wares, not extending a consciousness of God to any great extent because their attention was not on this great flow. But here was one who had placed his attention on God and therefore increased the size of his aura.

We are taught how to increase the aura by increasing the consciousness, by strengthening the arc of our attention upon God. And this, as we have discussed, is accomplished in a number of ways through the seven chakras, through the science of the spoken Word.

Q: Mrs. Prophet, you often talk about the prophets of Israel having the foundation of ascended master teachings. Did they have anything to say about the aura?

A: Doug, the understanding of the Old and New Testaments and the scriptures of the East comes with the gift of the Holy Spirit.

When the prophets and great teachers wrote of their mystical experiences, they had to describe them in certain concrete terms. Some of these terms become abstract, for instance, in the writing of Ezekiel. But nevertheless, when one is experiencing these manifestations of the expansion of the inner flame, one recalls the words of Ezekiel, who beheld God as the "fire infolding itself"—the same revelation as the I AM THAT I AM that Moses beheld.

I was recently impressed by a psalm of David, Psalm 46, in which he gives a mystical understanding of the Tree of Life as the I AM Presence and the flow of the crystal-clear energies of the crystal cord. He says, "There is a river, the streams whereof shall make glad the city of God, the holy place of the tabernacles of the Most High."

This verse is seen by the secular person as a commentary on outer conditions, but the mystic understands that the river is the river of consciousness. It is the river of life that emanates from the Source.

"The streams whereof shall make glad the city of God." The streams of this great river of life, which is spoken of in the last chapter of the Book of Revelation, have to do with the coming forth of the great river of life from the I AM Presence, the descent of that river into the heart and then its distribution, in what you might call rivulets, to the seven centers of being.

And therefore we have the "making glad of the city of God." The city denotes the state of consciousness. It denotes the space of one's self-awareness, hence the aura. *City* is the dwelling place. The flow of the river of God's consciousness makes glad the city of God, or the manifestation of God that is the aura. This is right in line with our discussion of the intensification of the aura.

"The holy place of the tabernacles of the Most High." These tabernacles of the Most High are the chakras, the seven centers that are referred to by John in the Book of Revelation as the seven churches.

The message of the Lord Christ to the seven churches given to John the Revelator is actually a release of a certain frequency of energy and consciousness for the quickening of the seven centers within the temple of being. These seven churches were also, of course, physical places that could be named and that had people who were forming a nucleus of Christianity in the early Church. We find that the mystic in every faith always sees that which is described outwardly in scripture as that which is concurrently taking place on a parallel line within.

Looking at this psalm further, we see that David is describing the entire experience of God coming into his being, occupying his four lower bodies, and the great flow of the river taking command of the disturbances, the discord, the day-to-day problems that register in these vehicles of consciousness. He says, "God is our refuge and strength, a very present help in trouble." This in itself is a decree. It is an affirmation that God is in the midst of the trouble, the troubled waters of the emotions and the water body.

"Therefore will not we fear, though the earth be removed and though the mountains be carried into the midst of the sea." He is speaking about the great conflict that occurs in the mind, the emotions (the desire), the physical body and their interaction—the cataclysm that occurs in consciousness when we contact God, because when God comes into our being, he rearranges our atoms and molecules.

David speaks of the raging of the forces of anti-Reality within. He says, "The heathen raged, the kingdoms were moved: he uttered his voice, the earth melted." This melting of the elements of rebellion, of stubbornness, of disobedience is accomplished by the alchemy of the Holy Spirit and its descent into the heart of David.

46

The Aura of Oneness

∞

- *How can we call forth light in our aura?*
- *What does it mean to flow with the great river of life?*
- *How do we feel our oneness with God?*

Mrs. Prophet, how do we call forth light in our aura?

A: Jesus demonstrated how to expand the light of the aura for the healing and the transformation of consciousness so that we would go and do likewise. John the Beloved, the disciple who was so close to our Master, has given us the understanding that we are sons and daughters of God. As sons and daughters of God with Jesus, we can call forth this light and, according to our faith in the God who lives within us, we can move the mountains of adversity in our lives.

Kuthumi's "I AM Light" mantra (see page 252) can be the alchemy for change in your life such as you never believed or dreamed possible. The mantra is the Word of God. As you meditate upon the mantra, you realize that God himself is the mantra singing in your soul, coming forth with the authority of the Christ and the power of the everlasting Word. This God within, who is the mantra, who is the speaking of the mantra, is also the fulfillment of the Word. For he has said, "My Word shall not return unto me void."

Feel God giving the mantra through you. When you give a mantra, it is as if God drops a portion of himself as a pebble in the pond of your being, and the ripples in concentric rings go forth from you. And when they reach the shore, they return to the center. This returning to the center is like the echo of God. As his voice has gone forth from you, so it will return to you with that fulfillment and that supreme joy of living on earth here and now in the great flame of the I AM THAT I AM, which you are.

Sometimes people feel that a mystical understanding of Jesus Christ and of Gautama Buddha is beyond their ability. Perhaps they feel that they are not educated enough to understand. If you think that you are one of these people, or if you feel you do not have the intelligence to understand God's laws—perish the thought —know that God lives in you and his mind is in you. And it will open in answer to your prayer and by your flowing with the great river of life, with the stream of God's consciousness.

You will find that *The Human Aura* is written simply. Kuthumi appeals to the simple folk, to the common people, to those of us who understand God innately, who do not want to be confused by complex theological doctrine and dogma but who live in the basic awareness that God loves us, that we are his children and that he has placed within our souls the understanding of how we must return to him. Can you imagine that God would create us without that innate formula of understanding?

The ascended masters' teachings show us how to read what is already within, the law that is written in our hearts. I do not suppose that I can teach you anything but only that I can remind you of the great storehouse of truth that God has placed within you.

I would like to give a short prayer now:

I call in the name of Jesus Christ, in the name of Kuthumi, to all the saints and the heavenly hosts to go now to each soul and touch the heart of each one who would be closer to God and closer to the reality of his own individualized I AM Presence. I call for the great light of understanding of the Cosmic Christ, Lord Maitreya; of Jesus Christ and Kuthumi, the World Teachers; of Gautama Buddha and all who are serving with the evolutions of earth for the advancement of consciousness.

Beloved heavenly Father, we know that whatsoever we ask in Jesus' name and according to thy will, it shall be fulfilled in this hour. Therefore touch these hearts and let them know thy indwelling presence and let that presence be for the healing of soul, mind and body and for the healing of the nations. In his name, we accept the answer to our call this hour. Amen.

Q: Mrs. Prophet, a lot of people don't feel this oneness that you talk about so often. Could you tell us more about it?

A: It saddens me that those who are a part of the body of God upon earth do not know one another, that they have been separated by those who have sought to come between their great love for one another and for God. Sons and daughters of God, his children, people of light everywhere, are one. They are one by love but also by the mathematical formula that states that things equal to the same thing are equal to each other.

Every son and daughter of God upon earth has within his aura a certain charge of the Christ consciousness, of oneness with Jesus and Gautama. Every son and daughter of God knows within himself that he is the beloved of God. And yet from every side he is told the contrary—that he is a miserable sinner, that he is not able to raise himself up and approach the altar of the living God because he is a thing of shame. Often people feel alone and separate from God.

It is my desire to provide the open door for that great friendship between all who understand the oneness of life, the heavenly hosts and all who have espoused the same cause—who understand that we came to earth to set the children of God free, to draw all of our brothers and sisters out of false theology, the doctrine and dogma of the false Christs and false prophets who have come to divide us with their schemes of darkness.

The penetration of the great teachings of the LORD's hosts within our midst is like the coming of the sun as the morning mist disappears and we feel this friendship, this liaison with ascended masters, heavenly hosts, saints who have gone on, loved ones. And we know that in every community, in every town and city upon earth there are those who have this same calling to intensify the light of the aura, to expand the aura, to be step-down transformers for the consciousness of Elohim.

God has placed us in every religion, in every church, in every government to be focal points of light, to meditate upon his law night and day and to transmit that law. We all are receivers and transmitters, like radio stations, and we are sending waves from the aura daily.

Above all, let us now promise that we will send to each other waves of love and that we will thereby strengthen the body of God upon earth and our unity with the body of God in heaven. Being part of this mystical body of God, we can truly say, "God is one." For we have become cells in that body and we experience the oneness of the person of God, the "pure son" of God, of which we are all a part.

In this mystical awareness, we can truly understand there is only one Son of God, "the only begotten of the Father, full of grace and truth," Christ the Lord, who lives within us all. We share, then, his table, his Communion cup. This is the great teaching, the true teaching of Christ revealed through his servants the ascended masters and the messengers in this age.

47

Creativity

∞

- *What is the pathway to the stars?*
- *What is the key to creative mastery?*
- *How can you increase the flow of perfection in your aura?*

Mrs. Prophet, what actually happens when we use Kuthumi's "I AM Light" mantra?

A: The light that comes forth fills our cup of joy to overflowing and we are led to the pathway of the stars. The stars are the symbol of each one's I AM Presence, the focal point of each one's causal body of light. Jesus referred to these causal bodies as the "many mansions" of his Father's house. We each have a mansion, a dwelling place in the secret place of the Most High God, and the light of the aura comes to us over the thread of contact between heaven and earth.

Man has so often been concerned with the concept of the human aura—how to protect it, how to direct it, how to increase it, how to see it, how to interpret it—that he has seldom taken into account the simple words of Jesus: "Let your light so shine before men."

Let your light so shine before men—this is true religion. This is the fulfillment of Kuthumi's mantra, "I AM Light!" We have to affirm that light in order to confirm it; we have to give it our vow, our trust, our life so that the light can give itself to us.

The light Jesus spoke of is the light we can magnetize through the human aura. He teaches us that God wants us to become like him. In order to become like God, we must go through the alchemy of the Holy Spirit, the sacred-fire change, the putting-off of the old man, the putting-on of the new.

Q: Can you tell us about Jesus' aura?

A: Often it is depicted in paintings as a halo, but I tell you that the aura of Jesus literally filled the entire planet Earth, so great was his extension of God's consciousness through that aura. His base of God Self-awareness enabled him to proclaim himself the Son of God and to realize his own innate divinity. Thus, he is called the Saviour of the World.

We can begin right where we are. Though our aura may extend only an inch from the body, it can be expanded—first to fill the house where we are and then to fill an entire community or neighborhood and then to fill an entire city with the light of the Holy Spirit. God himself, through his Son Jesus Christ, will come into our body temple by the LORD's Spirit and expand our aura.

Jesus' entire effort was to demonstrate what man can do and what man can be when he unites with the God flame. Jesus determined to come to earth and give us the teaching of our innate Christhood by example, not simply by academic instruction. So perfectly did he become the full example that we have forgotten that his mission was to demonstrate what we can do also, and thus we have fallen down to worship the person of Jesus instead of emulating that likeness of God that he outpictured for us.

The key to creative mastery is "to be," is *be-ness,* is to understand that each of us is a ray of intense light that cometh from the Central Sun into the world of form. And so, the key is to realize that the energy and the consciousness for that mastery are already within us.

Our challenge is to unlock that creativity and that mastery by unlocking the energy and consciousness of God, to discover God-being within and to expand it rather than to attempt something that is utterly impossible—the grafting upon ourselves of that God who is without. We cannot be anything except that which we already are, and by God's grace we are created in his image and likeness.

Q: How can we apply this teaching?

A: We can consecrate our aura as a vessel of the Holy Spirit. Because we have being and *are* being, we can take the "sling of enlightened fortune" and fling into the world our cup of joy that runneth over in simply being a manifestation of God. Kuthumi tells us:

> You must increase your understanding of the magnificence of flow—the flow of the little electrons in their pure, fiery state that seem to dance with total abandon and then again to march like little soldiers in precision formation— now disbanding as they assume what at first may seem to be erratic shapes, now regrouping in their intricate geometric patterns.
>
> Purposefully man pours out into the universe the healing balm that is his Real Self in action. Its flow is guided by the very soul of the living God, by an innate and beautiful concept of perfection steadily emanating to him and through him. Does man do this? Can man do it of himself? Jesus said, "I can of mine own self do nothing; but the Father that dwelleth in me, he doeth the works."
>
> Understand that the inner fires banked within yourself by the fire of the Holy Spirit can be expanded by your own desire to be God's will in action. Understand that these fires will act as a divine magnet to increase the flow of perfection

into your aura and thence into the world. Understand that you must therefore wax enthusiastic about daily expanding your light through your meditations upon the Holy Spirit.

Beloved sons and daughters of God, we are born to be co-creators and co-workers with the infinite Spirit. A co-worker is one who has the flame of God within himself, who sees himself as the servant of God, the instrument of God, because God lives in him, not because he is a miserable sinner.

What you have done yesterday, if it is not of the light, can be put into the flame by a simple call to God the Father in the name of the Son Jesus Christ or Gautama Buddha or Mary the Mother.

In the name of our own I AM Presence let us therefore invoke the sacred fire, the great crystal river of life, to wash through our consciousness now. As this great flowing stream of water/fire moves within us, let us know that the fulfillment of the promise of God—the transmutation of sin, the balancing of karma, the washing clean of our garments—is taking place and that we are coming today, through the law of forgiveness, before the great throne of God.

Let us know that God will receive us through his blessed Son, the Christ, who lives in us all—that we can be forgiven and therefore also receive these fires of transmutation of the Holy Ghost and be renewed and be born again through the true under-standing of the teaching of the law of the Christ.

God bless you and be with you as you pursue your own state of God consciousness.

48

The Colors of the Aura

- *What do the colors in the human aura mean?*
- *Is the aura an extension of the self?*
- *How does fear affect the aura?*

Mrs. Prophet, what is the specific meaning of colors in the aura?

A: Color is a manifestation of frequency, and frequency is a manifestation of consciousness, or one's state of consciousness. Therefore when reading the aura, you can determine the state of consciousness if you know what colors correspond to particular states of consciousness.

For instance, Kuthumi says, "As the intensity of the white and the violet light is increased in the aura, especially those shades which are pale and ethereal, one notes the enlarging of man's perceptions and an increase in spirituality."

Just as color reflects consciousness, so color amplifies consciousness. Thus, if we increase the light of purity and of the violet flame through our mantras and our prayers to God, we will also accelerate our consciousness on the white and violet rays.

We have discussed the seven rays of God as the prism of the Holy Spirit and as the seven paths of Christhood that we can walk. We have also correlated these seven rays with the seven chakras.

The violet light is focused in the seat-of-the-soul chakra and the white light is focused in the base-of-the-spine chakra. These chakras amplify the frequencies of consciousness that manifest as the violet light and the white light.

The violet flame, or light, is the color of freedom and has the quality of mercy. It is the energy of transmutation. Violet light in the aura, then, denotes that the soul is free to commune with God. The aura always reflects whether man is maintaining the crystal-clear stream of God's consciousness released through the seven chakras or whether he is misqualifying that energy and thereby producing a muddied stream.

The base-of-the-spine chakra, the Mother center, gives forth the pure white light when its energies are held in the purity of Alpha and Omega—Alpha and Omega being symbolical of

the divine polarity of the masculine and feminine energies that are concentrated in each chakra.

Although not everyone is capable of reading the aura directly, at subconscious levels within the soul and at the level of the Christ mind we all have perceptions of one another, and we register these perceptions. There are certain characteristics that we read in one another at these levels of consciousness that can tell us much about a person before we even know him.

We are usually aware when we are in the presence of someone who is holy, and often we have a warning when we are in the presence of someone who is dangerous. This indicates that although we may not have mastered the science and art of reading the aura, the God within us is aware of the God within others and the uses or misuses of that consciousness by individuals.

If there is a pale yellow, almost golden, light in the aura of an individual, especially around the head, we know that there is flooding through that one's mind, as Kuthumi says, the "fingers of cosmic intelligence." This energy present within the aura enables the mind of man to contact the universal Mind of God. We can make this contact through meditation upon the Buddha or the Christ, both of whom have given us the key to unlocking the crown chakra, which is the yellow center.

Then there is the pink fire of divine love that comes forth through the heart chakra. When it is not misqualified by the human sense of possessiveness, attachment or inordinate desire, it produces within the aura a billowing cloud of pink energy, denoting that the individual is infused with an awareness of God as love.

If there is a purple fire flecked with gold and ruby in the aura, we know it comes forth from the solar-plexus chakra. This tinge-ing of the purple flame with the gold denotes the mastery of the light of peace within the solar plexus and is an indication that the individual is active in service to life.

The green, or emerald, fire comes forth from the third-eye chakra and indicates a manifestation of truth and abundance. Those who have green in the aura are devoted to science and to the practical application of that science.

When one's pursuit of science becomes tainted by a materialism and ignorance of God's laws, then the green of the aura no longer reflects the pure emerald hue of the stone by that name, but it becomes muddied—an olive drab, even a brownish green. Those who have pure emerald green within the aura are healers, and through them and through their chakras flow the healing currents of the Elohim and of the cosmos.

The electric blue color that flashes in the aura of Archangel Michael and the devotees of the will of God denotes the presence of purity and power and the alignment of the inner blueprint with the cosmic blueprint of the will of God. It also denotes mastery of the throat chakra in the spoken Word.

Reading the aura will always tell us where there is mastery or attainment in the use of the chakras and where there is a perversion or a willful misuse of the chakras.

Q: Mrs. Prophet, does Kuthumi teach that the aura is an extension of the self?

A: Yes, but he also teaches that the tone of the divine aura is an extension of God, just as the mode of thinking and feeling is the extension of the human consciousness. He explains that the interference with the aura in its natural, pure state by the mortal consciousness and by the misqualification of light creates negative colorations.

The muddying of the pure colors of the aura occurs whenever there is a mingling of the emanations of imperfect thoughts and feelings with the pure colors released through the prism of the Christ. This marked change in color and vibration is obvious to the trained eye.

For instance, the aura of someone who is in a state of contemplation, study or meditation might have the presence of a yellow light, a violet light and even a blue light—the blue indicating faith in God. In a sudden emergency, such as a fire or a calamity within the household, the quietness of the aura would be disturbed. There could be a burst of fear from the solar plexus, accompanied by feelings of butterflies and extreme tension. Such stress would produce a muddying of the violet light of the aura as well as explosions, perhaps, of great energies of fear recorded as brown, black and gray substance.

Depending on the calamity, there could also be grief, resulting in a further darkening of the aura. Or people might begin shouting at one another, causing jagged lines of force to come forth from the throat chakra. So you can see that the aura can change instantaneously.

The aura changes moment by moment. You can master the flow of energy in your aura by maintaining a calm state of equilibrium in the midst of whatever happens within your environment, all the while maintaining contact with your source, the I AM Presence. You have the capacity to draw enormous quantities of energy from your I AM Presence to stabilize conditions that might, for instance, be burdening others within your household.

When you are conscious of your energy field and you zealously guard it as the habitation of God, then you are able to retain your reservoir of light and not constantly be like a cork bobbing upon the sea. You will not be milked of your light and your energy. You will not spill the cup as soon as it is filled and fail to make any permanent progress on the path of discipleship.

With his usual good humor, Kuthumi writes:

> Always remember... that those who fall in the swamp may come up covered with mud; for the quicksands of life, by their very nature, always seek to drag man down. But man can and does escape these conditions, overcoming through the same glorious victory that brings forth the

lotus in the swamplands of life.

I want you to understand, then, that by a simple act of invoking the light of the Christ consciousness, man can overcome the ugly chartreuse green of jealousy and resentment, the muddied yellow of selfish intellectualism, the crimson reds of passion, and even the almost violet-black attempts of self-righteous justification.

Then Kuthumi gives us his supreme advice:

To see others clearly, beloved hearts, remember that man must first perceive in himself the beautiful crystal of cosmic purity. Then, casting the beam out of his own eye, he can see clearly to take the mote out of his brother's eye.

By the purification of your perceptions, you will be able to enjoy the entire process of beholding the Christ in self and others, as one by one the little disturbances of the aura are cleared up through the natural manifestation of the childlike beauty of cosmic innocence.

49

The Aura, a Giant Beacon

- *What did Jesus teach about the aura?*
- *What should we do about guilt?*
- *What is the value of repentance?*

Mrs. Prophet, what did Jesus teach about the aura?

A: Jesus taught quite a bit about the aura, but one thing that comes to mind is his statement "Ye are the light of the world. A city that is set on an hill cannot be hid. Neither do men light a candle and put it under a bushel but on a candlestick; and it giveth light unto all that are in the house."

Jesus left us this timeless advice as a means of inculcating into the consciousness of the race the inner formula for the proper employment of the human aura. What Jesus is saying, of course, is that we cannot hide ourselves, because the aura is a giant beacon. It's a signal to God and to man of what we are. It's impossible to hide our light under a bushel; rather we put what we are on a candlestick.

This gives to us a tremendous sense of responsibility because we realize that we are lighting the world for others. And if we are going to strew the world with misdeeds and betrayal and dishonor, then we are going to be responsible for influencing many people in the downward way of self-destruction.

Consider the looting that occurred in the 1965 blackout in

New York. It was as if people thought that God could not see at night or that the registration of their auras upon the Cosmic Mind went out with the blackout. But the Law is that every jot and tittle must be fulfilled. And the recording by the recording angels of all that we do registers not only in the book of life but also in the living book that we are walking around with, our own human aura.

Q: Mrs. Prophet, is the sudden appearance of darkness in the aura always cause for alarm?

A: Not necessarily. Kuthumi says that "the aura is the sum total of the emanation of individual life in its pure and impure state." We all have several streams flowing through us simultaneously. We may be experiencing feelings of love at the same time that we have anxiety, at the same time that we are planning or thinking about our business of the day. All of these emanations are registering simultaneously on the great stream of consciousness that is life, which is reflected in the aura. Kuthumi says:

> Often gently concealing from public view the darker side of human nature, the aura puts forth its most beautiful pearly-white appearance before men as if mindful of the words of God that have come down from antiquity: "Though your sins be as scarlet, they shall be as white as snow."
>
> Occasionally the aura will momentarily turn itself inside out, and the more ugly appearance of a man's nature will come to the fore and be seen by those who are sensitive enough to perceive the human aura. This shouting from the housetops of a man's errors ought not always to be deplored, for when the gold is tried in the fire of purpose, the dross often comes to the surface to be skimmed off.
>
> Therefore, when from time to time some negative influence appears in yourself or in someone else, consider it

not as a permanent blight, but as a thorn which you can break off and remove from the appearance world. The fact that the within has thrust itself to the surface is an application of the principle of redemption, and when properly understood, this purging can mean the strengthening of your aura and your life.

Kuthumi brings the process of redemption right to the level of the psychology of the subconscious and its coming to the fore by the reflective quality of the aura itself. He teaches that as a part of the blotting-out process in the stream of time and space, God, in his greater wisdom, often exposes to public view the undesirable elements of our nature as a means of helping us get rid of them.

Kuthumi is a master psychologist. In his last life, as a Kashmiri Brahman, he spent considerable time in Dresden, Würzberg, Nürnberg and finally Leipzig. There he visited Dr. Gustav Theodor Fechner, one of the founders of experimental psychology.

Kuthumi's mastery in psychology can be seen in his in-depth understanding of the teachings of Jesus. He says:

> Suppressing evil or driving it deep within, tucking it away as though you would thereby get rid of it, does not really do the trick; for all things ought to go to God for judgment—willingly, gladly and freely.

This is why God purges the aura, bringing to the fore that substance which is impure. But often man misunderstands the judgment and so fears it that he runs and hides from his own sin and thereby postpones the day of his redemption. For he has been taught that the judgment brings damnation and eternal burning in the fires of hell, when actually it is simply the daily assessment by the God within of right and wrong.

The "right" becomes a permanent part of one's being and

personality and aura, and the "wrong" can be passed through the sacred fire of the Holy Spirit. That energy can literally be transmuted. This means that that very substance—the particles thereof, the nucleus, the electrons—is stripped of man's overlay of hatred and darkness and fear and anxiety. The energy is washed by the Word and returned to the individual as a resource that he can use again, this time with a better qualification of light.

Allowing the conveyor belt of the consciousness to daily conduct our energy and our life to God for judgment—willingly, gladly and freely—is the best way that we can keep on top of ourselves and maintain communion with Christ, which is our inheritance.

Q: **Mrs. Prophet, what should we do about guilt in our aura?**

A: Kuthumi says:

> Men ought not to remain burdened by the inward sense of guilt or nonfulfillment that the suppression of truth often brings. For the cleansing of the human aura of these undesirable conditions need not be a lengthy process. Just the humble, childlike acknowledgment that you have made an error and the sincere attempt to correct it will do much to purify your aura.
>
> God does not angrily impute to man that which he has already done unto himself through the misuse of free will; for man metes out his own punishment by denying himself access to the grace of God through his infringement of the Law.

This is a stupendous definition of God's judgment. It is the understanding that with free will we have full responsibility for our actions. God does not punish us, but we punish ourselves by depriving ourselves of his grace when we separate from him through sin, or the negative qualification of energy.

The gentle drops of mercy and of God's kindness to man are offered as the cleansing agent of man's own self-condemnation.

Condemnation never comes from God, but it comes from our own acceptance of the carnal mind, or the anti-Christ forces within our being. To call for forgiveness means to establish contact with God and his grace and to receive the purifying sacred fires of the violet flame that wash us and make us clean. Kuthumi describes these as "a heavenly rain, refreshing and cool, that is not denied to any."

In my many years of work with students at Summit University, I have noticed that the one overwhelming factor and burden of life is guilt—guilt that comes from many incarnations, as the sense of failure and the misuses of life pile up within the subconscious layer upon layer like sedimentary rock.

Instead of daily bringing our misuses of life and of the Law to God for forgiveness, for transmutation and for a baptism of the sacred fire, we accumulate all of our past misuses and our misdeeds. We become more and more burdened and we develop psychological problems—splits in the personality, psychoses, neuroses—and islands of darkness that deprive us of a wholeness and a unifying factor of identity.

Kuthumi teaches us how we can be free from these schisms and summon our forces to be the God-free beings, the sons and daughters of God that we are. He tells us to fill our consciousness with God-delight and observe how the purification of the aura brings joy unto the angels. And he reminds us of the words of Jesus: "Joy shall be in heaven over one sinner that repenteth, more than over ninety and nine just persons, which need no repentance."

To conclude this series of our studies on the human aura with Kuthumi, I would like to invite all to give with me again Kuthumi's "I AM Light" mantra:

I AM LIGHT

I AM light, glowing light,
Radiating light, intensified light.
God consumes my darkness,
Transmuting it into light.

This day I AM a focus of the Central Sun.
Flowing through me is a crystal river,
A living fountain of light
That can never be qualified
By human thought and feeling.
I AM an outpost of the divine.
Such darkness as has used me is swallowed up
By the mighty river of light which I AM.

I AM, I AM, I AM light;
I live, I live, I live in light.
I AM light's fullest dimension;
I AM light's purest intention.
I AM light, light, light
Flooding the world everywhere I move,
Blessing, strengthening, and conveying
The purpose of the kingdom of heaven.

50

The Divine Mother

∞

- *What is the true meaning of "Mother"?*
- *What is the role of woman today?*
- *What is the purpose of Mary's new scriptural rosary?*

Mrs. Prophet, what does "Mother" really mean?

A: Mother is a fountain of life that is deep inside, and it is awakened in our life by our earthly mother. The tie that we have to mother on earth is intended to be a tie to Mother in heaven. Unfortunately, not all earthly mothers reflect our heavenly Mother, and sometimes we carry a deep-seated ambivalence regarding Mother and the meaning of Mother in our life.

Regardless of experiences that we have had, positive or negative, beyond the earthly veil of the one we call mother is the Divine Mother shining through, playing hide-and-seek with us. In her laughter, in her sternness, in her eye we find the compassion of our Father.

You have heard me say I am in love with the Buddha. Well, I can also tell you that I am in love with the Mother.

The Divine Mother takes many forms. I can remember discovering Mother Mary when I was in college in Boston. Having been brought up outside of the Catholic faith, I was alienated from Mary. This alienation was based on ignorance and misunderstanding and that inbred prejudice that we find in our culture regarding many aspects of life.

One day I received a communication from The Summit Lighthouse—a dictation from Mary, the Mother of Jesus, given through the messenger Mark Prophet, who later became my husband. I remember walking down the street on my lunch hour reading her dictation, and all of a sudden that fountain within me was quickened and I knew the presence of the Motherhood of God for the first time in this life. I knew it through that contact with the Blessed Virgin. Suddenly the whole earth and the sky and everything around me was filled with the presence of Mother Mary.

I felt Mary speaking directly to my heart. She was saying, "I am here. I am real. I am your Mother." And I knew such a comfort and such a flame of oneness with the soul of one who magnified the LORD—one whom I had known before. I knew that Mary was not only the Mother of God but also a friend, an intimate of all who would seek her.

I later learned, as she explained it to me, that the appellation "Mother of God," which men have given to her, is not something that should be an offense to us. The correct understanding of this title enables us to realize that the role of all feminine beings is to mother, or to nourish, the God flame incarnate on earth.

What does this mean? It means that in our role as mothers, as sisters, as daughters and as wives we are on earth to exemplify a spark of God, as God is the universal Mother. Mother Mary came to give birth to Jesus Christ, and therefore she nourished the flame of God that burned upon the altar of his heart and provided the form that cradled the infinite Spirit. She did this not as an exception to the rule but as an example for all womankind to follow.

In this age of the rise of the feminine ray on earth and of

woman coming into her own, we must examine our role as women. We must realize that whether we have a business or a household, children or a husband or a large project in the community, the flame that God has given us is the flame of Mother.

God is in every part of life and in order for that God to come forth, to blossom, to be realized by everyone, it must be nourished. We fan the flame with our love and with our devotion. And it is the God whom we worship in heaven whom we must give life to on earth.

I began to see, then, that Mother Mary was not merely an exalted being, high and seemingly apart from us, but a friend who walks with us every day. From that moment on, I knew that Mother Mary was a part of my life and, indeed, that I had come to be her instrument to give her teachings to the world and to convey her understanding of our true role.

I ran down the street, entered a Catholic Church and knelt before her statue. I realized that her statue was not an idol but a focus of her own Electronic Presence, her own being. I called on the law of forgiveness for myself and all others who had ignorantly misunderstood her name, her role and her mission.

Ever since that day, I have walked in her service. And by and by after I was trained to be a messenger for the Great White Brotherhood, Mother Mary began to release dictations to me concerning the woes of earth, the problems within the Church and her concerns about the rise of conspiracy East and West in politics and economics.

Mother Mary is a realistic, down-to-earth executive and administrator. She works hand in hand with us and wraps us in her mantle of living flame as we pray to her as the intercessor before the Father.

It is not at all difficult for me to understand both the role of the heavenly saints of the West and the great gurus of the East, for all are a part of the great mystical body of God. All contribute a certain focal point of consciousness to us whereby we on earth can be the step-down transformers for the cosmic energy that is our very life and yet must be translated through our consciousness, through our free will and through the threefold flame of life within our hearts.

After many years had passed, Mother Mary appeared to me one fall morning in 1972 in the prayer tower of our retreat in Colorado Springs and she said:

> I want to give you a ritual of the rosary for sons and daughters of God. It is to be a scriptural rosary for those who adhere to the true teachings of Christ as taught by the ascended masters. This rosary will be for the bringing in of the golden age.
>
> It is to be used as a universal adoration of the Mother flame by people of all faiths. For, you see, the salutation "Hail, Mary" simply means "Hail, Mother ray" and it is an affirmation of praise to the Mother flame in every part of life. Each time it is spoken, it evokes the action of the Mother's light in the hearts of all mankind.

Q: Mrs. Prophet, can you tell us more about the rosary?

A: Mother Mary has explained:

> The rosary is a sacred ritual whereby all of God's children can find their way back to their immaculate conception in the heart of the Cosmic Virgin. The New Age rosary is the instrument for mankind's deliverance from the sense of sin and from the erroneous doctrine of original sin. For every soul is immaculately conceived by Almighty God, and God the Father is the origin of all of the cycles of man's being.

This is a most startling concept, Doug. Mary says:

That which is conceived in sin is not of God and has neither the power nor the permanence of Reality. All that is real is of God; all that is unreal will pass away as mankind become one with the Mother flame. The daily giving of the rosary is a certain means to this oneness.

When I pondered in my heart the meaning of our origin in God, I saw that God the Father and God the Mother have indeed created the soul immaculately. It is our sense of sin that has placed upon us this doctrine of damnation, this doctrine of original sin whereby from the moment we are born, without even having uttered a word or having had a thought or a feeling, we are considered to be miserable sinners.

I realized that man's true identity and origin in God are much more powerful than man's sense of sin and his misuse of God's sacred fire that resulted in what is known as the Fall. The Fall actually was the sin of disobedience to God, and for that disobedience we daily pay a great price. That price is our separation from God with all of the attendant pain and suffering, travail and disease that is upon the human race.

But Mother Mary came to show us the way back to the state of grace through the giving of the Hail Mary and through meditation upon her blessed Son, Jesus. The rosary that she gave me was to eliminate the sense of sin and the sense of death. And therefore we give the Hail Mary as follows:

HAIL MARY

Hail, Mary, full of grace
the Lord is with thee.
Blessed art thou among women
and blessed is the fruit
of thy womb, Jesus.

> Holy Mary, Mother of God,
> Pray for us, sons and daughters of God,
> Now and at the hour of our victory
> Over sin, disease and death.

Catholics will note that the traditional Hail Mary says, "Pray for us *sinners*," rather than, "Pray for us, sons and daughters of God." Mother Mary wants us to understand that God does not hold us in a death grip of sin and the sense of sin, but he holds us in the immaculate vision of his All-Seeing Eye as the son and the daughter who are the fruit of the union of the Father-Mother God.

Mother Mary said to me:

> People must begin to understand and know that they are created in the image and likeness of God and to affirm that "Now are we the sons of God," as John the Beloved said. And therefore, let the children of God look up to heaven and in dignity and nobility and sense of self-worth, give the call as the true son and the daughter of God. Let us then pray for that Mother ray, not at the hour of death, for there is no death. My own Son proved that death is unreal, and therefore call for my intercession at the hour of your victory over sin, disease and death.

Mother Mary asks that we appeal to her in the hour of our victory over sin, disease and death because in that hour we must do battle with the forces of our own subconscious that resist the coming of the light of the Son of God into the temple of our being.

51

A New Age Rosary

- *How do we put on the consciousness of Mother Mary?*

- *How does ritual help us realize ourselves as one with the rhythm of the universe?*

- *How can we overcome alienation from God as Mother?*

Mrs. Prophet, can you tell us more about the new scriptural rosary?

A: Doug, all people, men and women alike, should meditate upon the Mother flame, which is a fountain of living fire within us. It is a fountain of purity that must be quickened, raised and released.

When the Mother comes into prominence and into dominance within the temple of our being, she quickens God the Father, God the Son and God the Holy Spirit within us. We see, then, that the Mother on earth is the one who helps us to understand the Father and teaches us his laws. She enables us to understand the wisdom of the Son and she shows us how the love of God is the action of the Holy Spirit in our lives through our sacred labor.

Mother Mary taught me that giving the rosary is not an idolatrous adoration of her person. It is simply the giving of our energy through the science of the spoken Word to the Mother of the universe and the Mother force, the life force that is in us. The quickening of this energy leads to the soul's reunion with the Father. Mother Mary said, "I am but a representative of the Cosmic Virgin and there are many mothers in heaven and on earth who follow in this service."

Mother Mary is our friend and our helper. She has become Mother so that we might understand that it is also our mission to become Mother and to mother life. Mother Mary was, is and ever shall be the handmaid of the LORD. She stands with us as we prove the same science that she proved, as we give birth to the Christ within the cradle of our own evolving soul consciousness.

Mother Mary is a great presence on earth and when we call to her in the rosary, as so many Keepers of the Flame are doing all over the world, we feel the energy of God rising within us. We feel Mother Mary wrapping our auras in a mantle, a swaddling garment of grace.

Indeed, when we give the Hail Mary, Mother Mary enters our heart and we feel her place around us her own aura, the Electronic Presence of her ascended light body. Then we go through our day as the hands and feet, the heart and head of Mother Mary. We allow her to use us as her instrument and we become living incarnations of the Mother flame.

This overshadowing is the hallmark of hierarchy. Hierarchy is the vast chain of being of sons and daughters of God stepping down the consciousness of the Father all the way from the center of the cosmos to a tiny electron in a blade of grass. As we meditate in the ritual of the rosary, we are putting on the consciousness of Mother Mary and of every ascended being who ensouls the feminine ray of God.

Q: Mrs. Prophet, how does the ritual of the rosary help us realize our place in the scheme of things?

A: I think we have to understand the meaning of the term *ritual,* because it has become a dirty word in some circles. People feel that they have been cheated by a phony hierarchy in the Church that has used ceremony and pomp to entertain the congregation but keep them in ignorance.

Ritual is the very rhythm of the cosmos. It is in our body temple. The daily assimilation of energy, the partaking of food, of sleep, of work—all of this is the ritual of life. On the seven days of creation, God released the seven rays of his consciousness. On the seventh day, he released the seventh ray, which is the ray of transmutation and freedom. It is also the ray of ritual.

Ritual is the means whereby we go from point A to point B in consciousness. We are here, let us say, feeling sorry for ourselves, burdened, weary. We have problems with our family that seem insurmountable. In a state of anguish, we cry out to the LORD God to help us. God can help us only if we are willing to move our consciousness from that point A of our desperate pleading to point B of "taking dominion over the earth" and feeling the mastery of the Christ within us.

To move from point A to point B we engage in ritual—the ritual of prayer, the ritual of meditation, the ritual of saying, "Let us be up and doing." The best way to change consciousness is to start doing something constructive. The activity itself is the flame of the Holy Spirit that carries us and buoys us up and gives us a joy and a sense of hope that God will deliver us from crisis.

God himself delivers us through a process that is a ritual. When we call for help, the answer doesn't often manifest instantaneously, but we go through a certain pattern and cycle of time and space and then we find suddenly, lo and behold, we have moved from that point A to that point B and thus prayer has been answered.

Ritual, then, is a code word for the term *right-you-all.*

God says to us, "You must right all wrong by invoking the sacred fire through this ritual of prayer, meditation and decrees."

You must right all wrong of the past. This means the balancing of karma. It means the transmutation of sin by the love of Christ, by the law of forgiveness, by the alchemical presence of the Lord Christ, the Blessed Mother and other saints of East and West.

Ecclesiastes had the great sense of ritual being the means whereby God performs his sacred alchemy within us. We read in Ecclesiastes 3:14, 15:

> I know that whatsoever God doeth, it shall be forever: nothing can be put to it nor any thing taken from it; and God doeth it, that men should fear before him. That which hath been is now; and that which is to be hath already been; and God requireth that which is past.

By using God's sacred rituals, infusing them with a flame of love and not merely performing them mechanically, we meet the requirement of God to bring that which is past to the fore into the crucible of the sacred fire. And there our God as a consuming fire will actually transmute the elements of base consciousness into the great glory and the full radiance of his Presence.

In this alchemy, we come to realize that "that which hath been is *now*"—meaning that from the very beginning of creation the eternal Presence of the Christ is, and is unchanging. And "that which is to be" in the future—the fullness of his manifestation within us, which we long for—has already been. It will be *here and now* if we can retain the vision of our victory and at the same time perform the ritual necessary for arriving at the manifestation of that vision in our life.

The rosary is a ritual whereby through meditation we move from the plane of the lesser self to the plane of the Greater Self.

The rosary is the most healing energy of life because it puts us once again into harmony with Mother.

Do you realize how alienated the people of earth have become at subconscious levels from the heart and flame of God as Mother? There is an intense hatred of Mother and there is a hatred of the children of the Mother.

The twelfth chapter of the Book of Revelation depicts the Mother coming forth within us to give birth to the Divine Manchild. She figures as the Woman clothed with the Sun, with the moon under her feet and a crown of twelve stars upon her head. She comes to give birth to the Christ in all of us but she is rejected by the carnal mind, which figures as the dragon in all of us. And the dragon within us comes to make war with the Woman, "to devour her child as soon as it is born." Our own carnal minds are ready to devour this infant child, the Christ that is in the cradle of the heart waiting to grow to the fullness of the stature of Jesus Christ.

We see, then, that the meeting of Mother in the way is a tremendous challenge, and it requires the alchemy of consciousness of which the psalmist spoke when he said, "The heathen raged, the kingdoms were moved: he uttered his voice, the earth melted."

We need the sacred-fire baptism of the Holy Ghost to consume what I call anti-Mother and anti-Christ forces within our subconscious; for the heathen, the alienated parts of our own subconscious, are raging. The kingdoms, or the planes of consciousness at sublevels of awareness, are being moved. But God within us is uttering his voice, and by his voice the elements of earth are melted and we are formed and re-formed once again in the image and likeness of our God.

52

Ritual Drama

∞

- *What's happened to drama in our lives?*
- *What can we learn about our own destiny from the life of Jesus?*
- *What is the true meaning of destiny?*

Mrs. Prophet, when you talk about ritual, it seems that what you're really talking about is the drama of life itself. Drama is one of those elements that has been taken out of so many people's lives. Why has that happened?

A: I think that people have replaced the great drama of God's appearing with the melodrama of their own carnal minds parading on the stage of life. When God and Job were discoursing and God answered Job out of the whirlwind, he said:

> Who is this that darkeneth counsel by words without knowledge? Gird up now thy loins like a man; for I will demand of thee, and answer thou me. Where wast thou when I laid the foundations of the earth? declare, if thou hast understanding.

The point is: Who is man that he can stand and declare that we must eliminate ritual from the universe, when all of life is the great ritual drama of life unfolding—when, as God said, "the morning stars sang together, and all the sons of God shouted for joy"?

Ritual is the alchemical ingredient of life. It's the chemistry whereby God becomes man and man becomes God. And this is the goal of the entire flow of creation over the magnificent figure-eight spiral of infinity whereby Spirit becomes Matter and Matter becomes Spirit continuously in the nucleus of the atom.

Q: Mrs. Prophet, it seems to me that Shakespeare and other great playwrights were actually telling us in their dramas how to move from one plane of consciousness to the next, which sounds very much like what you describe when you talk about ritual. Is this the work of the masters themselves?

A: The soul needs the ritual drama of life and her meditation upon the stars to transcend the mundane and reach for the great Macrocosm of being. On earth today people want instant religion, instant God—like instant pudding. And they want it to replace a process, an alchemical process that must include redemption, that must include the kneeling before Almighty God and confessing, "I have erred. I have gone out of the way of the Tree of Life and I desire to return. I call on the law of forgiveness and I accept the living God in the presence of his Son, the Lord Christ, as my Saviour."

God answers our prayer with a whirlwind action of the sacred fire that is the coming of the Holy Spirit, the coming of the Comforter. The Comforter gives us the original teaching of Jesus Christ and of the Cosmic Virgin, and we learn of the science of the Word, which is our means of taking dominion over the earth.

When I go to the altar of God, I realize that that altar is a place where I may alter, or change, my consciousness through the great alchemy of the sacred fire. I know God is the Great Alchemist, even as I see him as the Great Dramatist writing the script of my life. And if I can follow this script and make my will become the will of God, wedded in the alchemical marriage of my soul's reunion with the Spirit, then I can live my life as the instrument of the LORD.

In her ritual of the rosary, Mother Mary teaches us to follow the greatest ritual drama that has ever been written and portrayed. It is the life of Jesus Christ. In this drama we see the incarnation of the infant Child become the World Saviour. We see him putting on the consciousness of God layer by layer—passing through his initiations, giving forth the teachings and then going through the great betrayal, the crucifixion and the ultimate glory.

There is no finer rendition by any dramatist anywhere of the metamorphosis that must occur whereby that which is conceived of the "earth, earthy" becomes the living Son of God—from the first man, Adam, to the last man, Christ, the Son who is the Real Self of each and every son and daughter of God.

Q: **Mrs. Prophet, would you explain exactly how giving the rosary relates to this ritual?**

A: The rosary is our soul's meditation upon God as we rise to the level of the Christ within the heart. And we meditate alternately upon Mary the Mother as the focal point of our own incarnation of the Motherhood of God and upon Jesus Christ for our realization of the fullness of that divine Sonship within us. Through the Mother and the Son we reach the Father, and in the Father we are reborn according to his immaculate design.

The rosary, then, is for the balance of the masculine and feminine polarity of being. And this is achieved by our contemplation of the life and the experiences of Jesus as we give the adoration of the Hail Mary.

Our meditation upon the events in the life of Jesus and the stations of the cross enables us to also pass through the experiences that Jesus passed through and therefore to participate in this drama—to become the drama with him, walking the stations of the cross. God thereby reenacts within us these most sacred events in Jesus' life, which is to become our very own life. When we finally are able to totally equate with the life of Mary and Jesus and other saints, then we ourselves will be able to put on their consciousness of victory, of the resurrection and of the ascension.

As we are willing to enter this path, Mary and Jesus, the hosts of the LORD, Archangel Michael and the angels come to us each day. And each day becomes a little ritual whereby we are given an important lesson in cosmic law through a circumstance in our life created by our own karma. This path is called the path of initiation because our souls are being initiated.

We no sooner conclude our rosary in the morning than we are beset with all of the problems of the day and the challenges that life joyously presents to us. We do not walk the *via dolorosa* because we are not sad, we are not in a sinful sense, we are not in a sense of shame. But we are in a sense of glory because from glory unto glory we know that we are putting on the consciousness of God.

Q: Mrs. Prophet, what is the outcome of this ritual that you describe?

A: New consciousness, new life—a joy that is indescribable!

Q: If we are denied the ritual, are we denied the outcome of the ritual?

A: Precisely. This is why the fallen ones have entered into the churches, into the governments and into the economies of the nations and stripped us of the great ritual drama of life, which is such a necessary process. In its place, they offer that old instant pudding—that one-two-three formula and you've got salvation. It deprives us of the entire path of overcoming and working toward a goal. It destroys initiative and leaves us absolutely impotent as sons and daughters of God.

Q: So there's no "salvation made easy" course?

A: There is no instant pudding at the altar of God. There is a working out of our salvation "with fear and trembling," as Paul said. And that fear is the tremendous awe of the Almighty and of his power and what this power can do if we misuse it.

Many sons of God have shown us by their example the ritual of becoming one with God. Take Mohandas Gandhi. In his life we see the great ritual drama of his soul moving from childhood closer and closer to God until so much of God is in him that he can move all of the people of India into one united effort for independence.

In his salt march, Gandhi started walking to the sea with seventy-eight of his followers. It became a gathering momentum. He went from village to village and more and more people followed him, until there were thousands. After reaching the coastal town of Dandi, he went down to the water and picked up a pinch of salt from the sand.

This gesture signaled the Indian people to gather salt in direct disobedience to British law, which forbade them to gather or make their own salt. He thus declared the independence of the soul to forge its own God-identity without the superpowers governing it and controlling it, dominating it until it becomes a vegetable.

Q: This is the true meaning of destiny, then, is it not?

A: *Destiny* means *Deity-est*ablished-*in-y*ou. It is a process, a ritual whereby we begin with an opportunity given to us by God. By free will we choose to become that opportunity. And working the works of God daily and letting the Father work through us, we fulfill our destiny as one with the immortals, as sons and daughters of God reuniting with him in the glorious ritual of the ascension.

The ascension is our destiny. It is the goal of life whereby we accelerate consciousness, moving from the lesser self to the Greater Self, and find ourselves one with God, hence one with eternal life.

53

The I AM Lord's Prayer

∞

- *What does it really mean to be a Son of God?*
- *What is Jesus' I AM Lord's Prayer?*
- *How does God pray through you when you pray?*

Mrs. Prophet, Mother Mary's scriptural rosary contains a version of the Lord's Prayer very different from the one most of us are familiar with. Can you explain?

A: First of all, let's take the Lord's Prayer as it is recorded in the Book of Matthew. Jesus counsels us that we ought not to use "vain repetitions as the heathen" but to pray "after this manner" and then he gives the Lord's Prayer.

Students of the ascended masters' teachings understand the word of God through Isaiah: "Concerning the work of my hands, command ye me." They see that Jesus and many of the saints spoke with the authority of God—God the Father, who lives within the Son and without whom the Son can do nothing.

The Lord's Prayer is not the prayer of a sinner groveling on the ground like an animal before a tyrannical or whimsical God, but it is the prayer of the Son to the Father, and it is a command. Every verse of the Lord's Prayer is actually a command that we give by the authority of the Christ within us to the flame of God, the I AM THAT I AM, the source of our energy and life.

"Our Father who art in heaven..." We address him, confident that he hears us. "Hallowed be thy name." This is a command. We are commanding God's energy that is in heaven to be manifest on earth. And our first desire is that the name of God, I AM THAT I AM, be sacred on earth. We must pray this prayer because God has given us the authority for the earth. He said, "Take dominion over the earth," and he gave us free will and an energy resource to do so.

The next command is "Thy kingdom come." We are commanding it because it is the will of God and because he has given us the authority to pray in this manner. When Jesus told us to pray "after this manner," he meant we must confirm by the science of the spoken Word God's will on earth as it is in heaven.

The next command we give is "Thy will be done in earth as it is in heaven." And then: "Give us this day our daily bread. And forgive us our debts as we forgive our debtors."

The more we read and understand this matrix of the Son commanding the flame, the essence, the energy of God to do the Father's will on earth, the more we understand our role as the instruments of the Great Alchemist, of God himself. God desires to move in manifestation on earth but he cannot do so unless we open the valve of consciousness, the valve of the heart and the valve of the sacred centers and let his energy flow. We do this by the command.

The final command is "And lead us not into temptation but deliver us from evil." Then follows: "For thine is the kingdom, and the power, and the glory, forever. Amen."

It is my understanding that Jesus taught the disciples the science of the spoken Word in the Upper Room, in the Essene community and at the home of Mary, Martha and Lazarus in Bethany. He taught that the command of God is reflected in the Son by the voice of the Son giving affirmation of God's being.

How many people have ever thought of the Lord's Prayer as our command to God, literally our demand upon the cosmos, upon the energy of cosmos to coalesce on earth in this supreme matrix of our Father's will?

Q: Well, as an ex-fundamentalist Christian, I have to tell you that it is a revolutionary concept. Wouldn't you agree?

A: Indeed it is. In fact, it is earth shattering. It's like discovering the mathematical formula for the splitting of the atom. All of a sudden we realize that we were created by God to be his sons and daughters, that in fact we can say with Christ, "Before Abraham was, I AM." And we understand that the eternal Christ that is our own identity has always been and will forevermore be.

We understand that the challenge of life on earth is for our own soul to come into alignment with that only begotten Son, that eternal Christos. And to do this we use the ritual of the science of the spoken Word. "After this manner therefore pray ye" —marvelous teaching!

And listen to this teaching from John: "As many as received him, to them gave he power to become the sons of God, even to them that believe on his name." The power to become a Son of God is conveyed to us by the Ascended Master Jesus Christ.

That power could not be conveyed if it were not already inherent within us, within that potential of the threefold flame in the heart. But it requires the igniting by the Son of God Jesus or by Saint Germain or by any one of the ascended masters or avatars of the ages. The one who has become the Christ incarnate has the power to transfer that flame to us, for we are also intended to become Sons of God.

Q: But what is the I AM Lord's Prayer?

A: The I AM Lord's Prayer is an advanced form of the Lord's Prayer. Jesus gave the I AM Lord's Prayer to his inner disciples, who had a deeper understanding of the mysteries of God. They understood that God is within the temple and that the affirmation of that God is the highest form of prayer and even the highest form of the command.

We have this prayer today because the Ascended Master Jesus Christ has dictated it to the messenger Mark Prophet. Mother Mary asked to have this prayer included in the daily rosary.

Q: How does it go, Mrs. Prophet?

A: Bear in mind that the name I AM has the inherent meaning "God in me is." When we say "I AM THAT I AM" we are affirming God above/God below where we are. This prayer uses the name I AM to amplify God's energy within us:

I AM LORD'S PRAYER

Our Father who art in heaven,
Hallowed be thy name, I AM.
I AM thy kingdom come
I AM thy will being done
I AM on earth even as I AM in heaven
I AM giving this day daily bread to all
I AM forgiving all life this day even as
I AM also all life forgiving me
I AM leading all men away from temptation
I AM delivering all men from every evil condition
I AM the kingdom
I AM the power and
I AM the glory of God in eternal, immortal manifestation—
All this I AM.

Q: Mrs. Prophet, don't you think that a lot of people will see this as the ultimate ego trip?

A: Precisely. And therein lies the danger. The one who declares that his untransmuted, unredeemed self is one with God is one who blasphemes. But the one who has actually felt the Presence of God enter him as the descent of the Holy Ghost and who has that Presence in his temple can unite his energy, his consciousness and his being with that God of very gods who lives within his temple.

He can make his voice one with the voice of God. Indeed, he can become the mouthpiece of God, who is answering the first prayer, which says: "Our Father who art in heaven, hallowed be thy name. Thy kingdom come. Thy will be done in earth as it is in heaven." Now he can say, "Our Father who art in heaven, hallowed be thy name, I AM," and he can hear God speaking through him: "I AM thy kingdom come. I AM thy will being done. I AM on earth even as I AM in heaven."

This is the tremendous authority of the Trinity within us—God the Father as the one who releases the Law and the decree, God the Son as the wisdom of that decree, and God the Holy Spirit as the action of that decree. This Trinity within us takes over our prayer and instantaneously, simultaneously becomes the answer to the call or the fulfillment of the demand that we place upon life.

And so when we pray and when we understand that we are praying as sons of God, we know that we have the authority to cast out demons, to exorcise evil spirits, to command "Peace, be still!" to the waters. This is not something that we attribute to man or to the carnal mind or to the lesser self. There is only one power that can act and it is the living God. There is only one God and without him we can do nothing. It is the Father in us who doeth the work.

A part of this great work is the decree itself. The decree sets the energy in motion. It's a fiat, it's a blueprint, it's a matrix of life. And so we say, "I AM giving this day daily bread to all. I AM forgiving all life this day even as I AM also all life forgiving me." We are simply saying, "God in me is giving this day daily bread to all.

God in me is forgiving all life this day even as God is all life forgiving me."

This constant affirmation of oneness with the one God is the only means to salvation. And the affirmation itself is the ritual through the science of the spoken Word whereby we do inherit immortality.

Q: It is the true mystic's prayer, isn't it?

A: Indeed it is and it must be correctly understood or else it will be misused.

The Sermon on the Mount by Gustave Doré

54

Mary, the Mother

∞

- *What's wrong with the stereotype images of Mother Mary?*
- *Why was Mary chosen to be the mother of Jesus?*
- *What was Mary's mission for Alpha and Omega?*

Mrs. Prophet, there seem to be a lot of stereotypes of Mother Mary. What is your reaction to these?

A: The stereotypes concerning Mother Mary are just so many masks that fall from her face when our souls contact the real, living soul of this Virgin of God, who truly does magnify the LORD within us. One concept, that Mary was just a human mother and therefore needs no special veneration, would tear from her the very veils of her divinity. The other extreme, where Mary becomes an idol so far removed from us as to be even more remote than God himself, is just as false.

I think the only way that we are going to derive the heavenly and the earthly example from Mother Mary is to discover what we ourselves are in relationship to God. Then we will understand her role and her relationship to God. We will understand that Mother Mary is not an exception to the rule but rather the full manifestation of a daughter of God, made in the image and likeness of the Son, the Christ, as we all are.

It is not because of the miraculous but it is because of

the fulfillment of the law of truth that we revere Mother Mary. We realize that because she has chosen to be the incarnation of God we also can choose to be the incarnation of God. This is not blasphemy, for it is our calling to be one with God and therefore to be instruments of his grace.

Mother Mary once said in a dictation: "I am Mary. I have chosen to ensoul the Mother ray for a cosmos." Likewise, each one of us, knowing ourselves to be sons and daughters of God, can say in this moment, "I am...," and then give our name and state what we have chosen, by the gift of free will, to be for God—what virtue, what grace, what quality of the Godhead we have chosen to bring forth.

Mary chose to be the incarnation of the Motherhood of God and she has achieved her goal. When people do not understand that they have the freedom to do the same, they tear down the very one who has proven what all can do—the one who has proven by example the way of the soul's liberation.

If individuals like Mary or Jesus or Moses or Muhammad or any of the great beings who have come to earth had not proven that God can dwell in man, then there would be no hope for us. So I would like all of us to look at Mother Mary as a simple woman— very much like women who are living today in this century—who embodied on earth with a calling from God, who knew she had that calling and who was willing to work to achieve it, to pray without ceasing and to give herself totally as the instrument of God.

Mary has told us:

> I am the handmaid of the Lord Alpha and the instru-
> ment of Omega. I am the awareness of the Father-Mother
> God extending even unto the planes of Mater, that the
> children of the One might know the sanctity of commu-
> nion—of the marriage of the daughters to the Holy Spirit,
> of the vows of the sons unto the Cosmic Virgin.

What does all this mean? Mother Mary teaches us that we are living in time and space in the planes of Matter—or of *Mater,* which is the Latin form of "Mother." *Mater* means "Matter," or the "Mother universe." Mary teaches us that we can conceive

of our own souls as wed to God. If we are women, we are wed in heaven to the eternal Son, the Christ. If we are men, we are wed in heaven to the Mother of God, to the being we refer to as the Cosmic Virgin.

This concept establishes our unique polarity with a point of contact in heaven. And it establishes the flow of energy from God to man —from God the Father to womanhood, from God the Mother to manhood. And thus the polarity of God reinforces our own polarity, and by that polarity there is a fusion of life that occurs.

On a more concrete level, Mother Mary tells us that she was called by Alpha and Omega to embody on earth to bring forth the Christ. Alpha and Omega are the beings who personify the Father-Mother God. They are referred to in the Book of Revelation as "the beginning and the ending." (*Alpha* and *Omega* are the first and last letters of the Greek alphabet.)

Q: Mrs. Prophet, why was Mother Mary chosen for this role?

A: Remember that Mother Mary is of the angelic evolution. In her initiations in the orders of angelic beings she became an archeia, which is the divine complement of an archangel, the highest attainment one can achieve in the evolution of the angelic order. Her divine complement is the archangel Raphael.

Archangel Raphael and Mother Mary serve together to ensoul the fifth ray of science and healing. The fifth ray, as we've said before, is the ray of truth, logic, mathematics and music—the music of the spheres. It is the ray of emerald green, which is focused through the third-eye chakra and is always for the concentration and precipitation in Matter of the energies of Spirit through the sacred science.

Scientists, musicians, mathematicians and doctors embody on this ray. It is a precise ray. Mother Mary was chosen because of her high attainment on this ray—because she was an angelic being and because she had the momentum in her causal body of aeons of evolution in heaven in the attainment of the mastery of precipitation.

She tells us:

> Because the flame of the fifth ray relates to precipitation in Mater and because the feminine aspect of the flame is directly involved in the spirals of God-realization descending from the formless into form, I was chosen by Alpha and Omega to incarnate in this system of worlds, to set forth in time and space the example of the Divine Woman reaching full self-realization in and as the Divine Mother.

Mind you, coming forth into Matter to bring forth the Christ (an individual who would ensoul the Second Person of the Trinity, the Son of God) was a very important calling. And related to this calling was something that we do not always hear about: the fact that Jesus himself embodied to focus the archetypal pattern, to set the blueprint in Pisces, for the image and the likeness of Christ—that Christ that we ourselves were to bring forth and embody.

In this two-thousand-year dispensation, followers of Jesus

and devotees of Mother Mary have attempted to imitate their role as the Christ and the Mother. This imitation of Christ is wholly acceptable within the teachings of our Church. We realize that in order to walk in the footsteps of Christ we must imitate that Christ.

It was the great concern of Alpha and Omega, of Almighty God himself, that the avatar who was to embody for the Piscean age be the fullness of the representative of the Christ so that all souls coming under his dispensation might follow and emulate him. Thus, Mary was chosen rather than any other of the personages of heaven. She recalls for us the moment:

> How well I remember that moment when I was bidden by heralds of the king and queen, our own beloved Alpha and Omega, and I came escorted by the beloved Raphael to stand before the throne of the twin flames of a cosmos!
>
> "You called, my father and my mother, and I have come."
>
> "Yes, our beloved, we have called. Unto you and to Raphael is given the opportunity from the heart of the Solar Logoi to manifest the balance of the flow of truth 'as Above, so below' over the spirals of the figure eight of our cosmos—opportunity to be on earth as in heaven the ensoulment of the Mother ray."
>
> "What does this mean, my father and my mother?"
>
> "It means that you have been chosen, Mary, to incarnate in the planes of Mater, to take on the feminine form that the errant souls of the children of God now wear, to live and serve among them, to adore the Christ flame within their hearts—as Sanat Kumara and Gautama have done and as the Christed ones, the avatars and Buddhas who have gone before, and the many angels who have volunteered to work through the forms of flesh and blood to save the lost sheep of the house of Israel who have taken on the ways of the idolatrous generation."

I heard the words of our dearest Father-Mother and I looked into the eyes of Raphael, my beloved. And for a moment—only a moment—the pain of the anticipated separation was too much to bear. Instantly I was strengthened by the beauty and nobility of his countenance and the sternness of his eye disciplined in the Law. He had, as it were, almost greater courage than I to descend into the planes of Mater.

But when I felt his hand press my own and the charge of the will of God and our dedication to eternal truth flowed into my being and soul, I faced the beloved Presence of God now pulsating in utter formlessness as cloven tongues of fire where a moment before the personages of the Divine Polarity had stood. I knelt in utter surrender to the call of hierarchy and in silence before the Holy of holies gave my life that the Word might become flesh and dwell among the inhabitants of Terra, that the Christ, the eternal Logos, might incarnate, the Incorruptible One.

55

The Soul of Mary

- *What were the early incarnations of Mother Mary?*
- *Do we also have a mission in this life?*
- *What is the connection between yoga and the rosary?*

Mrs. Prophet, how did Mother Mary prepare to play such an important role as ensouling the Mother flame for a planet?

A: The preparation of the soul of Mary began in heaven, where she evolved for aeons of cycles in God's own consciousness, increasing her awareness of God as Mother. Then came the moment when she was called before Alpha and Omega and sent forth to incarnate among earth's evolutions. From that hour, she prepared on earth through a number of lifetimes for the moment when she would incarnate in her final embodiment to be the mother of Jesus.

Mother Mary was embodied on Atlantis, where she served in the Temple of Truth as a priestess of the Most High God. There she tended the fires of the fifth ray and brought forth into the planes of Matter her soul's inner attainment, which she had achieved through thousands and thousands of years of service in heaven.

As she worked with the laws governing the flow of God's energy from the planes of Spirit to the planes of Matter, she learned in her outer consciousness what her soul already knew—

that disease, decay and death are caused by an arresting of the flow of light at some point in the four lower bodies and that this clogging of energy may result from man's misuse of the sacred fire with its attendant karma.

She also learned by her own experimentation in this laboratory of truth—for such was the ancient temple of Atlantis—that the cure for disease is the harmonization of the flow through the light centers in the lower bodies. She saw that the reversal of the processes of death and decay is effected by the initiation of spirals of the resurrection flame within the chalice of the heart.

Like Mother Mary, we all come with a mission, a calling from God. We have heard of Mother Mary's account of her going before our Father-Mother, Alpha and Omega. We must realize that we also were called before the great throne of Alpha and Omega and were given an assignment and a mission on one of the seven rays. We, too, began to incarnate and to serve in a position of service that would prepare us for the fulfillment of our mission in this age, in this century.

Now, in the Aquarian age, we as sons and daughters of God are called together to fulfill our vows, but many of us have lost the memory of the vow and of the inner experience with our Father-Mother God. We hardly remember that God is real or personable or that we can even talk to God.

And so Mother Mary comes to remind us of our vow and of our relationship with God—not to tell us that she is separated from us, that she is a goddess out of reach or an exception to the rule of life on earth. She shows us that she incarnated again and again and faced the same struggles and trials of overcoming that we now face. And yet Mother Mary, proving the way of victory, kept her soul inviolate and pure so that she might receive Jesus Christ in the hour of his appointed coming for the Piscean dispensation.

In the lifetime that Mother Mary was to be the mother of Jesus, she was born to Anna and Joachim. Anna and Joachim followed many of the teachings of the Essene community and had consecrated their lives to God. They were vegetarians and were schooled in the disciplines of the inner retreats of the Great White Brotherhood.

In their old age, after having prayed many years for a child, Anna and Joachim received a visitation from an angel of the LORD. He appeared to each one to tell them that they would give birth to this blessed child, a daughter who in turn would become the mother of the Christed One, the avatar of the age.

So Mary was born to them and when she was three years old she was consecrated in the temple, there to become a student of the sacred mysteries. It is said that her parents placed her on the first of fifteen stairs representing the initiations of the psalms of degrees (Psalms 120–134). She climbed the fifteen stairs one right after the other, showing that her soul had already passed these initiations in other lifetimes.

Q: Mrs. Prophet, were Mother Mary's parents chosen because of the rigorous life they led?

A: The rituals that were practiced by Anna and Joachim were by no means the reason that they were chosen. These practices were but the outer manifestation of their souls' inner commitment already made before the throne of Almighty God.

It is not practices or mechanical observances of prayer and ritual that give us the consciousness (or the 'kingdom') of God but rather that from the beginning we have chosen to be the will of God and we have responded to that will. The natural flow of our devotion to God that is manifest in spiritual exercises is but a sign of the inner calling. Outer practices and rituals cannot compensate for the human will that has not surrendered to the divine will.

Q: Mrs. Prophet, did Mary have any embodiments in between the time that she embodied on Atlantis and the time she embodied as the mother of Jesus?

A: I have noted in the book *My Soul Doth Magnify the Lord!* a number of Mary's incarnations. One of the most outstanding was in the days of the prophet Samuel, when Mary was called of the LORD to be the wife of Jesse and the mother of his eight sons.

Ever striving to fulfill her role in the Mother ray, Mary in this incarnation of her soul on earth magnified the light of the seven rays of the Christ in the first seven sons of Jesse. And in the youngest, David, she glorified not only the full complement of virtues of the seven rays but also the majesty and mastery of the eighth ray, which David exemplified in his reign and extolled in his psalms.

In the descent of our spiritual lineage, then, we find that the same flame of the Motherhood of God sponsored the Judaic tradition as sponsored the Christian dispensation. This once again teaches us that all rays of God in manifestation as the masculine and the feminine principles of life lead back to the One Source, the life, the all of our being.

Q: Mrs. Prophet, how does the rosary help us get back to this source?

A: The rosary is a balanced meditation on the masculine and feminine principles of life, on the Father and Mother energies within us, and thus it is a meditation on the cosmic caduceus. The goal of prayer and of the ritual of the rosary is to balance these energies, these cosmic forces within man and woman.

When we succeed in balancing these forces, we can attain to a state of wholeness; and in wholeness we can contact our Father-Mother God. No matter what our religion, the prayers of East and West, of every church and every calling are for this goal: the return to oneness, to wholeness.

In the rosary we give the Our Father for contact with God the Father and we give the Hail Mary for contact with God the Mother.

Q: **What is the connection between the practice of giving the rosary and the disciplines of yoga?**

A: The yogi, who is working to attain soul liberation and supreme reunion with God, lives in adoration of the Mother force, which is known as the Goddess Kundalini. It is the sacred fire that is locked in the base-of-the-spine chakra. Similarly, the energy of the Father force is locked in the crown chakra. When we have the union of these two forces within our being in the center of the heart, we then give birth to the Christ consciousness, or what some have called cosmic consciousness.

Making friends with Mother Mary, one who has realized and released the Mother force to the extent that she could ensoul the fullness of the Christ and bring forth the Son of God, enables us to go and do likewise. Contacting one member of the spiritual hierarchy who has attained on the Mother ray reinforces our own path of self-mastery.

Just as we apprentice ourselves on earth to masters of a particular trade or guild, so we may apprentice ourselves to the personages of heaven. If we want to become a great musician, we study under the world's greatest musicians. If we want to release the Mother flame, we apply to one who has already embodied that flame and who can guide and guard us in the release of this sacred energy.

Jesus said, "He that receiveth a prophet in the name of a prophet shall receive a prophet's reward." This is an important law. The point is that if we accept in Mary the Motherhood of God, we are also accepting our own potential to realize that Motherhood. If we deny it in Mary, we deny it in ourselves. If we deny that she is the Mother of Christ, we deny our opportunity to receive her reward, which is the gift of the Christ consciousness.

We find an anti-Mother force working in the world today, which is parallel to the force of anti-Christ, the force that opposes the Son of God coming to the fore of being. The anti-Mother syndrome makes us deny the Mother and therefore prevents us from raising up the Mother energies within, which would give us the full creativity and use of our soul faculties and the ultimate opportunity for soul liberation.

Mary is the supremely liberated woman. She shows each one of us how we can raise the Mother energy for the liberation of men and women and children. Mother Mary shows us that through meditation we can be free to liberate the Christ consciousness within ourselves.

Each time we say the Hail Mary we are giving the salutation to the Mother ray within our own being, to the energy—the pure white light of God—that is focused in the base-of-the-spine chakra. When we say, "Hail, Mother ray," it activates that light and by and by, increment by increment, the light slowly rises, naturally and in consonance with the laws of God, without being forced and without endangering the soul's evolution.

Mother Mary, then, becomes our own personal mother, our spiritual mother who is guarding our initiations on the path to becoming the fullness of all that Jesus became. As Mary sponsored Jesus, so she will sponsor us if we call to her. And she will show us not a relationship dependent upon her but an independent relationship whereby through union with our own Mother light we can become the fullness of the Motherhood of God and thereby nourish life on earth.

56

Anti-Mother

∞

- *How is the Mother force active in today's world?*
- *How can we distinguish between the real Mother and the counterfeit Mother force?*
- *And how do we harness the "fountain of life" within us?*

Mrs. Prophet, how is the Mother force active today?

A: Since the Mother principle is that which nourishes life, we can think of Mother and the Mother flame as the energy inherent in education, in great works of art—music, paintings, sculpture and drama—in science that pursues the mastery and conquest of time and space. All of this is the Mother force nurturing life. It is God within us who is releasing the energy that tutors the soul in the way it must go.

But we find that the presence of Mother—as all of the beauty and all of the goals that we see in life—is beset by a counterforce. This is depicted in the twelfth chapter of the Book of Revelation as the dragon that comes forth the moment the Mother is going to give birth to the Manchild. This Mother is the Mother within us all giving birth to our own Christ consciousness. And the dragon seeks to tear from us that Manchild as soon as it is born.

This anti-Mother, anti-Christ force manifests as child pornography, the desecration of woman, the tearing down of true educational values, even the tearing down of individual nation-hood and of our own history and the understanding of God-government. There are many forces active in the media and in the world today that tear down the true values of the Real Self of all.

We call this Real Self the Christ. You can call it the Buddha. You can call it whatever you like, but it is our true, inherent reality. And the Mother force of a cosmos is what protects this emerging identity within us all.

When we experience alienation from Mother or we allow the forces of anti-Mother to encroach upon our family and our life, we find that everything that we try to do is torn down. It disintegrates and there is chaos, there is confusion.

But what do we find as the antidote to this? In the twelfth chapter of the Book of Revelation, God sends his emissary Michael the Archangel to challenge the dragon. And there is war in heaven and Michael and his angels defeat that dragon and cast him out of heaven into the earth.

And so if we are going to raise up the light of Mother, which is such a cosmic force for creativity within us, we must enlist that emissary of God, Archangel Michael, to come to our aid and protection. This we can do by giving a simple call to Michael the Archangel that goes like this:

> Lord Michael before, Lord Michael behind,
> Lord Michael to the right, Lord Michael to the left,
> Lord Michael above, Lord Michael below,
> Lord Michael, Lord Michael wherever I go!
>
> I AM his love protecting here!
> I AM his love protecting here!
> I AM his love protecting here!

We find that it is often necessary to call forth the intercession of the angelic hosts of light in our daily lives. We call to Archangel

Michael because it is his office to defend our faith and to defend the flow of Father, Mother and Son within our consciousness.

Q: When you talk about Mother, are you talking about an impersonal force or something more personal?

A: I am talking about both the impersonal force of a cosmos, an energy frequency, and a very personal manifestation. The impersonal force becomes personal when a son or a daughter of God decides by free will to ensoul that force. This Mother Mary did; this we can do. But we have to overcome our antipathy to the concept of God as Mother.

Until we do, we will find ourselves unprotected as a people and as a nation from the forces of anti-Christ and anti-Mother, which are waging the spiritual warfare of Armageddon against our souls and against our souls' emergence into the fullness of that maturity whereby we can anchor the light of God and bring forth the victory in this age.

Q: Mrs. Prophet, how can we distinguish between the real and the counterfeit Mother force that you describe?

A: The difference is like the difference between Eve before the Fall and Eve after the Fall. It all hinges on obedience to the laws of God. The sin of Eve was the sin of disobedience against the Lord Christ. Obedience simply means being in harmony with your inner blueprint, being in harmony with the forces of cosmos that govern your life.

The Woman clothed with the Sun is the woman who has magnetized the light of cosmos to the glory of the feminine ray of God. That Woman in the Book of Revelation can be every woman on earth. But in order to be clothed with the Sun, she must be willing to surrender all that is unlike that Sun consciousness. And then the flame within her heart will become the magnet of Great Central Sun energies and she will become so filled with light that she can hold the flame on earth for the Christ consciousness to be exalted in all sons and daughters of God.

Inasmuch as we have seen centuries upon centuries roll by without too much manifestation of this cosmic consciousness, we can surmise that there have not been many women who have been able to ensoul the Mother force and to sustain it in the face of the dragon of the carnal mind within the self and within the mass consciousness.

And so today Mother Mary comes to the fore, gives us a science, gives us a new rosary and a new way to use the spoken word to coalesce energy. She is doing this not because she desires personal adoration but because she desires to transfer to us our rightful and lawful inheritance as sons and daughters of God.

Men as well as women must exalt the Mother principle because we are all seeking the balance of Father and Mother. Men ought to pray to Mother just as naturally as women pray to Father. And in the fusion of the twain, we would have happy, harmonious, healthy families and offspring, healthy communities, healthy states and nations.

It all begins with the resolution within ourselves of the Father and Mother principles. This is really the basis of modern psychology. Our schisms and the problems we have in dealing with our earthly mothers and fathers are what generate in us the alienation from God the Father and God the Mother.

Q: The real Mother and the counterfeit Mother force are as different as night and day, then, aren't they?

A: It's like the difference between the sun and the moon. The moon energies are identified with the figure of the great whore in the Book of Revelation, who is the personification of that anti-Mother force. It is a death energy because it always seeks to tear down and to lower the energies of man and woman until they are entirely spent upon a pleasure cult and a success cult instead of upon the true culture of the Mother whereby we are raised up.

Q: Mrs. Prophet, what does this have to do with our daily lives?

A: The energy locked within us is like the lightning that has flashed across the sky for a million years. It is like the white-fire core of the atom that is in the heart of the mountains and the rocks. Suddenly man discovers this energy, he harnesses it and a whole new era of life and civilization occurs. The energy of Mother locked within all of us can be released. When it is released we experience the joy of living! We discover who we are. We become truly worthy sons and daughters of God.

The moment we begin to salute the light of Mother and the light of Father within ourselves this energy is unlocked. It comes to the fore and gives us joy, dominion, purpose and understanding of our reason for being. It unfolds the path of the ascension whereby we can reunite with God.

Whatever we are doing in this moment—washing the dishes, cleaning the house, preparing the evening meal—can become a sacred labor that we charge with the energies of Father and Mother within our being. And suddenly Matter is endowed with

Spirit! This is the materialization of the God flame. It is crystallization. It is the spiritualization of our consciousness.

It means that a new energy, a new life comes into us and by this life we can experience the atonement, the redemption, the resurrection and the reunion with God. This is the goal of life but it is also a daily goal. Paul said, "I die daily," and what this really means is that we are born and reborn daily as we recontact this source, this fount of life, that God has placed within us.

We need this energy. Our lives are dead without it, and this is why people meditate. Meditation is but the first step of the science of the spoken Word. When we meditate upon God or the Inner Self or the great void, we contact that energy source. In order to draw it down and make it practical in our lives to solve every single problem we have, we must vocalize—we must let our praise burst forth as a song, a decree, a fiat from our throat chakra. Then it crystallizes and we find that that energy becomes charged, literally *charged* with a new life. And we are no longer the living dead but we are alive and buoyant with life!

The Virgin of the Globe

Life takes on a new freedom, and we realize that this freedom is meant for all peoples and all nations. We become excited about transferring the Word and the flame we have discovered in our heart. This becomes the flame that leaps heart-to-heart across the earth with that awakening, quickening energy that is the New Age.

57

The Mystery of Surrender

- *How can we make our bodies "hum"?*
- *Is the adoration of Mother unmanly?*
- *How do we let go of our mortality?*

Mrs. Prophet, when you give the rosary you seem to give it with so much more feeling than we hear in the churches. Why?

A: Some have made of the rosary a hypnotic charm, a superstition, an exercise in rote, a dead ritual, a vain repetition of words. But this does not mean we cannot go to the core of the teaching and discover the fount of Mother life that is within us.

Giving the Hail Mary becomes the salutation to an energy source that is paralleled in nature. It is as powerful as nuclear energy. It is like the oil that rushes from the center of the earth. The rushing of the energy of Mother from the base of the spine up to the crown of the head is like that very phenomenon but even more intense—it is like a volcano erupting.

The harnessing of the energy of this intense cosmic force is what makes life in Matter hum. Our bodies do not hum if we have not tied in to our own natural resource.

When we release the spiritual fire within our own microcosm, we are also setting up a meditation forcefield that extends throughout the earth because Mother Mary always magnifies that forcefield. Mother Mary said, "My soul doth magnify the

LORD." LORD is a term for "Law." Mary is magnifying the Law of God, the inner blueprint, the inner design of all the sons and daughters of God on earth. And therefore we say in the Hail Mary, "Pray for us, sons and daughters of God, now and at the hour of our victory over sin, disease and death."

As we take the hand of the angels and the hosts of the LORD, we take Mother Mary's hand and we know that she is leading us in the path of dominion over the earth. The Great Law states: as Above, so below—as without, so within.

The salutation to the Mother within always parallels the salutation to the Mother above, or the Mother who is in heaven. This is not only Mary the Mother but every saint of East and West who has realized oneness with the great Mother force.

Q: **Mrs. Prophet, how do you answer those who say that this kind of adoration for Mother is somehow or other unmanly?**

A: Well, it's just as silly as thinking that it is unwomanly to pray to God the Father. All of us need Father, all of us need Mother, all of us need the balance of these forces within.

Q: **How can we get this energy, Mrs. Prophet, and get it quickly?**

A: We cannot pour old wine into new bottles. So the secret is to get rid of the old wine and the old bottles, which means not only the old doctrine and dogma that we have been fed as gruel for a couple of thousand years but also the misqualified substance within our own subconscious.

The best way to do this is to surrender to the reality of the Real Self within. We do not surrender to an outer tyrannical god that we have manufactured by our anthropomorphic sense of God, but we surrender to the Law, or the Lord, of our own being. We surrender to the alchemy, the very chemistry, of our cells and atoms, to the harmony of the stream of life that is flowing within us.

This surrender is the alchemy whereby we receive the influx of the light of God and can attain to that power, wisdom and love that all the saints have known. To help us do this, Mother Mary has dictated the Fourteenth Rosary: "The Mystery of Surrender."

Q: Mrs. Prophet, what can we learn about surrender from the Fourteenth Rosary?

A: It's a known fact that we kill ourselves with what we eat, not with what we don't eat. Americans are overfed materially and they are overfed spiritually with so much stuff that there is literally a spiritual constipation and the life of a cosmos cannot flow through the chakras. The Fourteenth Rosary helps us get rid of all the debris so that the light of God already within us can simply flow.

Mother Mary tells us:

> Surrender! Surrender to this law within, all that which is anti-Mother, anti-God, anti-the-Real-Self—all of these schisms and divisions that are fabricated within the subconscious. Let go of everything! Give everything to God and understand that it's like carrying your dirty wash to the laundromat. You put it in, it comes out clean. You give to God everything that you are and he gives back to you everything cleaned and purified.

If we can just open our hands and let go and let all of our energy, our life, our successes, our failures, our desires, our not-desires flow into the flame, then we will find that a great purge of the Holy Spirit will come upon us. We will be relieved of momentums of lifetime upon lifetime of incorrect consciousness.

As God flows in, his energy flushes out the impurity and we find ourselves standing in the very midst of this central sun of being that is our own I AM Presence. The mystery of surrender is the moment of our dying unto unreality. It's the moment of letting go of each justification of the human ego—our false sense of responsibility, our false pride, our false humility, all of the burdens of sophistication with which we have cloaked the soul, the fad consciousness, the herd consciousness, which takes us farther and farther and farther from the center of our own reality.

Mother Mary says: "Let go of the things that you think you must have. Let go of the things that you think in your pride you will never do or the things that you think you will always do. Let go of all human attachments. Let go of every ambition except God's desiring within you to be God."

Why let go? Because it is freedom. It's the only freedom we will ever know—the freedom of nonattachment that the Buddha teaches. As soon as we let go of something, it returns to us—not as it was but in a purified form, in the form in which it ought to be for us to live our life according to the inner divine plan.

Q: Mrs. Prophet, I remember that once you said, "Surrender the mortal and God returns the immortal." This is what you're saying now, is it not?

A: It's really true, Doug. If we are willing to see that this mortal will die in any case and that God gives us the option of surrendering it now so that he can return to us our immortality, we really begin to realize what is this game of life.

Why are we on earth? What are we doing here? What are all of these experiences for? They are for precisely this: God wants us to show him within this crucible of our experience that we are willing to give back to him all that he has given us, and in that willingness he bestows upon us immortal life.

58

Higher Consciousness

∞

- *What is the Coming Revolution in Higher Consciousness?*
- *What is the guru-chela relationship?*
- *What is Saint Germain's message today?*

Mrs. Prophet, would you tell us what you mean when you talk about the Coming Revolution?

A: The Coming Revolution is a revolution in higher consciousness, but it is a revolution that will affect every part of our lives—because at its core is the unlocking of the energy of God that is the spark of life within the heart, the threefold flame of the Real Self.

When the individual makes contact with that Real Self, it is like the bursting forth of a fountain of light and of an energy coil that envelops the entire being and becomes a spiral of a higher self-awareness. Through this higher self-awareness we can join forces for a revolution, which is really a turning around of our way of life on earth.

Civilization today, even in America, is in a downward spiral of moral decay and degeneration. This is accompanied by a lessening sense of self-worth and the worth of life. We see this evidenced in the liberalization of abortion laws and in the controversy over euthanasia. People seem to think that human life is no longer as valuable as it was esteemed to be in our early history.

This is because they have not yet discovered that their life is God, that God is life within them.

They have projected their awareness of God outside of themselves and accepted the condemnation that they are sinners, and so they experience a lessening of their individual self-worth. Hence we find a movement toward socialism, a mass consciousness, a welfare system, where the individual gets lower and lower and lower until all are finally reduced to the lowest common denominator of the human consciousness. We are told we are animals instead of sons and daughters of God made in his image and likeness.

Q: How widespread do you think the Coming Revolution is going to be?

A: I think that the spark of this revolution, once it ignites our consciousness, is going to leap city to city around the earth, because I believe that everyone is just on the verge of contacting that inner light and that Inner Self. And contact with that Inner Self is what made Jesus the world figure that he was and is.

That same contact gave Gautama Buddha a following, a religion, an enlightenment, an energy. Energy is the key. That energy has enabled Gautama to have to this present day millions and millions of followers.

All of the great lights of history, whether scientists, artists, statesmen or doctors, have had the essential key of reverence for life. We see this, for example, in the lives of Albert Schweitzer and Mohandas Gandhi. The moment such individuals have discovered the spark of life to be within (instead of something removed) is the moment they have become effective on the world scene.

And this is why the movement that we call the Coming Revolution in Higher Consciousness is so explosive. It is not explosive in the outer revolutionary sense; it is an inner revolution.

But the inner revolution cannot help but change our entire way of life on earth because it liberates the soul force.

Q: **What does Saint Germain have in mind?**

A: Saint Germain comes to initiate us. And this gets into an interesting subject: What is initiation?

Let's say that you, as a disciple of Jesus Christ, of Gautama Buddha or of any of the ascended masters, desire to come up higher in your state of consciousness. You desire to understand more of God and to be more of God within your heart and mind and soul. It takes an ascended master to convey that necessary light, to convey an increment of energy, an increment of the mind of God that will give you that expanded self-awareness. This is the meaning of the term *initiation.*

The guru-chela, or master-disciple, relationship has been going on for thousands of years. It is the means of the transfer of God's energy that the guru, or teacher, has concentrated within his being through contact with the Inner Self. As he has a greater concentration, or reservoir, of that energy than ordinary people, he has become the one in hierarchy who is called the guru and can transfer that energy to those seeking the same attainment and the same contact.

Saint Germain is one such ascended master guru. He served the flame of freedom throughout his embodiments on this planet—for at least a hundred thousand years. He made his ascension in 1684 after his incarnation as Francis Bacon and has been serving as an ascended master, the chohan of the seventh ray. In this century he has come forward to release his teaching on the I AM Presence and the violet flame.

And so, the master Saint Germain is coming to personally contact his chelas. He is not coming physically, although some do see him. He is coming in his finer bodies, as we call them. His presence will be felt, his light will be felt, his energy will be transferred.

Those who have concentrated a greater manifestation of light within their chakras do see the ascended masters. Others do not see but they feel. Others do not feel but they hear the word and they gain a new understanding. So all are at different levels of awareness, hence different levels of initiation.

Q: Now, what does this have to do with the Coming Revolution?

A: Saint Germain is the one who sponsored America and he sponsors freedom in every nation today. He has taught us that those whom he calls the spoilers, or the fallen ones, have invaded every area of life in our civilization. They have interfered with the economic policies of the nations, with politics, with education, with religion. And they have taken from the people their just and rightful inheritance of the abundance of God's grace and his gifts and even material supply.

Therefore, Saint Germain comes to teach us the science of the spoken Word. He comes to assist us in unlocking our own energy source, which is God, so that we can right these wrongs, not by violent revolution but by a revolution that comes through the flow of cosmic consciousness, of tides of light from the Central Sun, of energies that are a literal alchemy for the transformation not only of the individual soul but of society as a whole.

Q: Mrs. Prophet, what is your personal contact with the master Saint Germain?

A: Saint Germain is the master who sponsored me in this life. When I saw his picture when I was eighteen, it reminded me of the inner vow I had made to him before coming into embodiment. I recall standing before him and making my vow that I would take up the torch of freedom and serve him. A few years after I saw his picture, Saint Germain contacted me through the

Ascended Master El Morya and saw to it that I was trained as a messenger. And today he is releasing his teachings through me.

You can read these teachings in the *Pearls of Wisdom,* which are weekly releases from our headquarters. The *Pearls of Wisdom* contain the basic teachings of the ascended masters. Saint Germain's discourses, published in the *Pearls,* are a vital message for all who cherish freedom as an inner flame as well as a way of life in America. It was freedom for which this nation was founded, and freedom ought to be the motivating light of all our decisions, public and private.

Q: Mrs. Prophet, I think that Saint Germain is probably an unfamiliar figure to many. How can they overcome the sense of unfamiliarity?

A: Saint Germain is Uncle Sam. And Uncle Sam is more than a picture on a billboard, more than an advertisement to join the armed forces. When we think of Uncle Sam we think of the spirit of America, and that is indeed who Saint Germain is. He is the very person, the very essence of our culture and of all that we stand for—not in the sense that we are exclusive but in the sense that we have a gift, a great gift from Almighty God that is ours to give to all the nations of earth.

Saint Germain teaches us what that gift is and how we can implement it. He teaches us how we can take that gift as a precious energy, as well as an understanding, and protect the freedom we have been given and save this nation for another round of opportunity. America was founded so that those who came here might experience this soul liberation, this reunion with God that comes as we walk the path of initiation under Saint Germain, the master of the Aquarian age.

Q: Mrs. Prophet, is Saint Germain's message for all Americans or just the few who are into mystical teachings?

A: Saint Germain's message is basic and is for every man, woman and child. Far from being metaphysical speculation or mysticism, it is a practical, down-to-earth statement of the master of the flame of freedom.

It is entirely in agreement with the tradition of Jesus Christ. You will recall that Saint Germain was embodied as Saint Joseph, the protector of Jesus and Mary. Saint Germain is one with Jesus Christ, and there is no conflict from the standpoint of either religion or politics in our finding out more about this wonderful person, this "pure son," who has individualized the God flame, attained mastery in time and space and ascended to be one with the immortals.

He tells us how to live, how to restore our birthright, how to regain control of our money and our money system, how to overcome the problems of taxation and what is happening in the administration as tax upon tax is leveled upon the American people.

Saint Germain speaks to us of the evils of abortion. He warns us that abortion is the killing of God, or the potential for God, within the womb. Abortion is bringing an enormous karma upon our nation through disruption in the weather and the plagues foretold in the Book of Revelation.

Saint Germain is truly the voice of the seventh angel, who comes to warn us of the dangers to our heritage if we do not fulfill our destiny and our calling as representatives of the sons and daughters of God and the twelve tribes of Israel.

59

The Master of Aquarius

- *Who is the ascended master of the Aquarian age?*
- *What is the purpose of religion in the modern world?*
- *Can anybody learn to be an alchemist?*

Mrs. Prophet, would you tell us more about Saint Germain as the master of the Aquarian age?

A: Quite a movement has been going on in America—the search for the guru, the search for the teacher. It seems that we as a people understand that we need a teacher. Somehow we sense that the place we want to go, but can't quite get to, can be reached through a teacher.

So the imported gurus of India have come and played their parts on the stages and theaters of the nation. And some have remained and sustained a following and others have gone with the wind.

We are entering into a spiral of the blending of East and West, of the understanding of God as consciousness that comes down from the ancient traditions of the masters of the Himalayas as well as from the Lord Christ and the prophets of Israel and from all that has gone on in our Western culture.

I think that America knows it needs its leader. And at no time in its history has it needed its leader more. We see the dearth of leadership in government and in society today and we all say, "Where are our leaders?"

There was a time in the period of the development of Israel when there were no kings but only judges in the land because none were worthy to be king. The word *king* is a code word, or an abbreviation, for "the one who holds the *k*ey to the *in*carnation of the *G*od flame"—*k-in-g*.

The one who holds the key for our incarnation of the God flame in America today is the Ascended Master Saint Germain. This does not make Jesus Christ of any less importance in America. It means that what we have learned from Jesus Christ as our great teacher of the Piscean age and as the World Saviour has prepared us to meet our next teacher, our next master.

Beloved Jesus the Christ has prepared the way for us to follow Saint Germain. Saint Germain, who was embodied as Saint Joseph, protected Jesus as he was preparing for his mission. America is in her childhood today and Joseph, the protector of the infant child (the Divine Manchild who is brought forth by the Woman clothed with the Sun) is Saint Germain.

Saint Germain has a special message for this seventh age and this seventh dispensation. And this is why he is referred to in the Book of Revelation as the seventh angel. The seventh ray is the ray of alchemy, of science, of freedom, of transmutation and transformation. It is also the ray of the royal priesthood of the Order of Melchizedek.

All of these components go into making up the energy of the seventh ray and the violet flame. The violet flame is the gift of the Holy Spirit that Saint Germain unlocks for us and teaches us how to use in the laboratory of the soul. The soul becomes the scientist in her own laboratory—in her own subconscious mind and in her own superconscious mind—working with the energies that Moses discovered to be the I AM THAT I AM, working with the energies that Jesus defined as the Christ, or the eternal Word, the Logos, by which the creation was framed.

This two-thousand-year cycle, then, is a period of learning, a period of transition, a period when we must secure our freedom: freedom in America and freedom for oppressed peoples everywhere. If we do not pass this initiation as individuals, gaining our freedom from personal tyranny, and if we do not pass this initiation as a community and as a nation, we will not be able to continue in the path of initiation over the next two thousand years. Instead, we will find ourselves at the mercy of some sort of superstate or supereconomy, where the nations of the world are utterly controlled by the elite through their control of the money and the money system. We see this happening today both through government and through the multinational corporations.

So, even when the little people of the world lift up their heads in outrage, nothing can be done because power (and money is power) is vested in the hands of the few. And the few are representing their own vested interests rather than the real interests of the children of God on earth.

Q: What can the little people do, Mrs. Prophet?

A: We can begin right where Saint Germain begins. He has written *Saint Germain On Alchemy: Formulas for Self-Transformation,* a paperback book that

contains vital information on how we can begin right where we are, right with what we know, and go into the secret chamber of the heart and find there the flame of life.

This flame of life right within us has the unlimited

power, wisdom and love of God, which when invoked and released can bring forth that precipitation of energy, of enlightenment, of all that we need to know to be in action for the Coming Revolution—all that we need to know to turn around what is happening in the downward spiral of civilization and create an upward spiral.

Saint Germain comes, as Jesus did, to overturn the money-changers in the temple. He comes in this age for the redress of grievances being practiced against the people, even as Jesus came in his time to correct the darkness of the Sadducees and Pharisees, even as Gautama Buddha came in his time to challenge what was happening in a decadent Hinduism.

The thing we have to realize is that the way religious thought goes is the way government and the economy will go. This is because religion, even if it is rejected, forms the basis of the culture and of the self-awareness of a people. If people do not have the correct understanding of their rightful and lawful relationship with God through Christ, through the Great White Brotherhood, they are not free to act with the full power and authority of God behind them. They fear to act for fear of the consequences, and therefore they do nothing.

And the fallen ones, who have wrested the secrets of the universe, manipulate God's energy and manipulate the masses through the media. They move in and take more and more and more, even while they lead the people down the primrose path of a pleasure cult and a self-indulgence whereby they neglect the important details necessary to their survival, both spiritual and material.

Saint Germain is concerned about our material survival in America and in every nation, because the material foundation of life is the basis for all spiritual preoccupations. We cannot completely lose ourselves in the spiritual, in meditation, in the enjoyment of God, but we must bring back—as Gautama Buddha did from the planes of nirvana, the planes of bliss and enlightenment—that which we have gleaned. And we must take practical measures right down here on the city council, right here on the school board, right here with the problems of integration. This is where life is happening. This is where policies are being made that affect the future of our children and our nation.

We don't know how to analyze because we have not been given the standard of the Christ consciousness. Saint Germain comes to bring us that standard.

In his book *Saint Germain On Alchemy,* Saint Germain begins telling us right in chapter one how Jesus walked on the water. And he explains that it was a transfer of energy from the body of Jesus to the body of Peter that enabled Peter to also walk on the water. Saint Germain illustrates for us a basic law of alchemy that can be demonstrated in this magnificent guru-chela relationship he is offering us today.

Saint Germain says:

> The law of transfer of energy is vital to the science of alchemy; for without it, it is impossible to "create" Matter. It is a law that nothing cannot create something.

Q: Is it possible for someone with lesser attainment than Jesus or Saint Germain to use the laws of alchemy?

A: It's possible for you and for everyone who puts his mind to it. Anyone who is capable of a basic grammar school education is capable of studying this book by Saint Germain. It is written in simple English, and it is a conveyance of Saint Germain's heart flame. Saint Germain has said that he overshadows and stands over each individual who reads this book to sponsor that soul if the soul responds to his call.

You will remember that when Jesus called his disciples, they were fishing. They were going about the business of the day, the economic affairs of life. Jesus said, "Come, and I will make you fishers of men."

Those who want to be disciples of the real guru of the age can respond to Saint Germain's heart call by receiving the *Pearls of Wisdom,* which are our manna in the wilderness. They come to us each week as the daily bread from the ascended masters. I would also encourage all to consider reading *Alchemy,* which Saint Germain has given as the gift of his heart to all who would bear the light in the Aquarian age.

60

Spiritual Alchemy

∞◇∞

- *What is the real meaning of the science of alchemy?*
- *Is it possible to change base metals into gold?*
- *What is the secret of the white stone?*

Mrs. Prophet, we've talked about Saint Germain and the science of alchemy. What really is alchemy?

A: In his book *Saint Germain On Alchemy,* the master writes:

> The inner meaning of alchemy is simply *all-composition,* implying the relation of the all of the creation to the parts that compose it. Thus alchemy, when properly understood, deals with the conscious power of controlling mutations and transmutations within Matter and energy and even within life itself. It is the science of the mystic and it is the forte of the self-realized man who, having sought, has found himself to be one with God and is willing to play his part.

Q: Does this mean that the law of alchemy can only be used for good?

A: All people use alchemy all the time because alchemy simply is the use of God's energy. And a lot of people are misusing God's energy. Saint Germain even tells us that there are those who have wrested the secrets of the universe from certain of the adepts of the ages and that these can and do use this science for evil purposes. But he says that none can escape accountability for the misuse of the sacred fire and the energy of life.

The true scientist is a priest at the altar of the sacred fire. He is in the laboratory of the forces of Spirit and Matter. Saint Germain cautions us about approaching this altar. For the way in which we as scientists use the flow of Spirit and Matter for precipitation will determine whether we evolve in the consciousness of God-freedom—which will ultimately propel us into our own ascension in the light and our eternal freedom—or whether we are bound to the shackles of our own tyranny, that same tyranny that we have attempted to impose upon nature.

Q: Does this mean that everybody will eventually be able to turn base metal into gold?

A: As you know, Saint Germain was embodied among the medieval alchemists of Europe. And as the Wonderman of Europe he did exactly that. Many of the nobility were fascinated and astounded when this man who wore diamonds on every finger and who moved about in court circles would take their flawed gems and return them flawless and priceless.

So Saint Germain has demonstrated that science, but he is concerned that we first understand the science of self-transformation whereby we can transform the human consciousness into the divine consciousness through the invocation of the gifts and graces of the Holy Spirit.

In *Alchemy*, he does teach us, however, how to meditate on the molecular structure of the amethyst to precipitate an amethyst Maltese cross. He gives a step-by-step seven-part meditation whereby we can study the chemical composition and the formula of crystals in Matter and, by our meditation on these, actually focalize intense cosmic energies for the good of life on earth.

Q: Does that mean we should all practice the precipitation of physical objects?

A: Our whole life is a precipitation! If you believe the ancient maxim that we have created ourselves, you realize that what you look at in the mirror in the morning is the product of your own personal alchemy with the forces of the universe. We have been in the process of creating ourselves for thousands of years. Our very facial characteristics, our body structure, our lifestyle are the results of our past uses and misuses of God's energy. And therefore, alchemists we are, like it or not.

Saint Germain comes to tell us that we can be alchemists of the Spirit with the goal of ennobling the race and becoming benefactors of the race in the highest sense of the word. We can be disciples of Christ Jesus and true followers of his example who believe in his words: "He that believeth on me—i.e., the Christ in me—the works that I do shall he do also; and greater works than these shall he do." It is interesting that the very first miracle that Jesus wrought in Cana of Galilee was the changing of the water into wine, marking him clearly as one of the great alchemists of all time.

Saint Germain in his embodiment as Merlin the Magician at the court of Arthur was also the alchemist. And you will recall that important scene in the square in London when the archbishop of Canterbury and the kings and nobles were on hand, and many tried to remove the sword Excalibur from the stone. The stone was inscribed with the words: "Whosoever pulleth this sword from this stone is rightwise born king of all England." It was Merlin who saw to it that the sword was there, and it was Merlin who gave to the lad Arthur the key to removing the sword from the stone.

Thus we see Merlin as the one who anointed the king of the Britons. And we see him again in the role of anointer of kings in his incarnation as the prophet Samuel. So too, our Saint Germain, as the sponsor of America, did anoint our first president,

George Washington. As the story goes, this took place just out-side of Philadelphia.

Q: Mrs. Prophet, since it seems that we are destined to be alchemists, where do we start?

A: Saint Germain starts with defining the purpose of our al-chemical experiment. The title of chapter two in *Alchemy* is "The Purpose of Your Alchemical Experiment." As you know, Saint Germain was embodied as Francis Bacon, and anyone who has ever studied Francis Bacon is truly impressed with his skill as a writer. And those who know his secret realize that he also authored the Shakespearean plays and encoded in those plays certain mys-teries of the Brotherhood as well as the mysteries of his own life.

We can hear the ring of that writer and of that thinker in this alchemy book. It is a book that is tremendously loved by lovers of Shakespeare. In chapter two Saint Germain says:

> Void is unfruitful energy. The alchemist must develop a sense of the value of time and space and the opportunity to manipulate both. Freedom is won by quest and con-quest, but mainly by the conquest of the finite self. True mastery of the finite comes through the indrawing love, the compelling, almost magnetic heart call of the soul to its Divine Source.
>
> Only the great inflow of the cosmic light of God can release the soul from the imprisoning shadows of its human creation. Summon, then, the purity of purpose that will make your creative design good; relentlessly challenge the base elements that arise like hobgoblins to disturb and try the plan you have begun; then patiently evolve your God-design—the purpose of your alchemical experiment.

Q: Mrs. Prophet, what does Saint Germain have to say about the white stone and the elixir that we associate with the early alchemists?

A: The white stone is the philosophers' stone that has been talked about and around, but few have discovered its secret. Saint Germain says, "Know thy Self as the white stone." And this is the Self with a capital *S,* meaning the Real Self, the Inner Self, the God Self. And so we consider that this white stone is a focal point of tremendous cosmic energy.

What is this Great Self? There is really only one Great Self. And if you visualize the universe as a giant piece of white paper with little circles drawn on it like the monads of Leibniz,* you can see each of us as one of the little circles, one of the monads. And when the little circle realizes that its real identity is this vast piece of paper, it is discovering the Real Self, which is the Real Self of all. And it discovers that there is only one Self, and that Self is God.

Saint Germain comes to say that when we find this out and when we really know it and can really understand it, then we will get to the key of alchemy, that white stone or that energy that is this Great Self, this great God Source.

Now, as long as that little monad, drawn like a circle on the vast piece of paper, thinks that *it* is the Real Self, it will have no real energy except the tiny portion upon which it is drawn, which is not sufficient to work the works of alchemy.

That tiny portion is not sufficient unto itself to transform itself or to experience the great alchemy of which we are speaking. And therefore we need to understand that the surrender of that little circle to the larger piece of paper on which it is drawn is the key to the discovery of the Inner Self. We also need to understand that nothing is lost in that surrender but everything is gained. This is the true path to oneness. It is the true path to brotherhood—the

*German philosopher, statesman and mathematician Gottfried Leibniz (1646–1716) theorized that the universe is composed of countless centers of spiritual energy known as monads. While each monad is unique, has soul-like essence and mirrors the universe, it develops independently and interacts with other monads solely as a result of a harmony preestablished by God.

principle upon which the Great White Brotherhood was founded.

The ascended masters realize that they themselves are simply circles drawn upon the infinite mind of God and that as they are one in that mind they have the all-power of the universe. But if they were to think of themselves as separate monads, they would lose their power. In fact, if they so thought, they would never have become ascended masters in the first place—because the definition of *ascended master* is one who overcomes time and space by relinquishing himself as that finite little circle drawn upon the Infinite. He does not fear the loss of identity by the bursting of that membrane but realizes that as he is one with the All, he is then the All-in-all.

So, on this subject of the white stone, Saint Germain says: "Know thy Self as the white stone from whence all thy creation must proceed in orderly fashion." When we have that Self-awareness, we are ready to work and to walk as the alchemist. When we have it, we've got the basic key. It simply takes that practice that makes perfect. Saint Germain says:

> If the key ideas are not created from within thee who art the alchemist, then the whole act is either hapless or an imitation of the work of another.
>
> Now, if it be God thou wouldst imitate, then "Well done!" may truly be spoken of thee; but if the vanity of mankind, then piteous let thy consciousness remain. The True Self of man, from whence cometh every goodly design, is worthy to be consulted as to what it is desirable to create. Therefore, the true alchemist begins his experiment by communing with himself in order to perceive the inspiring thoughts of the radiant mind of his Creator.

We can readily see that Saint Germain's voice rings with the psalmist, who said, "Ye are gods, and all of you are children of the most High."

61

The Science of Precipitation

∞∞

- *How do the alchemist's experiments affect the law of supply and demand?*

- *Is it possible to draw anything we need directly from the Universal?*

- *What does the Book of Revelation have to say about the alchemy of our time?*

Mrs. Prophet, how does the practice of alchemy affect the law of supply and demand?

A: In *Saint Germain On Alchemy,* the master says:

> It is well for the would-be alchemist to realize that this is an exact and true science whose illumination is conferred upon man by God himself. Its purpose is to teach mankind how to obtain for themselves every gracious gift and virtue that their lifestreams might require in finding the way back Home to God's heart.

I think we misunderstand the law of supply and demand because we do not understand the interaction of cosmic forces over the figure eight, which is the symbol of infinity. It is also the symbol of the transfer of energy from Spirit to Matter and from Matter to Spirit.

We think that we live in a material universe but actually we live in a spiritual-material universe. And the interchange of energy over that figure eight, or over the T'ai Chi, is the interchange of the yang and yin of cosmic forces and of the masculine and feminine principles.

Saint Germain's teachings on alchemy help us understand how this interchange of energy works. He says:

> I conceive nothing wrong in the idea, nor do I look with disfavor upon your having a divine source of supply to meet all your needs. I do feel it is needful for you to keep constantly humble and grateful as God places within your hands the key to the control of natural forces.
>
> Again, and second to no idea contained herein, is the constant need to understand the universal scheme or plan of creation so that all that you design and do will be harmonious with eternal Law and cosmic principles.

Q: **Mrs. Prophet, does this mean that we can immediately draw from the Universal anything that we need?**

A: It is the Law that we can draw forth from God, the Universal, every good and perfect gift, all of our daily needs. But we do not always see the results of our alchemy immediately, because we are no longer in the garden of paradise. We are outside of Eden and subject to God's edict that we earn our daily bread by the sweat of the brow.

We find, then, that alchemy has been immensely slowed down on earth and that the fruit of our effort comes not instantaneously like magic but day by day, cycle by cycle, as the reward for our service and our application.

We talk about the law of precipitation whereby spiritual energies are drawn forth out of the Universal and coalesced in Matter. In direct precipitation, a person can hold out his hand and the desired object instantaneously appears. In indirect precipitation, we bring about the desired results gradually, through meditation, visualization and physical work as we apply ourselves directly to a project.

In the sense of indirect precipitation, millions among mankind today are practicing certain laws of alchemy. We find in America, where there is that peculiar creative genius for work, for science, for invention and for building a material civilization, that many individuals excel in the natural uses of alchemy. However, many of these very ones who would and could become master alchemists need the key and the precious ingredient of Saint Germain's "all-chemistry" of God. This missing ingredient would lend to their material accomplishments that broader dimension of spiritual alchemy that brings the soul to an intensified contact with the Spirit of the living God. It is this science that Saint Germain would confer and that he has actually given to many of his disciples on earth.

Q: Mrs. Prophet, why of all things is Saint Germain, the master of the Aquarian age, teaching us a course on alchemy?

A: For one reason—he is the Master Alchemist! He says in *Alchemy*:

> Alchemy was originally intended to be a means of enriching individual destiny by making available the technique of changing base metals into gold, thereby producing opulence in the affairs of the successful practitioner. The dedication of the early alchemists to the cause of ferreting out its secrets was complete, and it was sanctified by the coordination of their minds with the works of their hands.
>
> These alchemists pursued their experiments under the duress of persecution led by the entrenched reactionary forces of their day, and it is a tribute to their lives and honor that they persisted in the search. Thus they brought forth and bequeathed to humanity the bona fide results of their efforts as acknowledged scientific achievement and annotated philosophic knowledge to bless the culture and archives of the world order.

Saint Germain sees that the world today requires alchemy. He sees that we need to pursue the path of becoming the alchemist in order to change the course of our civilization. He tells us: "The key to alchemy, to change, that must precede all other keys is the mastery of yourself, to a greater or lesser degree. For self-mastery is the key to all self-knowledge."

Saint Germain says that we must acknowledge without question that we ourselves are the alchemists who will determine the design of our creation and that we must know ourselves as the Real Self and our creation as coming forth from that Self. This point is the real foundation of the teachings of the seventh dispensation, the Aquarian age.

And when you reflect upon the Book of Revelation and the fact that it refers to the voice of the seventh angel, you see that the Book of Revelation is a book of alchemy. It prophesies the alchemy that will occur at the end of the Piscean dispensation.

We're at that moment right now. The cycles are turning. We have completed a two-thousand-year cycle and we as individuals on our personal path of initiation must go through everything that is described in the Book of Revelation. We must go through it within our own consciousness. Furthermore, the planetary body as a whole, passing through its evolutionary initiations, must also go through this testing. And so, to both the mystic and the alchemist, the Book of Revelation is a key to the alchemy of self-transformation.

We have all heard about the beast, the false prophet, the dragon and other figures in the Book of Revelation. Saint Germain comments on their inner meaning:

> Seething vortices of humanly discordant thoughts and feelings daily impose a hypnotic effect upon almost everyone on earth. These tend to nullify the great concentration of intelligent, creative power that is the birthright of every

man, woman and child on this planet, though it is consciously employed by far too few.

While increasing numbers among mankind seek after freedom, the reactionary elements, either with or without purpose, attempt to burden the race with new shackles each time deliverance from one form or another of human bondage is secured.

We see the soul, then, walking in the midst of a menagerie or a jungle of the beasts that appear in the Book of Revelation. We see that soul having to become an alchemist in order to get through this path of initiation, through the house of horrors that the subconscious realm of the mass mind has become.

This house of horrors is also much apparent in many of the countries of the world where tyranny and a totalitarian state are a way of life and mass executions and concentration camps are still in existence this very day. It is the alchemist wedded to his own inner Christ mind who is able to come forth from those conditions, as Daniel from the lion's den, unscathed.

We see that Saint Germain is giving us the tools to deal with the tyranny of the beasts of mass control that exist on earth in big government, big business, the manipulations of an international economy, and so forth.

Saint Germain says that the alchemist, who is really your soul and my soul, in order to be successful—to be the overcomer, to master time and space—"must be consciously aware of his God-given freedom to create." Do you realize that today men and women do not understand that they have been given the power by God to create and to be co-creators with him, and therefore they do not use that power? Saint Germain says:

> Those restrictions and restraints imposed upon the soul as forms of human bondage must be shunned. Yet in every case these must be distinguished from the necessary

laws that structure society. Beauty and righteousness must be emblazoned upon the left and right hand to remind the would-be alchemist of his responsibility to God and man to behold his works before releasing them to see that they are indeed good, and good for all men.

What Saint Germain tells us in *Alchemy* is that we have the power to create. We have lost that science and the memory of that science because in many incarnations past we have misused it. We have not created for the good of all, but we have created an energy veil, an *e-veil,* or evil, which is the mass hypnosis that now blankets the consciousness of the people and separates them from the Real Self.

Saint Germain's message is: If you will create according to God's plan, his will and in his image and likeness, God will restore to you, when you prove yourself to be an alchemist with reverence for life, the full science that you had in the beginning when you were with God in the Garden of Eden.

Q: Mrs. Prophet, I guess without the freedom to create there really is no freedom, is there?

A: That is precisely what Saint Germain is awakening our consciousness to—the idea that we as the American people, as citizens of the earth and a cosmos, have actually lost this precious, sacred gift of the power to create. And this is what Saint Germain comes to restore as the master of the Aquarian age.

62

The Will of God

∞

- *How can we know God's will?*
- *Once we know it, what is the next step?*
- *How can we maintain contact with the higher invisible world?*

Mrs. Prophet, with all the talk about doing the right thing and following God's will, I think the question for most people is "How do you know what God's will is?"

A: I have found that God will never, never fail to reveal himself to us if we persistently seek him. The answer to the question "How do you know God's will?" is simply: "Ask." Ask God, "What is your will for me today?"

And when you have asked, go about your daily duties. You will find that in the alchemy of the day—in its unfoldment, in the blending of forces, in the movement of your mind with the mind of God—God will reveal his will not so much by a spoken word but by the very action of his Spirit in and through you.

God's will is like the unfolding rose. It unfolds like a spiral, and we come to understand it proportionately as we keep ourselves attuned to the mind of God and as we keep active, doing the best we know how to do each day for him, for our family and for our community.

Q: How can we put this knowledge of the will of God to work for alchemy and for change in our lives?

A: The will of God is power. When you are aligned with the will of God it is as if you and God were each a colander: you put the two together, you get the holes lined up and then the cosmic energy of the universe flows through those holes. You find yourself literally charged and bristling with God's energy. As soon as you are out of alignment with God's will, it is as if your colander had moved, causing a total block to the flow. You don't know what to do with yourself and you don't know what to do with your life.

So, if we find ourselves in that predicament of not knowing which way to go, we have to pause a moment—maybe for a day or longer—and say, "If I don't have the fulfillment in my life that I am seeking, it has to be because somewhere along the way I have gotten out of alignment with the will of God."

Saint Germain reveals the path of freedom and how to get back into alignment with the will of God. Saint Germain's guru is the Great Divine Director, whose causal body contains the energy concentration for divine direction. In other words, he keeps the flame of divine direction for life on earth. It is from the Great Divine Director that Saint Germain learned the alchemy of self-transformation.

Saint Germain teaches us how to give certain mantras and decrees to the flame of divine direction held in the heart of the Great Divine Director. By doing a series of these mantras and decrees daily, we can come into a greater alignment with the cosmic consciousness of the Great Divine Director.

I would encourage those who are seeking divine direction, the will of God and the alchemy of self-transformation in their lives to read Saint Germain's teachings. (See page 366.)

Q: OK, once we have identified the will of God and made up our minds that it is going to be our will, what's the next step?

A: Things really start happening when you decide that the will of God is the center of your life. Saint Germain tells us that since his ascension he has maintained contact with one or more lifestreams on earth. He talks also about Jesus visiting his disciples even in this age.

The moment you can say, "Not my will but thine be done," with a full understanding that you have free will to accept or reject God's will, you realize that that is all the ascended masters are waiting for. When you accept God's will as Jesus did in Gethsemane, immediately an angel comes and ministers unto you as the angel ministered unto him.

Alignment with the will of God is what will give us conscious cooperation with the invisible world and with the invisible hierarchy. Saint Germain tells us that "the creation of the visible is wholly dependent upon those essences that are not visible to the unaided eye." This is an important point in alchemy. It means that to draw forth from the Universal, from the energies of Spirit, we must be able to visualize these realms and establish contact with them.

Because we have not yet mastered time and space, we do not come and go in infinity as the ascended masters do. However, we have need of the energies and resources of infinity to take dominion over the earth. And so, the next best thing is to make contact with those who have access to those resources. When you need money, you go to the bank for a loan.

So, Saint Germain says that in the process of alchemy we should follow the path of what he calls "enlightened self-interest." Enlightened self-interest is interest in the Self, the Real Self, the God Self. He explains to us that this is not selfishness but it is actually doing what is best for and good for the Self. He says that unless we pursue this enlightened self-interest we will never be able to do the things that Jesus did.

Before Jesus became the Master of Galilee he studied these very laws of alchemy in the retreats of the Great White Brotherhood. Having mastered them before taking embodiment, he brushed up on this sacred science before beginning his mission. Jesus then became the greatest alchemist of all time.

Saint Germain is saying, "If you are going to help the world, help yourself first and do it according to the teachings of alchemy I am giving you." He explains: "Ignorance with its defilement of the Law deprives the individual and society of enlightenment. The only cure is illumined obedience, together with scientific attentiveness to the detail of the Law."

We practice illumined obedience when we seek to understand God's will, to know that it is good and that it is really the foundation and structure of our identity—and by conscious free will we accept and obey that will. Obedience does not mean that one becomes a zombie, a puppet on a string or a jellyfish. The goal is to become a strong individual and then to yield that strength to the creativity of the mind of God.

Q: Mrs. Prophet, some people use their subconscious minds to enhance their creativity. What does Saint Germain have to say about this?

A: Saint Germain gives us the following teaching:

> Let the sincere student who would ponder and practice methods of mind and memory control, which are the methods of God himself, acquire the habit of consciously giving to the blessed Higher Mind, or Christ Self, the responsibility for designing and perfecting the embryonic ideas and patterns of his creation. Many of these patterns

which at first appear to be consciously conceived by the alchemist frequently have their origin within this higher portion of the blessed Self.

He explains to us that twenty-four hours a day the Higher Mind is active in expanded dimensions. We are not always aware of what this Higher Mind is doing. But if we meditate upon something that we desire to draw forth, even wisdom itself, and we release that as a matrix into the Higher Mind before we retire at night, then in the morning we can be filled with inspiration and divine direction.

Saint Germain counsels us that it is important as we pursue his studies in alchemy to have a pad of paper and a pencil next to our beds so that if we are awakened in the night we can write down immediately what we are thinking and what the Higher Mind is impressing upon us. Otherwise, invariably we will not remember in the morning.

This is because those moments, which often occur in the middle of the night, are moments of a higher contact and an experience in higher consciousness. Many times we say, "Well, I'll pick it up in the morning," but in the morning we do not remember because we are not capable of sustaining in our full waking consciousness the contact with the Inner Mind.

We find that the Great Alchemist himself, God the Almighty One, is working in and with and through our soul—from the superconscious mind, the highest source, through the conscious, subconscious and unconscious levels of our being, which contain the memories of our past achievements, even from previous incarnations. Alchemy, then, becomes the science of a total integration of the soul with the forces of her own microcosm, her own being, as that being is in contact with the one universal Source.

In *Alchemy*, Saint Germain gives us much instruction on

alchemy before he releases the following basic outline of how to pursue the process:

> First design a mental matrix of the desired object, then determine where you wish it to manifest. If you know the material substance of which it is composed, memorize its atomic pattern; if not, call to the Divine Intelligence within your Higher Mind to register the pattern for you from the Universal Intelligence and to impress it upon your memory body and your mind.
>
> Recognize that light is an energy substance universally manifesting on earth, thanks to the sun center of being, the focal point of the Christ in this solar system. Call for light to take on the atomic pattern you are holding, to coalesce around that pattern, and then to "densify" into form. Call for the multiplication of this atomic structure until molecules of substance begin to fill the void occupying the space in which you desire the object to appear.
>
> When the total outline is filled with the vibratory action of the fourth-dimensional substance representing the desired manifestation, ask for the full lowering of the atomic density into three-dimensional form and substance within the pattern established by the matrix of your mind; and then await results.

There is a core of information in Saint Germain's writings for the individual who perceives himself as a part of the avant-garde who will carry earth's evolution from the old order to the new. The symbol of this new order of the ages sponsored by Saint Germain is the eye in the capstone of the pyramid, which appears on the one-dollar bill.

That eye is the All-Seeing Eye of the inner alchemist, your own Higher Mind, your own Real Self. When you make contact with that inner eye of God, you can precipitate the great pyramid of Self and find yourself one with a cosmos.

Glossary

Words set in italics are defined elsewhere in the glossary.

Adept. An initiate of the *Great White Brotherhood* of a high degree of attainment, especially in the control of *Matter,* physical forces, nature spirits and bodily functions.

Affirmation. A positive statement, usually beginning with the name of God, "I AM," that affirms and strengthens the qualities of God within oneself, helping to bring those qualities into physical manifestation.

Akashic records. The impressions of all that has ever transpired in the physical universe, recorded in the etheric substance and dimension known by the Sanskrit term *akasha.* These records can be read by those with developed *soul* faculties.

All-Seeing Eye of God. See *Cyclopea.*

Alpha and Omega. The divine wholeness of the Father-Mother God affirmed as "the beginning and the ending" by the Lord Christ in Revelation (Rev. 1:8, 11; 21:6; 22:13). Ascended *twin flames* of the Cosmic Christ consciousness who hold the balance of the masculine-feminine polarity of the Godhead in the *Great Central Sun* of cosmos.

Angel. A divine spirit, a herald or messenger sent by God to deliver his *Word* to his children. A ministering spirit sent forth to comfort, protect, guide, strengthen, teach, counsel and warn.

Aquarian age. The 2,150-year cycle following the age of Pisces. The age of Pisces gave us the understanding of God as the Son, exemplified by the sponsor of that age, Jesus Christ. The age of Aquarius brings us the awareness of God as the Holy Spirit and as the Divine Mother. It is sponsored by the Ascended Master Saint Germain and his divine complement, the Ascended Lady Master Portia. During this cycle, the opportunity will be given to humankind to apply the laws of freedom and justice, the science of precipitation and transmutation, and rituals of invocation to God that can bring in an age of enlightenment and peace such as the world has never known.

Archangel. The highest rank in the orders of *angels.* Each of the *seven rays* has a presiding archangel who, with his divine complement, or *archeia,* embodies the God consciousness of the ray and directs the bands of angels serving in their command on that ray.

Archeia (pl. **archeiai**). Divine complement and *twin flame* of an *archangel.*

Archangel Michael. The angel of the LORD who stands in defense of the *Christ consciousness* in all children of God; also known as Prince of the Archangels and Defender of the Faith. As the archangel of the first ray, Michael embodies the qualities of faith, protection, perfection and the will of God. He is the most revered angel in Jewish, Christian and Islamic scripture and tradition.

Archangel Raphael. Archangel of the fifth spiritual ray (green ray) of science, healing and vision. Archangel Raphael, together with Mother Mary, his divine complement, brings great healing energy to the evolutions of earth.

Ascended master. Enlightened spiritual beings who once lived on earth, fulfilled their reason for being and have ascended and reunited with God in the ritual of the *ascension.* The ascended masters are the true teachers of mankind. They direct the spiritual evolution of all devotees of God and guide them back to their Source.

Ascension. The ritual whereby the *soul* reunites with the *Spirit* of the living God, the *I AM Presence,* through the acceleration by the *sacred fire* at the natural conclusion of one's final lifetime on earth. It is the process whereby the soul, having balanced her karma and fulfilled her divine plan, merges first with the *Christ consciousness* and then with the living Presence of the I AM THAT I AM. Once the ascension has taken place, the soul—the corruptible aspect of being—becomes the incorruptible one, a permanent atom in the body of God, free from the round of *karma* and rebirth.

Astral plane. A frequency of time and space beyond the physical, yet below the mental, corresponding to the *emotional body* of man and the collective unconscious of the race; the repository of mankind's thoughts and feelings, conscious and unconscious. Because the astral plane has been muddied by impure human thought and feeling, the term "astral" is often used in a negative context to refer to that which is impure or psychic.

AUM. See *OM.*

Aura. A luminous emanation or electromagnetic field that surrounds the physical body. The atmosphere surrounding and interpenetrating the *four lower bodies* of man and his *chakras* upon which the impressions, thoughts, feelings, words and actions of the individual are registered, including his *karma* and the records of past lives.

Avatar. From Sanskrit *avatara,* literally "descent." A Hindu term for an incarnation of God on earth. The incarnation of the *Word.*

Base-of-the-spine chakra. A four-petaled white *chakra* located at the base of the spinal column. It is associated with the fourth ray and the expression of purity, hope, joy, self-discipline, integration, perfection, wholeness and nurturing.

Bodhisattva. (Sanskrit, "a being of *bodhi* or enlightenment.") A being destined for enlightenment, or one whose energy and power is directed toward enlightenment. A bodhisattva is destined to become a Buddha but has forgone the bliss of *nirvana* with a vow to save all children of God on earth. An *ascended master* or an *unascended master* may be a bodhisattva.

Carnal mind. The human ego, human intellect and human will; the animal nature of man.

Causal body. Interpenetrating spheres of *light* surrounding each one's *I AM Presence* at spiritual levels. The spheres of the causal body contain the records of the virtuous acts we have performed to the glory of God and the blessing of man through our many incarnations on earth.

Central Sun. Whether in the *microcosm* or the *Macrocosm,* the central sun is the principal energy source, vortex, or nexus of energy interchange in atoms, cells, the heart center of man, amidst plant life and the core of the earth. The Great Central Sun is the center of cosmos, the point of integration of the Spirit-Matter cosmos, and the point of origin of all physical-spiritual creation.

Chakra. (Sanskrit, meaning "wheel," "disc," "circle.") Term used to denote the centers of light anchored in the *etheric body* and governing the flow of energy to the *four lower bodies* of man. There are seven major chakras corresponding to the *seven rays,* five minor chakras corresponding to the five secret rays, and a total of 144 light centers in the body of man.

Chela. (Hindi *cela* from Sanskrit *ceta* "slave" or "servant.") In India, a disciple of a religious teacher or *guru.* A term used generally to refer to a student of the *ascended masters* and their teachings.

Chohan. Lord or master; a chief. Each of the *seven rays* has a chohan who focuses the *Christ consciousness* of the ray for the earth and her evolutions.

Christ. (From the Greek *Christos* "anointed.") Messiah (Hebrew, Aramaic "anointed"); "Christed one," one fully endued and infilled—anointed—by the light (the Son) of God. The *Word,* the Logos, the second person of the Trinity.

Christhood. The individual expression of the universal Christ consciousness. On the spiritual path, the individual *Christ Self,* the personal *Christ,* is the initiator of the *soul.* When the individual passes certain initiations on the path of Christhood, he or she earns the right to be called a Christed one and gains the title of Son or Daughter of God.

Christ consciousness. The consciousness or awareness of the self in and as the *Christ;* the attainment of a level of consciousness commensurate with that which was realized by Jesus, the Christ. The Christ consciousness is the realization within the soul of that mind which was in Christ Jesus.

Christ Self. The Higher Self; our inner teacher, guardian, friend and advocate before God; the Universal Christ individualized for each of us; the Real Self of every man, woman and child, to which the soul must rise. The Christ Self is the mediator between the individual and God.

Cosmic Law. The law that governs mathematically, yet with the spontaneity of mercy's flame, all manifestation throughout the cosmos in the planes of *Spirit* and *Matter.*

Crown chakra. A golden-yellow *chakra* of 972 petals located at the crown of the head. It is associated with the second ray and the expression of illumination, wisdom, self-knowledge, understanding, humility, open-mindedness and cosmic consciousness.

Crystal cord. The stream of God's *light,* life and consciousness that nourishes and sustains the *soul* and her *four lower bodies.* Also called the silver cord (Eccles. 12:6).

Cyclopea. Masculine Elohim of the fifth ray, also known as the All-Seeing Eye of God or as the Silent Watcher. See also *Elohim; Seven rays.*

Decree. A dynamic form of spoken prayer used by students of the *ascended masters* to direct God's *light* into individual and world conditions. It is the authoritative *Word* of God spoken in man in the name of the *I AM Presence* and the living *Christ* to bring about constructive change on earth through the will of God.

Dharma. An individual's dharma is his duty to fulfill his reason for being. It is his divine plan, which runs as a thread through all his lifetimes. When the dharma is fulfilled and sufficient karma is balanced, the *soul* is eligible for the *ascension.*

Dictation. A message from an *ascended master,* an *archangel* or another advanced spiritual being delivered through the agency of the Holy Spirit by a *messenger* of the *Great White Brotherhood.*

Eighth ray. The ray of integration, where we integrate the mastery of the *seven rays* through the flame of the *Christ,* the *threefold flame.* The eighth ray corresponds to the *secret chamber of the heart,* an eight-petaled *chakra* behind the *heart chakra,* where the threefold flame is sealed.

Electronic Presence. A duplicate of the I AM Presence, which holds the pattern of the *Real Self;* a powerful replica of an *ascended master,* the fullness of his tangible light body, which can be focalized in time and space within the aura of a disciple. A devotee who calls to an ascended master, in the name of the I AM THAT I AM, may be blessed with his Electronic Presence.

Elemental life. Nature spirits who are the servants of God and man in the planes of *Matter* for the establishment and maintenance of the physical plane as the platform for the *soul's* evolution. Elementals who serve the fire element are called salamanders; those who serve the air element, sylphs; those who serve the water element, undines; those who serve the earth element, gnomes.

Elijah. The Israelite prophet who was taken up into heaven in a chariot of fire (II Kings 2:11). He later embodied as John the Baptist, who prepared the way for Jesus' mission (Matt. 17:10–13). Elijah was a rare exception of a man who ascended and then reembodied in physical form. After his lifetime as John the Baptist, he returned to the ascended state.

El Morya. The *ascended master* who is the teacher and sponsor of the *messengers* Mark L. Prophet and Elizabeth Clare Prophet and the founder of *The Summit Lighthouse; chohan* of the first ray.

Elohim. (Hebrew; plural of *Eloah,* "God.") The name of God used in the first verse of the Bible: "In the beginning God created the heaven and the earth." The Seven Mighty *Elohim* and their feminine counterparts are the builders of form. They are the "seven spirits of God" named in Revelation 4:5 and the "morning stars" that sang together in the beginning, as the LORD revealed them to Job (Job 38:7). In the order of *hierarchy,* the Elohim and cosmic beings carry the greatest concentration, the highest vibration of *light* that we can comprehend in our present state of evolution.

Emotional body. See *four lower bodies.*

Enoch. According to the Bible, Enoch was a prophet who predicted the judgment of the ungodly (Jude 4–19). The Bible says that "Enoch walked with God and he was not, for God took him" (Gen. 5:24). This has been interpreted as the record of his ascension; he is now known as the Ascended Master Enoch.

Etheric body. See *four lower bodies.*

Etheric plane. The highest plane in the dimension of *Matter;* a plane that is as concrete and real as the physical plane (and even more so) but is experienced through the senses of the *soul* in a dimension and a consciousness beyond physical awareness. It is the world of *ascended masters* and their *retreats,* etheric cities of *light* where *souls* of a higher order of evolution abide between embodiments. It is the plane of reality.

Etheric retreat. The spiritual home of an *ascended master* or heavenly being. Retreats are located chiefly on the *etheric plane,* or heaven-world, and serve many functions for the spiritual *hierarchy* as they minister to souls on earth. Some of the retreats have been opened so that souls can travel there in their finer bodies during sleep to study at universities of the Spirit.

Fallen angels. The fallen angels are those angels who followed Lucifer in the Great Rebellion, whose consciousness therefore "fell" to lower levels of vibration. They were "cast out into the earth" by *Archangel Michael* (Rev. 12:7–12), constrained by the karma of their disobedience to God and his Christ to take on and evolve through dense physical bodies.

Father-Mother God. See *Alpha and Omega.*

Four cosmic forces. The four beasts seen by Saint John and other seers as the lion, the calf (or ox), the man and the flying eagle (Rev. 4:6–8). They serve directly under the *Elohim* and govern all of the *Matter* cosmos. They are transformers of the infinite light to souls evolving in the finite.

Four lower bodies. Four sheaths of four distinct frequencies that surround the *soul;* the vehicles the soul uses in her journey on earth: the etheric, or memory, body; the mental body; the desire, or emotional, body; the physical body. The etheric body houses the blueprint of the soul's identity and contains the memory of all that has ever transpired in the soul and all impulses she has ever sent out. The mental body is the vessel of the cognitive faculties; when purified, it can become the vessel of the mind of God, the Christ mind. The desire body houses the higher and lower desires and records the emotions. The physical body is the miracle of flesh and blood that enables the soul to progress in the material universe.

Gautama Buddha. Buddha means "the Enlightened One." Gautama attained the enlightenment of the Buddha in his final incarnation as Siddhartha Gautama (c. 563–483 B.C.). For forty-five years he preached his doctrine of the Four Noble Truths, the Eightfold Path and the Middle Way, which led to the founding of Buddhism. Gautama Buddha presently holds the office of Lord of the World and is the hierarch of Shamballa, an *etheric retreat* over the Gobi Desert.

Great Central Sun. See *Central Sun.*

Great White Brotherhood. A spiritual order of Western saints and Eastern adepts who have reunited with the *Spirit* of the living God; the heavenly hosts. They have transcended the cycles of *karma* and rebirth and ascended (accelerated) into that higher reality that is the eternal abode of the *soul.* The *ascended masters* of the Great White Brotherhood have risen in every age from every culture and religion to inspire creative achievement in education, the arts and sciences, God-government and the abundant life through the economies of the nations. The word "white" refers not to race but to the aura (halo) of white *light* surrounding their forms. The Brotherhood also includes certain unascended *chelas* of the ascended masters.

Guru. (Sanskrit.) A personal religious teacher and spiritual guide; one of high attainment. A guru may be unascended or ascended.

Heart chakra. A twelve-petaled pink *chakra* located in the center of the chest. It is associated with the third ray and the expression of love, compassion, beauty, selflessness, sensitivity, appreciation, comfort, creativity, charity and generosity.

Hierarchy. The universal chain of individualized God-free beings fulfilling the attributes and aspects of God's infinite Selfhood. This universal order of the Father's own Self-expression is the means whereby God in the *Great Central Sun* steps down the Presence and power of his universal being/consciousness in order that succeeding evolutions in time and space might come to know the wonder of his love.

Higher Self. The *I AM Presence;* the *Christ Self;* the exalted aspect of selfhood. Used in contrast to the term "lower self," or "little self," which indicates the *soul* that went forth from and may elect by free will to return to the Divine Whole through the realization of the oneness of the self in God. Higher consciousness.

Holy Christ Self. See *Christ Self.*

I AM Presence. The I AM THAT I AM (Exod. 3:13–15); the individualized Presence of God focused for each individual *soul.* The God-identity of the individual.

I AM THAT I AM. See *I AM Presence.*

Karma. (Sanskrit, meaning "act," "action," "work" or "deed.") The consequences of one's thoughts, words and deeds of this life and previous lives; the law of cause and effect, which decrees that whatever we do comes full circle to our doorstep for resolution. The law of karma necessitates the soul's reincarnation so that she can pay the debt for, or "balance," her misuses of God's *light,* energy and consciousness.

Karmic Board. See *Lords of Karma.*

Keepers of the Flame Fraternity. Founded in 1961 by Saint Germain, an organization of *ascended masters* and their *chelas* who vow to keep the flame of life on earth.

Kundalini. See *sacred fire.*

Lifestream. The stream of life that comes forth from the one Source, from the *I AM Presence* in the planes of *Spirit,* and descends to the planes of *Matter* where it manifests as the *threefold flame* anchored in the *secret chamber of the heart* for the sustainment of the *soul* in Matter and the nourishment of the *four lower bodies.* Used to denote souls evolving as individual "lifestreams" and hence synonymous with the term "individual." Denotes the ongoing nature of the individual through cycles of individualization.

Light. Spiritual light is the energy of God, the potential of the *Christ.* As the personification of *Spirit,* the term "light" can be used synonymously with the terms "God" and "Christ."

Logos. (Greek, "word," "speech," "reason.") See *Word.*

Lords of Karma. The ascended beings who comprise the Karmic Board. They dispense justice to this system of worlds, adjudicating karma, mercy and judgment on behalf of every *soul.* All souls must pass before the Karmic Board before and after each incarnation on earth, receiving their assignment and karmic allotment for each lifetime beforehand and the review of their performance at its conclusion.

Macrocosm. (Greek, "great world.") The larger cosmos; the entire warp and woof of creation. Also used to contrast man as the microcosm ("little world") against the backdrop of the larger world in which he lives. See also *Microcosm.*

Maitreya. Lord Maitreya ("he whose name is kindness") holds the office of Cosmic Christ and is known as the Great Initiator. He was the *guru* of Adam and Eve in the Mystery School known as the Garden of Eden and was also the guru of Jesus Christ.

Mantra. A mystical formula or invocation; a word or formula, often in Sanskrit, to be recited or sung for the purpose of intensifying the action of the *Spirit* of God in man. A form of prayer consisting of a word or a group of words that is chanted over and over again to magnetize a particular aspect of the Deity or of a being who has actualized that aspect of the Deity. See also *Decree.*

Mater. (Latin, "mother.") See *Matter; Mother.*

Matter. The feminine (negative) polarity of the Godhead, of which the masculine (positive) polarity is Spirit. Matter acts as a chalice for the kingdom of God and is the abiding place of evolving *souls.* Matter is distinguished from matter (lowercase *m*)—the substance of the earth earthy, of the realms of maya, which blocks rather than radiates divine *light* and the Spirit of the *I AM THAT I AM*. See also *Mother; Spirit.*

Memory body. See *four lower bodies.*

Mental body. See *four lower bodies.*

Messenger. One who is trained by an *ascended master* to receive by various methods the words, concepts, teachings and messages of the *Great White Brotherhood;* one who delivers the Law, the prophecies and the dispensations of God for a people and an age. Mark L. Prophet and Elizabeth Clare Prophet are messengers of the Great White Brotherhood for *The Summit Lighthouse.*

Microcosm. (Greek, "small world.") (1) The world of the individual, his *four lower bodies,* his *aura,* and the forcefield of his *karma.* (2) The planet. See also *Macrocosm.*

Mother. "Divine Mother," "Universal Mother" and "Cosmic Virgin" are alternate terms for the feminine polarity of the Godhead, the manifestation of God as Mother. *Matter* is the feminine polarity of *Spirit,* and the term is used interchangeably with *Mater* (Latin, "mother"). In this context, the entire material cosmos becomes the womb of creation into which Spirit projects the energies of life.

Nirvana. The goal of life according to Hindu and Buddhist philosophy: the state of liberation from the wheel of rebirth through the extinction of desire.

OM (AUM). The sacred syllable of creation, the *Word* that went forth in the beginning and from which all other sounds originated.

Omega. See *Alpha and Omega.*

Path. The path of initiation whereby the disciple who pursues the *Christ consciousness* overcomes step by step the limitations of selfhood in time and space and attains reunion with Reality through the ritual of the *ascension.*

Pearls of Wisdom. Weekly letters of instruction dictated by the *ascended masters* to their *messengers* Mark and Elizabeth Prophet for students of the sacred mysteries throughout the world. *Pearls of Wisdom* have been published by *The Summit Lighthouse* continuously since 1958. They contain both fundamental and advanced teachings on *cosmic law* with a practical application of spiritual truths to personal and planetary problems.

Physical body. See *four lower bodies.*

Real Self. See *Christ Self.*

Retreat. A focus of the *Great White Brotherhood,* usually on the *etheric plane* where the *ascended masters* preside. Retreats anchor one or more flames of the Godhead as well as the momentum of the masters' service and attainment for the balance of *light* in the *four lower bodies* of a planet and its evolutions. Retreats serve many functions for the councils of the *hierarchy* ministering to the lifewaves of earth. Some retreats are open to unascended mankind, whose *souls* may journey to these focuses in their *etheric body* between their incarnations on earth and in their finer bodies during sleep.

Sacred fire. The Kundalini fire that lies as the coiled serpent in the base-of-the-spine *chakra* and rises through spiritual purity and self-mastery to the crown chakra, quickening the spiritual centers on the way; also referred to as the light of the Divine Mother. God, *light,* life, energy, the *I AM THAT I AM.* "Our God is a consuming fire" (Heb. 12:29).

Saint Germain. The *ascended master* who is hierarch of the *Aquarian age* and sponsor of the United States of America; *chohan* of the seventh ray.

Science of the spoken Word. See *Spoken Word.*

Secret chamber of the heart. A spiritual chamber behind the *heart chakra* surrounded by great light and protection. It is the connecting point of the cord of light that descends from each one's *I AM Presence* to sustain the beating of their physical heart, giving life, purpose and cosmic integration. It is the place where one communes with their *Holy Christ Self* and fans the fires of the *threefold flame.*

Seven rays. The *light* emanations of the Godhead that, when invoked in the name of God or in the name of the *Christ,* burst forth as a flame in the world of the individual. The seven rays of the white light that emerge through the prism of the *Christ consciousness.* Rays may be projected by the God consciousness of ascended or unascended beings through the *chakras* and the third eye as a concentration of energy taking on numerous God-qualities, such as love, truth, wisdom, healing, and so on.

Silent Watcher. See *Cyclopea.*

Soul. Projected from the *I AM Presence* into physical evolution, the soul is the living potential of God. The soul is not immortal but can attain immortality through fusion with the *Holy Christ Self* and the *I AM Presence* in the ritual of the *ascension.*

Spirit. The masculine polarity of the Godhead; the coordinate of *Matter;* God as Father, who of necessity includes within the polarity of himself God as *Mother* and hence is known as the *Father-Mother God.* The plane of the *I AM Presence,* of perfection; the dwelling place of the *ascended masters* in the kingdom of God.

Spoken Word. The *Word* of the LORD God released in the original fiats of Creation. The release of the energies of the Word, or the Logos, through the throat *chakra* by the sons and daughters of God. Today disciples use the power of the Word in *decrees, affirmations,* prayers and *mantras* to draw the essence of the *sacred fire* from the *I AM Presence,* the *Christ Self* and cosmic beings to channel God's *light* for the purpose of transmutation, transformation and constructive change in the planes of *Matter.*

Summit University. A modern-day mystery school founded in 1971 under the direction of the *messengers* Mark L. Prophet and Elizabeth Clare Prophet. At Summit University, students study the teachings of the *ascended masters* delivered through their messengers.

The Summit Lighthouse. An outer organization of the *Great White Brotherhood* founded by Mark L. Prophet in 1958 in Washington, D.C., under the direction of the Ascended Master El Morya for the purpose of publishing and disseminating the teachings of the *ascended masters.*

Threefold flame. The flame of the Christ, the spark of life that burns within the *secret chamber of the heart* (a secondary *chakra* behind the heart). The sacred trinity of power, wisdom and love that is the manifestation of the *sacred fire.*

Transfiguration. An initiation on the path of the *ascension* that takes place when the initiate has attained a certain balance and expansion of the *threefold flame.* Jesus' transfiguration is described in Matthew 17:1–8.

Tube of light. The white light that descends from the heart of the *I AM Presence* in answer to the individual's call. About nine feet in diameter, it is a cylinder that originates in the *I AM Presence* and extends three feet below the person's feet. The tube of light acts as a shield of protection from negative energies and is sustained twenty-four hours a day as long as harmony is maintained in one's thoughts, feelings, words and deeds.

Twin flame. The *soul's* masculine or feminine counterpart conceived out of the same white-fire body, the fiery ovoid of the *I AM Presence.*

Unascended master. One who has overcome all limitations of *Matter* yet chooses to remain in time and space to focus the consciousness of God for lesser evolutions. See also *Bodhisattva.*

Universal Christ. The Mediator between the planes of *Spirit* and the planes of *Matter.* Personified as the *Christ Self,* he is the Mediator between the Spirit of God and the soul of man.

Violet flame. Seventh-ray aspect of the Holy Spirit. The *sacred fire* that transmutes the cause, effect, record and memory of sin, or negative *karma.* Also called the flame of transmutation, freedom and forgiveness. When the violet flame is invoked through the science of the *spoken Word,* it brings about constructive change.

Word. The Word is the Logos: it is the power of God and the realization of that power incarnate in and as the *Christ.* The energies of the Word are released by devotees of the Logos in the ritual of the science of the *spoken Word.* It is through the Word that the *Father-Mother God* communicates with mankind. The Christ is the personification of the Word. See also *Christ; Decree.*

Cosmic Consciousness
Corona Class Lessons
The Science of the Spoken Word
Mysteries of the Holy Grail
The Answer You're Looking for Is Inside of You

Climb the Highest Mountain Series:
The Path of the Higher Self
Foundations of the Path
The Path of Self-Transformation
The Masters and the Spiritual Path

Pocket Guides to Practical Spirituality Series:
Karma and Reincarnation
Alchemy of the Heart
Your Seven Energy Centers
Soul Mates and Twin Flames
Violet Flame to Heal Body, Mind and Soul
The Art of Practical Spirituality
How to Work with Angels
Creative Abundance
Access the Power of Your Higher Self
The Creative Power of Sound

FOR MORE INFORMATION

For more information about Summit University Press or
The Summit Lighthouse Library, to place an order or to receive
a free catalog of our books and products, please contact us at:

Summit University Press
PO Box 5000, Corwin Springs, MT 59030-5000 USA
Tel: 1-800-245-5445 or 406-848-9500
Fax: 1-800-221-8307 or 406-848-9555

Summit University Press: www.summituniversitypress.com
The Summit Lighthouse Library: www.tsl.org; tslinfo@tsl.org

Mark L. Prophet and Elizabeth Clare Prophet are pioneers of modern spirituality and internationally renowned authors. For more than 40 years the Prophets have published the teachings of the immortal saints and sages of East and West known as the ascended masters. Together they have given the world a new understanding of the ancient wisdom as well as a path of practical mysticism.

Their books, available in fine bookstores worldwide, have been translated into 20 languages and are sold in more than 30 countries.